PHILANTHROPY
AND
JIM CROW
IN AMERICAN
SOCIAL SCIENCE

Recent Titles in
Contributions in Afro-American and African Studies
Series Advisers: John W. Blassingame and Henry Louis Gates, Jr.

PHILANTHROPY AND JIM CROW IN AMERICAN SOCIAL SCIENCE

John H. Stanfield

CONTRIBUTIONS IN AFRO-AMERICAN AND AFRICAN STUDIES, NUMBER 82

GREENWOOD PRESS
WESTPORT, CONNECTICUT
LONDON, ENGLAND

Library of Congress Cataloging in Publication Data

Stanfield, John H.
  Philanthropy and Jim Crow in American social science.

  (Contributions in Afro-American and African Studies,
ISSN 0069-9624 ; no. 82)
  Bibliography: p.
  Includes index.
  1. Afro-Americans—Research—United States—History.
2. Racism—United States—History.   3. United States—
Race relations—Research—United States—History.
4. Endowment of research—United States—History.
5. Endowments—United States—History.   6. Social
sciences—Research—United States—History.   I. Title.
II. Series.
E184.7.S72   1985   308.8′96073   84-8995
ISBN 0-313-23894-4 (lib. bdg.)

Library of Congress Catalog Card Number: 84-8995
ISBN: 0-313-23894-4
ISSN: 0069-9624

First published in 1985

Greenwood Press
A division of Congressional Information Service, Inc.
88 Post Road West
Westport, Connecticut 06881

Printed in the United States of America

10 9 8 7 6 5 4 3 2 1

Copyright Acknowledgments

Specified excerpts from *An American Dilemma: The Negro Problem and Modern Democracy* by Gunnar Myrdal, Copyright 1944, 1962 by Harper & Row, Publishers, Inc., are reprinted by permission of Harper & Row, Publishers, Inc.

Archival sources of quoted materials are credited in the Preface. Every reasonable effort has been made to trace the owners of copyright materials in this book, but in some instances this has proven impossible. The publishers will be glad to receive information leading to more complete acknowledgments in subsequent printings of the book, and in the meantime extend their apologies for any omissions.

This book is dedicated to my mother, Almeda Lee Stanfield who though gifted to an extraordinary degree in human relations taught me through the rugged terrain of her life that inner strength is the most indispensable human virtue.

Contents

Tables

Preface

This book is composed of several interrelated case studies that illustrate the development of pre–World War II social science research on race relations. Such research was a product of the world views, consciousness, and organizational resources of philanthropists and foundation administrators interested in using social science to reinforce or modify the Jim Crow social order forged in the late nineteenth century. In presenting these cases, I show the importance of studying societal and funding factors in the development of the social sciences, particularly in shaping the social scientific interest in race relations. Such an analysis cannot help but lead to the conclusion that, historically, the sponsorship of social scientific and especially sociological research on the Afro-American experience has evolved more from questions of sociopolitical control than from a search for empirical truth.

Although the views expressed in this book are mine, numerous individuals contributed to the various forms and stages of its contents. The most important are Wendell Bell, John W. Blassingame, Scott A. Boorman, Maurice Clifford, Patricia Clifford, G. Franklin Edwards, Donald Fisher, Henry-Louis Gates, Edmund W. Gordon, Raymond L. Hall, Ira E. Harrison, Harriet G. McCombs, Charles C. Moskos, Jr., Joyce Ladner, James P. Pitts, Donald R. Ploch, Marcia Radosevich, Arthur Raper, John Shelton Reed, Albert J. Reiss, Jr., Daniel Rigney, Robert C. Weaver, and Carol Yeakey.

I wish to thank the archival collections staffs of the following institutions for giving me access to the invaluable documents in their care: Berea College, Carnegie Corporation of New York City, University of Chicago, Fisk University, Howard University, Library of Congress, National Archives, Rockefeller Archive Center, Shomburg Center for Research in Black Culture, University of Chicago, University of North Carolina-Chapel Hill, and Yale University. Titles and locations of all archival materials used are given in full in the Bibliography.

I wish to thank the following publishers for granting me permission to publish excerpts from several of my published articles: *Western Journal of Black Studies*, ''Veneral Disease Control Demonstrations Among Rural Blacks in the American South,'' Winter 1981; *Phylon*, ''The 'Negro Problem' Within and Outside the Institutional Nexus of Pre–World War I Sociology,'' September 1982; JAI Press, *Annual on Knowledge and Society*, Vol. 4, ''Leonard Outhwaite's Advocacy of Scientific Research on Blacks in the 1920s,'' 1983; and Gordon and Breach, ''Dollars for the Silent South: Southern Liberalism and the Julius Rosenwald Fund, 1928–1948,'' in Gordon and Breach, *Perspectives on the American South*, Vol. 2, 1984. I am grateful to Harper and Row for allowing me to quote extensively from Gunnar Myrdal's *An American Dilemma*.

The following diligent persons deserve praise for typing, editing, and proofreading the manuscript in its various stages of development: Paula Antrum, Donna Bigelow, Diane Johnson, Elizabeth Jones, Deanna McDermott, Marjorie Rich and Gayle White. Special thanks is extended to Kimberley Phillips for her research assistance.

Of all people and of all books, it would be inexcusable for me to ignore or downplay the roles of the funding agencies which have made my career and work possible through their generous and tolerant giving; namely, the Ford Foundation, the Rockefeller Foundation, and the National Science Foundation.

PHILANTHROPY
AND
JIM CROW
IN AMERICAN
SOCIAL SCIENCE

1

Racial Inequality in American Social Sciences: A Neglected Chapter in the Sociology of Knowledge

Sociologists and other sociologically oriented scholars have begun exploring at length societal conditioning factors which shape the origins and development of social science disciplines, communities, and institutions. Particularly valuable are societal conditioning perspectives which conceptualize and demonstrate empirically the synchronic links between contextual factors such as institutional settings, political economy, and patrons and internal factors such as great persons' biographies, theories, methods, and paradigms. Such analyses avoid reification which oversimplifies the examination of the origins and development of the social sciences as intellectual enterprises.

A variant of the social conditioning point of view is the "inequality in social science" perspective. This approach reminds us that the social sciences are relatively powerful intellectual enterprises which are microcosms of and reproducers of societal patterns of class, gender, and racial inequality.[1] Perhaps the least understood inequality in social science issues, which shall be the topic of this book, is the production of racial inequality in social scientific knowledge. How are the social sciences microcosms and reproducers of societal racial inequality? At best, this question has been entertained through documenting the lives and works of prominent race relations social scientists; through expounding on the operations of racially biased assumptions in social scientific research; and by reviewing paradigmatic trends in the race relations literature.[2] These traditional perspectives may have added to our understanding of how social scientists have grappled historically with racial issues and race relations research, but they promote internalistic perspectives that reify the race relations foundations of social science knowledge production from critical societal conditioning factors. Thus, little is known about how societal racial inequality patterns are reproduced in the institutional arrangements which materialize the social sciences and how resultant knowledge production reinforces hegemonic societal racial ordering.

I offer case studies that document a sociology of social science paradigm. It sheds light on the intrinsic linkages between the origin and development of race relations social science and historically specific societal racial inequality patterns. Given the tendency for contemporary social scientists to ignore or underestimate the historically persistent significance of race or to call it something else like class or gender, the central focus on racial inequality in American social scientific knowledge deserves justification.

What I have argued thus far leads to the conclusion that we must study the origins and evolution of the social sciences by first taking into account the material societal conditions which produce and institutionalize them, not the reverse. From the colonial era to the present post-industrial age, American elites, through their race/class consciousness and powerful social circles, have used race as a central tool for the construction of reality as well as for organizing and stratifying society. The taken for granted cultural rules and the formal policy procedures which govern the elite use of race have varied with historically specific material conditions such as demographic shifts, industrial developments, civil rights movements, and popular race relations ideas. But in diverse historical ways, there has been an unyielding tendency for race to continue to be a primary source of self-evaluation and evaluation of the Other. Race continues to be an important determinate of mate selection, church affiliation, quality of health, residence, occupational and educational attainment, and access to the core of corporate capitalism and key institutional decision-making circles.[3]

The dialetics of historically specific and historically persistent multiracial societal structures are the product of intergenerational socialization processes similar to those which reproduce class stratification. Americans, as well as members of other multiracial societies, learn ideas of race and class through the routines which form the premises of Schutzian "taken-for-granted" life worlds. This is why making sense out of the causes and effects of multiracialism is more complex than analyzing surface or intentional racist patterns of racial domination. In multiracial America, race, as an elite tool of reality construction, creates a normative taken-for-granted societal structure in which race is an integral aspect of the flow of everyday life.[4]

The observation that race is an integral aspect of the routine flow of American life encouraged me to look for societal conditioning factors which best illustrated how the material characteristics of this multiracial society shape the production of a race relations social science composed of researchers, concepts, methods, paradigms, and institutional settings which reflect and reproduce societal racial inequality patterns. This search led me to focus on historically specific financial patrons of social science research, in conjunction with other critical societal conditioning factors such as political economy, region, media, and societal race, class, and gender inequalities.

I chose to examine the role of financial patrons of race relations social science in their organizational and societal contexts because science in itself is a noncapitalistic phenomenon which is dependent upon external sources of capital for development. This is why an increasing number of historians and sociologists of science are turning their attention to the roles financiers play in the production of scientific knowledge. Specifically, they are studying the impact of research financing on the selection and careers of scientists, the formation of scientific disciplines, communities, and institutions, and the formulation of theories, methods, and paradigms.[5]

Most students of the financing of scientific research have concentrated on physical and biological sciences, with little regard for the social sciences. This secondary concern for the social sciences is due to the conventional sociology of science definitions of science which has promoted positivistic assumptions about science as a mode of knowledge. These positivistic world views take for granted that physical and biological sciences are the truest sciences and, therefore, are most worthy of sociological analysis. Also, given the greater prestige of physical and biological sciences in contrast to social sciences in capitalistic societies, more funds are made available to assess the historical development of the former rather than of the latter.

A third reason for the scant attention paid to the financial dimensions of the history and sociology of social science is more psychoanalytical than philosophical or socio-political. Being human, most social scientists experience grave difficulty in studying themselves. The alleged fact that social scientists are supposed to be value free and free agents makes it particularly difficult for social scientists to study the influences of finances in the development of their own disciplines. It has been easier, and less threatening, to mystify financiers of social science and their organizational contexts or render them completely invisible while stressing great persons' assessments of how social science disciplines originated and evolved.

Given the crucial participation of financiers in the history and sociology of science, it is important to bring them and their organizations into the analysis of how social sciences develop. To the slight extent to which such studies have been conducted, they have stressed what I call effect functionalism. Effect functionalism emphasizes the consequences of financial funding actions on the careers and work settings of social scientists. We have several excellent studies that plot the effects of financier activities with little regard for the biographical characteristics and organizational contexts of financiers. Effect functionalism helps to reinforce great persons' analyses of the social sciences through separating the development of social scientists and their intellectual enterprises from the contributions of those with the capital to create, institutionalize and, if need be, destroy their very professional existence.

There are distinctive methodological and ideological reasons why effective functionalism is the dominant financing of social science approach. Problems of data accessibility have prevented sophisticated inquiries into the biographical and organizational attributes of financiers and their interpersonal and institutional relationships with beneficiary social scientists. Especially in examinations of contemporary patterns of giving to social research, records needed for reconstructing financier consciousness, decision-making processes, and organizational settings have been quite difficult to collect. This is why most studies of social science financing studies are based upon published foundation or government appropriation reports, massaged for public consumption. Some financing of social research studies are dependent upon interviews with beneficiary social scientists who often are not aware of how and why financiers make funding decisions.

There is the ideological problem of the reluctance of social scientists in general, and those who study race relations in particular, to believe that power elites exist and are actively involved, mostly through the phenomenology of their social status, in designing and preserving societies to their own liking. It has been difficult for social scientists of science, especially social scientists of social science, to accept perspectives which explain the development of social sciences through locating causation in elite circles. This hesitancy magnifies when we turn to the literature on race relations social science. Historians and sociologists of the sociology of race relations have tended to label power and privilege perspectives that do not reduce race "down to something else" as "separatist," "conspiracy theory," "historical presentism," or in other ways ideologically tainted.[6] The lack of study of the role of financiers in the development of race relations research has been encouraged by moralistic intellectual traditions that fail to acknowledge that, most fundamentally, race is an elite tool of reality construction, and should be studied as such—even in the area of knowledge production.

Examining the emergence and institutionalization of race relations social science in power and privilege terms leads inevitably to a reconsideration of the careers and contributions of black scholars. At least since the 1920s, black social scientists and historians have been in greatest demand when white elites perceive a crisis in their racial authority. This was particularly apparent in between the world wars and during the 1960s when funding agency administrators, publishers, and academic mentors credentialled and published a significant number of black social scientists and historians. When elites resolve their racial crisis of authority or are distracted by other pressing national and international issues, as in the 1950s and post–1960s, the market for scholarship on blacks decreases along with the elite sponsorship of black entry into the social sciences.

No matter what the market demand is for black scholars, the prestige stratification of their contributions is relative to how much their ideas and even personalities are accommodative to the historically specific racial caste relations within and external to their disciplines. We find this to be the case in how pre–World War II philanthropic foundation administrators, white academic mentors, and elites in professional social sciences tended to select or ignore black social scientists and evaluate their work.

Recently, several archives have opened records of philanthropists, foundations, and benefiting social scientists involved in race relations research and policy development between the world wars. These records facilitate materialistic analyses of the synchronism of the internal and contextual dynamics of race relations research and Jim Crow social structure. In this book, I use archival materials and pertinent secondary works to reconstruct the biographies, race consciousness, organizational contexts and societal conditions of philanthropists, foundation administrators, and benefiting race relations social scientists.

Emphasis will be on foundation administrators and race relations social scientists affiliated with the following foundations: the Carnegie Corporation, the General Education Board, the Julius Rosenwald Fund, the Laura Spelman Rockefeller Memorial, and the Phelps-Stokes Fund. These men and foundations created a generation-specific sphere of knowledge production which in the main was accommodative to Jim Crow societal structure and helped to produce it. Stress will be on the biographical and organizational characteristics of philanthropists and foundation administrators who, through their interpersonal and institutional ties with agreeable social scientists, sponsored a race relations social science which they hoped would assist in resolving the rapidly changing characteristics of a most troubling barrier to Jim Crow societal stability: The Negro Problem.

In the unraveling of this major theme, several points that counter conventional ideas about foundations will become clear. First, philanthropists and the administrators of their foundations constructed an elite status culture which produced knowledge as a means of social control. They were not merely passive gatekeepers of knowledge waiting for ambitious researchers to submit their research proposals. More often than not (and contrary to the claims of official foundation histories), philanthropists and foundation officers had their own ideas about the world and sought accommodating beneficiaries to carry them out.

Second, pre–World War II philanthropic and foundation giving to race relations research was a phenomenon occurring within an organizational field composed of a network of financiers, researchers and worksettings. The network was maintained through different foundations having similar race relations interests, which created a cohort of foundation administrators and beneficiary social scientists who agreed broadly on the definition of research and the social place of blacks. The knowledge they produced was a sociopolitical construction, not a universal, value free intellectual product.

The network was preserved through patrimonial linkages which developed through the longevity of "giving and receiving" research funds and through various patterns of mentorship. Philanthropists and foundation administrators gave and still give most of their money to trustworthy individuals, not to impersonal institutions. We shall see that much of the financing of race relations research occurred "among friends" or more broadly, among a fraternally oriented social circle, which had some fascinating consequences. The patrimony of foundation giving raises doubts about the wisdom of considering such activities as merely rational contractual actions.[7]

Before ending this chapter, it would be instructive to give a precise definition of Jim Crow societal structure and to point out specifically how it relates to interwar philanthropy and race relations social science. Until the 1954 *Brown* decision and the major civil rights acts of the 1960s, the United States was officially a Jim Crow society. Jim Crow was a variant of apartheid which emphasized legal and psychological separation of the races: prohibition of interracial marriage; separate health, transportation, and educational facilities; racially defined occupations; highly ritualized racial etiquette in public spheres; and violent treatment and usurpation of the civil rights of racial minorities. An ideology and practice in social, economic, legal, and political spheres, Jim Crow was a reality construction created and maintained through a mixture of taken-for-granted and conscious biological and cultural ideas about race and the normative separation of the races in a rigid caste order.

From the end of Reconstruction to the end of World War I, biological explanations of black inferiority and Anglo-Saxon superiority were dominant in intellectual and political circles. Before the 1880 census, the post–Civil War decline in the black birthrate was used by biological determinists as evidence of the innate inability of ex-slaves to compete with whites. During the period between Reconstruction and World War I (approximately 1875–1915), the popular press and social observers commonly conceptualized blacks as a biologically fixed population and warned about the evils of race miscegenation. Popular literature and the emerging movie industry used black dialect as an indicator of the innate inferiority and ignorance of blacks.[8]

Biological determination, even with its cultural corollaries such as beliefs in racial antipathy and the inferiority of black language, was a stagnant world view. It fixed blacks eternally at the bottom of society and whites at the top. Even to begin to envision a society in which blacks were significantly upwardly mobile and competitive with whites was impossible for most biological determinists. There was no room for such occurrences in their paradigms of race relations.

Biologically deterministic rationalizations for a formally segregated society was phenomenologically relevant as long as blacks appeared to be permanently significant only in the South, especially the rural South. Thus it was not problematic for national magazine and newspaper editors, philanthropists, and southern liberals to support efforts like Booker T. Washington's educational philosophy, which were tailored to the rural South and discouraged blacks from migrating north. It was easy and convenient for northern elites to have paternalistic and biological attitudes about blacks as a southern problem while ignoring small black populations in their own communities.

The apparent immobility of southern blacks between the Civil War and World War I, compared to their mobility following World War I, converged with biological beliefs about black inferiority to make the Negro problem synonymous with the southern problem. Historically, northern subregions had only small black communities whose residents tended to be mulattoes from old families. This demographic background contributed to the myth that the North did not have a "Negro problem," which enabled guilt-free northerners to send missionary and foundation assistance south for the underdeveloped black masses.

Black migration north accelerated in the mid–1910s in response to a sagging plantation economy and northern capitalistic interest in replacing depleted European labor with cheaper black labor. This movement created an anomaly in the biologically deterministic view of Negro inferiority. Even though two-thirds of blacks remained in the South until the 1940s, the so-called Great Black Migration was so intensive that it rapidly changed white perceptions of the "place" of blacks in society. Blacks were no longer just southerners but were becoming a national racial group or, to describe more accurately the attitudes of white northerners, a more widespread problem. Blacks, like eastern and southern European immigrants a short time before, seemed to transform American cities overnight. In the late 1910s, well before the Harlem Renaissance, popular writers and others called the black migration north an indication of an emerging New Negro. The urban riots of the late 1910s gave evidence that the "New Negro" was now north and eagerly competing with whites in social, political, and especially economic spheres.

By no means did the dramatic black migration north, with its radical geopolitical, economic, social, and cultural consequences, completely destroy biological rationales for an apartheid society. Yet, the rapid demographic shifts of black populations and consequent flux in race relations created a demand for more flexible ideologies and practices in order to preserve Jim Crow. This explains the gradual popularity of culturally justified Jim Crow, which emerged and became dominant by the beginning of World War II. The institutionalization of intelligence testing and eugenic research in psychology; the financing of race research by foundations, the liberal perspectives on race of expanding civil rights organizations (such as the National Association for the Advancement of Colored People and the Commission of Interracial Cooperation), and the political and economic conditions of the Great Depression facilitated the growth of cultural determinism in racial thought and policy in the years between the wars.

Cultural determinism in the justifications for Jim Crow took two forms: natural history and sociocultural evolution. Natural historians optimistically stressed the benefits of allowing race relations problems to be resolved without state intervention. They believed that although racial groups in America had problems to work out due to social and cultural misunderstanding and divergent economic interests, the biracial organization of society was not to be tampered with. They explained patterns of race relations and resolution of race-relation problems in a society presumed to be permanently biracial, or more specifically, apartheid.

Sociocultural evolutionists argued that Jim Crow was an unfortunate evil whites and blacks had to put up with as they learned step by step how to get along. Social evolutionism was apparent in the great quantity of popular and academic scholarship promoting interracial cooperation and the positive accomplishments and virtues of blacks. Both its literary and organizational forms (the latter exemplified in the work of the Commission on Interracial Cooperation) were rooted in the educational premise that whites would gradually learn how to get along with blacks as they associated with the "best elements" of the black population and were exposed to a revealing literature on black experiences. Meanwhile, Jim Crow would persist.

Both these major cultural justifications for Jim Crow, along with minor ones such as cultural pluralism, legitimated limited black educational and economic mobility in a formally segregated society. Resolving interracial competition and conflict, supporting interracial cooperation efforts, and praising the unique contributions of blacks were not viewed as racial integration strategies. At most, blacks were to be incorporated into and ranked in strata (classes) and institutions (churches and small businesses) parallel to those of whites. A common rebuttal to criticisms of Jim Crow was the claim that blacks segregated themselves voluntarily. Another response was the accusation that critics were pushing for change faster than (white) society was willing to accept it.

The emergence and growth of the physical sciences in the late nineteenth and twentieth centuries cannot be divorced from the origin, evolution, and decline of Jim Crow as a variant of apartheid and its convergence with the evolution of corporate capitalism. The organizational and political events that reasserted rigid racial caste relations during the 1880s and 1890s represented attempts to keep blacks out of not only central political processes and institutions but also the emerging corporate ruling classes and the managerial levels of corporations and allied institutions, such as foundations, investment banks, and security-holding companies. By financing and supporting the design of marginal black industrial schools during this era and after, corporate ruling classes produced the channels needed for the systematic exclusion of blacks from the sciences and technologies crucial to the advancement of corporate capitalism.

In other words, the biological and cultural ideologies and practices that created and maintained Jim Crow also made normative the white exclusivity of scientifically based corporate development, which became the impetus for corporate capitalism around the turn of the century.[9] During this time, capitalists and philanthropists financed centers of high technology development and physical science experimentation and supported generously the operations for the Tuskegee Institute and the Hampton Institute. This same pattern of racial differentiation, which marginalized blacks in the emerging economic order, was reinforced in the racial exclusiveness of the first scientific engineering associations which were quickly absorbed into the structures of expanding corporations.

Prior to the 1920s, key capitalistic and philanthropic sponsors of scientific research were too preoccupied with searching for order in the physical and technological base of corporate capitalism to pay much attention to the development of the social sciences. Financiers interested in race relations supported social science research mostly in the areas of eugenics and intelligence testing; both means of scientifically justifying the subordination of eastern and southern European immigrants and rationalizing the low-caste status of ex-slaves.

When the American Social Science Association was established in 1865, we notice the preoccupation of scientifically oriented reformers with the turbulent post–Civil War industrialization in American cities. In the midst of this disorderly industrialization, which included a rapid influx of European immigrants and the initial stages of ex-slave geographic mobility, middle-class groups searched for order—a societal order defined in accordance with their own perceptions and vested interests. The American Social Science Association, progressive reform groups, leaders of elite academic institutions, and even nativistic and eugenic associations were included in this effort to make sense of the processes and events that were redesigning America. The American Social Science Association served as a clearinghouse of ideas about how sources of unprecedented social change were producing adjustment problems among immigrants and the poor. More abstractly, and more rhetorically, authors alluded to the South's "Negro problem."

The major support for social science before World War I came from sparse university financing and from progressive civic and social scientific associations such as the American Social Science Association. As seen in the work of William E. B. DuBois, George Haynes, Walter Wilcox, Thomas J. Jones, and anthropologists in the Bureau of Ethnology, federal agencies also sponsored numerous social science studies. But while the primary support for the social sciences before World War I was not directly tied to the roots of corporate capitalism, many of the ideas developed by social scientists were used to justify the biological and cultural degradation of racial minorities in the new capitalist society. This is apparent in the close links between biologically deterministic social scientists and major political figures. Edward Ross's anti-Asian thought, for instance, heavily influenced Theodore Roosevelt's anti-Chinese and anti-Japanese foreign policies. Before and after World War I, eugenic social scientists Robert M. Yerkes and Henry Fairchild influenced congressional efforts to restrict immigration. It is true that *The Polish Peasant* by William I. Thomas and Florian Znaniecki, which was begun well before World War I, was not a deliberate attempt to support the cultural and political demands of capitalism. But the authors' ideas about problems of ethnic adjustment converged with the capitalist imperative of a consensual social system which included well-assimilated immigrant groups.[10]

Radical changes in perception and real changes in black status, wrought by capitalist interest in black labor and the dramatic black migration north in the 1910s, sowed the seeds of the environmental paradigms that would dominate social scientific and race relations research. But before such seeds could germinate, massive financing of the meagerly supported social sciences was necessary. The blossoming of environmental views of blacks in the social sciences between the world wars can be completely understood only through assessing the interests, world views, and organizational resources of philanthropists and foundation administrators concerned about the Negro problem, and about the institutionalization of social science research.

Philanthropic and scholarly shaping of race studies in the social sciences may have been in tune with changing empirical realities, but it still adhered to numerous traditional assumptions about relations between the races. Even though urbanization of the black population, race riots, and the growing power of civil rights organizations made environmental explanations about black conditions more acceptable, the validity of a formally segregated society was still taken for granted. This was apparent in the foundation and academic popularity of natural history and sociocultural evolutionary race relations paradigms and the rejection of those that were more power and pluralistic oriented.

Chapter 2 offers a richer historical and sociological context of Jim Crow and the development of accommodative race relations research. Chapter 3 dissects the personal and racial ideology of the father of mainstream Negro Problem sociological research, Robert E. Park. Chapters 4, 5, 6, and 7 are case studies of the major philanthropists, foundation administrators, and social scientists who constituted the interwar network of sponsors and beneficiaries in the realm of race relations research. In conclusion Chapter 8 discusses the impact of philanthropy and Jim Crow on American social science and on the careers of black social scientists in a broad theoretical framework.

NOTES

1. Julia R. Schwendinger and Herman Schwendinger, *The Sociologists of the Chair* (New York: Basic Books, 1974), is a comprehensive analysis of how American political economy contexts shape sociological conceptions of reality.

Another area not mentioned is regionalism in social scientific knowledge production. The major works on regionalism in sociology, which emphasize the development of southern sociology, include: Michael O'Brien, *The Idea of the American South, 1920–1941* (Baltimore, Md.: Johns Hopkins University Press, 1979); Dewey W. Grantham, *The Regional Imagination* (Nashville, Tenn.: Vanderbilt University Press, 1979); Morton Sosna, *In Search of the Silent South* (New York: Columbia University Press, 1977); Paul M. Gaston, *The New South Creed* (New York: Alfred A. Knopf, 1970); and David J. Singal, *The War Within: From Victorian to Modernist Thought in the South, 1914–1945* (Chapel Hill: University of North Carolina Press, 1982). The most promising works about sexism in the social sciences include: William Leach, *True Love and Perfect Union: The Feminist Reform of Sex and Society* (New York: Basic Books, 1980); Rosalind Rosenberg, *Beyond Separate Spheres: Intellectual Roots of Modern Feminism* (New Haven, Conn.: Yale University Press, 1982); Margaret W. Rossiter, *Women Scientists in America: Struggles and Strategies to 1940* (Baltimore, Md.: Johns Hopkins University Press, 1982); and Marcia Millman and Rosabeth Moss Kanter, eds., *Another Voice: Feminist Perspectives on Social Life and Social Science* (Garden City, N.Y.: Anchor Press/Doubleday, 1975).

2. See James E. Blackwell and Morris Janowitz, eds., *Black Sociologists: Historical and Contemporary Perspectives* (Chicago: University of Chicago Press, 1974); Wayne Brazil, *Howard W. Odum, 1880–1930: The Building Years* (Ph.D. dissertation, Harvard University, 1975); Horace R. Cayton, *The Long Old Road* (New York: Trident Press, 1965); William E. B. DuBois, *Dusk of Dawn: The Autobiography of a Race Concept* (New York: Harcourt Brace and Company, 1940); Patrick Gilpin, *Charles S. Johnson: A Intellectual Biography* (Ph.D. dissertation, Vanderbilt University, 1973); Grace E. Harris,

The Life and Works of E. Franklin Frazier (Ph.D. dissertation, University of Virginia, 1975); Robert Hemenway, *Zora Neal Huston: A Literary Biography* (Urbana, Ill.: University of Illinois Press, 1977); Fred Matthews, *Quest for an American Sociology: Robert E. Park and the Chicago School* (Montreal: McGill-Queens University Press, 1977); Stanford M. Lyman, *The Black American in Sociological Thought* (New York: Putnam, 1972); Howard W. Odum, *American Sociology: The Story of American Sociology Through 1950* (New York: Longmans, Green, 1951); Daniel Perlman, *Stirring the White Conscience: The Life of George Edmund Haynes* (Ph.D. dissertation, New York University, 1975); Winifred Raushenbush, *Robert E. Park: Biography of a Sociologist* (Durham, N.C.: Duke University Press, 1979); Benjamin P. Bowser, "The Contributions of Blacks to Sociological Knowledge: A Problem of Theory and Role to 1950," *Phylon* 42 (1981): 180–193; Oliver Cox, Introduction, in Nathan Hare, *Black Anglo Saxons* (London, 1965); Butler A. Jones, "The Tradition of Sociology Teaching in Black Colleges: The Unhearalded Professionals," in James E. Blackwell and Morris Janowitz, eds., *Black Sociologists: Historical and Contemporary Perspectives* (Chicago: University of Chicago Press, 1975); Joyce Ladner, *The Death of White Sociology* (New York: Random House, 1973); and Michael R. Winston, "Through the Back Door: Academic Racism and the Negro Scholar in Historical Perspective," *Daedalus* (Summer 1971): 678–719.

Works that offer externalist explanations about the development of race relations social science include: John H. Stanfield, "Leonard Outhwaite's Advocacy of Scientific Research on Blacks in the 1920s," *Knowledge and Society: Studies in the Sociology of Culture, Vol. 4* (Greenwich, Conn.: JAI Press, 1983), pp. 87–101; Michael Banton, "1960: A Turning Point in the Study of Race Relations," *Daedalus* 102 (Spring 1974): 631–644; James Vander Zanden, "Sociological Studies of American Blacks," *Sociological Quarterly* 14 (Winter 1973): 31–52; Thomas Pettigrew, *The Sociology of Race Relations* (New York: Free Press, 1980); Edward Shils, "Tradition, Ecology, and Institution in the History of Sociology," *Daedalus* 99 (Fall 1970): 760–785; James T. Carey, *Sociology and Public Affairs: The Chicago School* (Beverly Hills, Calif.: Sage Publications, 1975); and Lewin M. Killian, "The Race Relations Industry, as a Sensitizing Concept," *Research in Social Problems and Public Policy* (1979): 113–137. For an interesting externalist perspective on race relations in the biological sciences, see Kenneth R. Manning, *Black Apollo of Science: The Life and Works of Ernest Everett Just,* (New York: Oxford University Press, 1983).

3. Two major works tht exemplify the significance of race debate in American sociology are William J. Wilson, *The Declining Significance of Race* (Chicago: The University of Chicago Press, 1978); and Dorothy Newman et al., *Protest, Politics, and Prosperity* (New York: Pantheon, 1978).

4. This social construction of reality perspective is derived from Peter L. Berger and Thomas Luckman, *The Social Construction of Reality* (New York: Doubleday and Company, 1967).

5. The following works are examples of how the financing of scientific research has been studied: E. Richard Brown, *Rockefeller Medicine Men* (Berkeley, Calif.: University of California Press, 1979); S. Cohen, "Foundation Officials and Fellowships: Innovation in the Patronage of Science," *Minerva* 14 (Summer 1976): 225–240; John Ettling, *The Germ of Laziness: Rockefeller Philanthropy and Public Health in the New South* (Cambridge, Mass.: Harvard University Press, 1981); Donald Fisher, "The Rockefeller Foundation and the Development of Scientific Medicine in Great Britain," *Minerva* 16 (1978): 20–41; Raymond Fosdick, *The Story of the Rockefeller Foundation*

(New York: Harper and Brothers, 1952); David Fox, "Abraham Flexner's Unpublished Report: Foundations and Medical Education, 1901–1928," *Bulletin of the History of Medicine* 54 (1980): 475–496; Frederick Gates, *Chapters in My Life* (New York: Free Press, 1977); Robert E. Kohler, "The Management of Science: The Experience of Warren Weaver and the Rockefeller Foundation Programme in Molecular Biology," *Minerva* 14 (Autumn 1976): 276–306; Michael D. Reagen, *Science and the Federal Patron* (New York: Oxford University Press, 1969); Alexandra Oleson and John Voos, eds., *The Organization of Knowledge in Modern America, 1860–1920* (Baltimore, Md.: Johns Hopkins University Press, 1979); Manning, *Black Apollo of Science*; Robert F. Arnove, ed., *Philanthropy and Cultural Imperialism: The Foundations at Home and Abroad* (Boston: G. K. Hall and Company, 1980); Martin Bulmer, "The Early Institutional Establishment of Social Science Research: The Local Community Research Committee at the University of Chicago, 1923–30," *Minerva* 18 (Spring 1980): 51–110; Richard Colvard, "Risk Capital Philanthropy and the Ideological Defense of Innovation," in George K. Zollschan and Walter Hirsch, eds., *Social Change: Explorations, Diagnoses and Conjectures* (New York: John Wiley & Sons, 1976), pp. 864–886; Lewis Coser, *Men of Ideas* (New York: Free Press, 1965); John F. Galliger and James L. McCartney, "The Influence of Funding Agencies on Juvenile Delinquence Research," *Social Problems* 21 (Summer 1973): 77–90; Hemenway, *Zora Neal Hurston*; Gerrit Huizen and Bruce Mannheim, eds., *The Politics of Anthropology* (The Hague: Marion Publishers, 1979); Dell Hymes, ed., *Reinventing Anthropology* (New York: Pantheon Books, 1972); Barry E. Karl, *Charles E. Merriam and the Study of Politics* (Chicago: University of Chicago Press, 1974); Richard S. Kirkendall, *Social Scientists and Farm Politics in the Age of Roosevelt* (Columbia, Md.: University of Missouri Press, 1966); Gene M. Lyons, *The Uneasy Partnership: Social Science and the Federal Government in the Twentieth Century* (New York: Russell Sage Foundation, 1969); James L. McCartney, "The Financing of Sociological Research, Trends and Consequences," in Edward A. Tiryakian, eds., *The Phenomenon of Sociology* (New York: Appleton Century Crofts, 1971), pp. 384–397; Michael O'Brien, *The Idea of the American South, 1920–1941* (Baltimore, Md.: Johns Hopkins University Press, 1979); Shils, "Tradition, Ecology, and Institution in the History of Sociology"; Michael Ussem, "State Production of Social Knowledge: Patterns in Government Financing of Academic Social Research," *American Sociological Review* 41 (August 1976): 613–629; A. J. Wilson, *Social Science Research in Industry* (London: Hawop, 1972); Albert R. Gilgen, *American Psychology Since World War II* (Westport, Conn.: Greenwood Press, 1982); James L. McCartney, Daryl Chubin, and John R. Hall, "Financing Sociological Research," *American Sociologist* 17 (1982); and Harold Orlans, *Contracting for Knowledge* (San Francisco: Jossey-Bass, 1973).

6. For instance, see R. Fred Wacker, *Ethnicity, Pluralism, and Race: Race Relations Theory in America Before Myrdal* (Westport, Conn.: Greenwood Press, 1983); and August Meier, "Black Sociologists in White America," *Social Forces* (1977).

7. The "traditional" pre–World War II foundation literature is comprised of official foundation histories and the biographies of philanthropists and foundation administrators. Emerson F. Andrews, *Philanthropic Giving* (New York: Russell Sage Foundation, 1950); Merle Curti, ed., *Philanthropy in the Shaping of American Higher Education* (New Brunswick, N.J.: Rutgers University Press, 1965); Wilma Dykeman and James Stokely, *Seeds of Southern Change: The Life of Will Alexander* (Chicago: The University of Chicago Press, 1962); Edwin R. Embree and Julia Waxman, *Investment in Peo-*

ple: The Story of the Julius Rosenwald Fund (New York: Harper Brothers, 1949); Abraham Flexner, *The General Education Board: An Account of Its Activities* (New York: General Education Board, 1915); Abraham Flexner, *I Remember* (New York: Simon and Schuster, 1940); Raymond Fosdick, *The Story of the Rockefeller Foundation* (New York: Harper and Brothers, 1952); Raymond B. Fosdick, *Chronicle of a Generation: An Autobiography* (1958); Raymond Fosdick, *Adventure in Giving: The Story of the General Education Board* (New York: Harper and Row, 1962); Frederick Gates, *Chapters in My Life* (New York: Free Press, 1977); Kenneth James King, *Pan-Africanism and Education* (London: Oxford University Press, 1971); Waldemar A. Nielson, *The Big Foundations* (New York: Columbia University Press, 1972); Anson Phelps Stokes, *Negro Status and Race Relations in the United States, 1911–1946: The Thirty-five Year Report on the Phelps-Stokes Fund* (New York: Phelps-Stokes Fund, 1948); Warren Weaver, *U.S. Philanthropic Foundations: Their History, Structure, Management and Record* (New York: Harper and Row Publishers, 1967); and Morris Werner, *Julius Rosenwald* (Glenview: Harper and Brothers, 1939).

8. George M. Fredrickson, *The Black Image in the White Mind: The Debate on Afro-American Character and Destiny, 1817–1914* (New York: Harper & Row, 1977); Richard Hofstader, *Social Darwinism in American Thought* (Philadelphia: University of Pennsylvania Press, 1944); Daniel J. Leab, *From Sambo to Superspade: The Black Experience in Motion Pictures* (Boston: Houghton Mifflin, 1975); and Rayford W. Logan, *The Betrayal of the Negro from Rutherford B. Hayes to Woodrow Wilson* (New York: Collier Books, 1965).

9. David Noble, *America by Design* (New York: Knopf, 1977).

10. For overviews on the participation of American social scientists in nativistic and eugenics research and their general racial attitudes, see John Higham, *Strangers in the Land* (New York: Atheneum, 1963); Richard Hofstadter, *Social Darwinism in American Thought*, rev. ed. (New York: Braziller, 1959); Hamilton Cravens, *The Triumph of Evolution* (Philadelphia: University of Pennsylvania Press, 1978); and George W. Stocking, Jr., *Race, Culture, and Evolution* (New York: Free Press, 1968).

2

Race Problems in Pre–World War I Professional Sociology

The period between the end of the Civil War and the beginning of World War I was difficult for old Anglo-Saxon elite families, the emerging urban middle class, and European immigrant laborers. The sudden influx of southern and eastern Europeans, particularly Jewish immigrants, induced a "status panic" among the Anglo-Saxon elite on the eastern seaboard. They responded by taking preventive measures against ethnic encroachment including the establishment of exclusive social clubs and preparatory schools and the support of nativistic, if not Americanization, movements.[1]

The emerging urban middle class of this period attempted to bring rapid and disorganized industrialization under its control. Professionalism, which in part is a means of bourgeois control over definitions of industrial society, shaped the development of organized social welfare, education, medicine, the social sciences, law, city reform, and mainstream religion. The super-rich gave legitimacy to this professional control but continued to own the means of production.[2]

As European immigrants flooded into urban areas between the 1880s and the mid–1900s, industrialists developed Americanization programs designed to create an efficient yet passive labor force. Exploitation by major industrialists, wretched working conditions, and the popularity of socialism among the immigrants contributed to increasing efforts to unionize workers. The well-known facts of the violent encounters between corporate capitalists and laborers during this period emphasize the difficulties eastern and southern Europeans had in blending into the American political economy and organizing against it. The anti-Semitism and nativism so prevalent among the Anglo-Saxon majority added to these difficulties.

Although the Anglo-Saxon elite, the emerging urban middle class, and the European immigrant classes occupied different niches in the political economy which often put them at odds, their common phenotypical traits and European background created an enduring racial bond: they were all white. Upwardly mobile European immigrants quickly learned the virtues of being white upon their arrival in America. Therefore, the status groups of European descent were very concerned about the consequences of the emancipation of African slaves. The hostility of European immigrants toward ex-slave economic competition and industrialists' use of blacks as strikebreakers has been well documented; what concerns us here are elite and middle-class responses to slave emancipation which clarify issues about the race consciousness of philanthropists and the discovery of the Negro problem in American sociology.

In order to understand the white elite response to the emancipation of slaves, we must consider briefly the origins and evolution of America as a multiracial, multiclass nation. Social and cultural histories inform us that British-Americans came to dominate the East Coast and pushed westward, disenfranchising native populations of their property and human rights in the process. As the nineteenth century progressed, America's multiracial character was enriched through the conquest and internal colonization of Mexicans and the inclusion of Asians who came as contract workers (the Chinese) and as voluntary immigrants (the Japanese). This period also saw the emergence, institutionalization and legal discrediting of African slavery.

Anglo-Saxons wished not only to create laboring classes to work in their railroads, fields, and factories, but also to maintain their own racial purity. They defined races through attitudes which correlated physical features with morality, values, intellectual abilities, behavior, and potential for assimilation. This phenomenology was racially exclusive. The "melting-pot" only included other people of European descent. It was never meant to include Asians, Mexicans, Native Americans, or especially Africans.[3]

Anglo-Saxon aversion to intimate contact with non-Europeans, which originated in the exclusively white power structure designed in the colonial era has remained in force to this day. Although race relations—intergroup attitudes, values, and interaction strategies—have fluctuated, racial inequality—power distributions, decision-making authority, and resource monopolization—has remained unchanged. From the colonial era to the present, America has been a society ruled by those of European descent.[4]

Anglo-Saxon and other elite status groups of European descent have used various means to legitimize their right to exploit and control non-European Americans. These myths, reproduced through intergenerational socialization, have emphasized the alleged laziness, immorality and low intelligence of non-Europeans, who have been viewed as sociopolitical problems of control rather than as normal human beings.

A most effective means of race myth making has been science. The Enlightenment brought a sense of liberation from religious dogma and an interest in exploring and explaining human nature in non-theological terms. Biological and social sciences began to flourish in the nineteenth century, which also marked the zenith of European nationalism and European expansion into Africa and Asia, as well as the defeat of the slave regime in the American south. The biological and social sciences became means through which European superiority could be "proven" and exploitation of non-Europeans justified. The quantitative perspective on "racial differences" has evolved from nineteenth century phrenology studies to twentieth-century psychological intelligence and achievement testing. Theoretical traditions have evolved from the racially biased rhetoric and social Darwinism of the nineteenth-century European nationalists, through anthropological functionalism and sociological natural history, to paradigms of pathology and asymmetrical assimilation.

Although the question of race and racial differences has been increasingly liberalized, the fact that biological and social scientists continue to study these phenomena reflects the continued importance of race as a factor in European nation-state building, colonialism, and neocolonialism. The use of "empirical data" to explain the causes and consequences of racial differences in income, educational attainment, intelligence, mobility patterns, family structures, and residence perpetuates the myth that race is relevant in defining human differences and therefore confirms the stratified racial order. In other words, American biological and social scientists have been preoccupied with the problem of race and racial differences off and on because they are part and parcel of a multiracial society and reconfirm if not reinforce its racial order by their very expressions about these phenomena as well as their sometime efforts to influence public policy.

In the aftermath of the Civil War, the emerging urban white middle class was quite concerned about the presence of emancipated African slaves and unassimilated European immigrants. This class relied on the state-sanctioned legitimation of their occupations in their search for "order" and for solutions to the threat to their cultural and racial purity. The professionalization of the social sciences and social welfare activities was central to this effort.[5]

In 1865, the American Social Science Association was organized by New Englanders interested in using the "science of society" to resolve ills in society such as disease, crime, poverty, and immigration. They believed that they could use quantitative data, particularly the U.S. Census and surveys, to persuade the government to eradicate social problems. These amateur social scientists, as historian Mary Furner has called them, differed from their professional counterparts, who were more concerned about reform than about an impassioned search for truth. Because of this difference in orientation, the latter group created more specialized assocations: the American Economics Association, the American Psychological Association, and the American Sociological Society.[6]

The founders of the American Social Science Association agreed with the more professionally minded members of their generation in the ideas and structures that constituted American culture. Their reformist efforts were directed at correcting aberrations which contradicted what America represented to them—liberal democracy and a land for and by the people. They believed that the structure of the nation-state had to be repaired for democracy to flourish. Thus, they developed a definition of social science oriented toward the status quo exemplified in the distinction its founders made between social science and socialism.[7]

Reformist social science and professional social science may differ in philosophy and objectives, but both have continued to emphasize reinforcement of sociopolitical and cultural hegemony rather than dismantling and restructuring society. Even the most radical paradigms advanced within the mainstreams of the disciplines have tended to be conservative, as seen in the extent to which American social science establishments accept Marxism as a plausible alternative perspective.

Due to their orientation toward the status quo, early reformist and professional social scientists viewed populations such as the poor, immigrants, and blacks as sociopolitical and cultural problems of control. Even before the massive immigration of eastern and southern European immigrants, members of the association spoke of the value of immigrant labor, but stressed the greater importance of federal laws to make sure immigrants did not disrupt American morals, culture, or health. As the dramatic influx of European immigrants continued, discussions emphasized the virtues of Americanization programs.[8]

Most reformist and professional social scientists assumed that the society the elite and middle classes were designing was right. These beliefs gave them confidence to define individual prosperity in terms of conformity and to develop asymmetrical ideals of cultural assimilation. The European "immigrant problem," then, was represented by foreign languages, religious orientations, rural time senses, and different fashions and food habits, all of which prevented the immigrants' ready blending into white Anglo-Saxon Protestant middle-class culture.

For non-European "races," the situation was more complicated. Not only differences in culture but more important, undesirable phenotypic traits—black skin, woolly hair, yellow skin, slanted eyes—inhibited the smooth stirring of the melting pot. Unlike the immigrant problem, the Negro problem, the Mexican problem, the Indian problem, and the "yellow peril" were more or less permanent problems because in these cases, in the minds of the whites, the cultural differences together with the "unpleasant" physical features of the non-whites symbolized pathology in urgent need of control. The Negro problem represents social scientists' assumptions about the impossibility of complete amalgamation, let alone assimilation, of non-European races in America.[9]

IMMIGRANT AND NEGRO PROBLEMS IN AMERICAN SOCIOLOGY

The first American textbook to include the word "sociology" in its title was a defense of slavery. Like Emile Durkheim's advocacy of new foundations for potentially pathological, industrializing societies, George Fitzhugh's *Sociology for the South* was a promotion of the "normal" state of human affairs—a society ruled by slave masters.[10] It is ironic that this mid-nineteenth-century study examined the potential chaos of the emancipation of African slaves, for even though Fitzhugh was long forgotten when professional sociology came into being at the turn of the century, sociologists at that time were greatly concerned about problems of assimilation and amalgamation of poor European immigrants, and, to a lesser extent, blacks. In 1905, the sociopolitical control premises of the new discipline were in accord with Fitzhugh's use of the term "sociology."

Associational sociology represented an effort by the urban middle class to gain authority in interpreting the changes created by rapid and disorganized industrialization, influxes of European immigrants, and the expansion of American colonialism. Its proponents assumed that science could be used to explain, if not repair, society. Albion Small founded the *American Journal of Sociology* in 1895 in Chicago, intending to capture the market for the growing interest in sociology by narrowing its definition and justifying specialized training. The establishment of the American Sociological Society, which used Small's journal as its official organ for thirty years, represented an effort by professional sociologists to extend their authority.[11]

The Schwendingers have shown convincingly that even reform-oriented professional sociologists were true believers in the American democratic ethos.[12] Lester Ward, Albion Small, and other critically minded sociologists believed that state intervention could help solve social problems. These views put them at odds with the proponents of social Darwinism. Nonetheless, their theories were congruent with the social and political needs of the evolving corporate state. Edward Ross's and Charles Cooley's respective conceptions of norms and the looking-glass self, for example, grounded acceptable behavior and self-esteem in the values and perceptions of the collective.

Professional sociologists' concern for contemporary society and its problems legitimized their conceptions of normal and abnormal human conditions that were given scant attention by the other professionalizing social sciences which were carving out their own territories. Thus, while all the social sciences have had some theories about "race and racial differences," sociologists have monopolized empirical inquiry into these matters. In the area of immigrant studies, for instance, we find sociologists of the Gilded Age taking the lead in creating an empirical base for immigrant problem research.

The earliest sociologists developed their theories and methods out of the midwestern and eastern urban milieu in which their universities were situated. The American Sociological Society, which was founded and monopolized by eastern and midwestern sociologists, institutionalized this sectional idea of society and cultivated it by providing a forum for issues related to the interests of easterners and midwesterners. *The American Journal of Sociology* further legitimized the sectional world view by publishing articles and book reviews preoccupied with issues related to political, economic, cultural, and organizational changes in the Midwest and East. Perhaps the apex of this concern was represented by the great number of articles and books which attempted to describe the causes and consequences of urbanization. The institutional symbol of mid-western/eastern sociology was the University of Chicago Sociology Department, which encouraged the development of paradigms concerning industrialization and urbanization, which were integral to the Chicago region.

The sociologists' refusal to look beyond their surroundings created gaps in sociological knowledge as the discipline became increasingly populated by highly technical journals and by specialized practitioners using standardized concepts, theories, and methods. For instance, the paradigm of urbanization developed by Gilded Age sociologists stressed the inevitable decline of the countryside and the dominance of the city simply because this is what they observed in their midwestern and eastern home bases. But this paradigm did not fit the plantation South, which remained highly dependent upon the countryside, even in the midst of industrialization and urbanization.[13]

The urban midwestern world constructed by professional sociologists inevitably included southern and eastern European immigrants as the most pressing "race problem" prior to World War I. Between the 1890s and mid–1910s, sociology textbooks, journals, book review columns, and professional meetings discussed widely the assimilation problems of immigrants. Many sociologists spoke for or against immigrant exclusion and eugenics. The more conservative, pro-exclusion and pro-eugenic sociologists such as Edward Ross and Henry Pratt Fairchild held sway. Edward Ross's anti-oriental and European immigrant views were especially popular. The book review columns of the *American Journal of Sociology* during this period likewise reveal a fascination with social Darwinism and eugenics.[14]

Even liberal sociologists valued the status quo. William Isaac Thomas and Florian Znaniecki's *The Polish Peasant in America*, a seminal work on the immigrant problem, was most representative of their views.[15] According to Thomas, the asymmetric assimilations of Poles was normative, but snags along the way created "adjustment problems." Thomas's liberalism was represented in his dismissal of social Darwinism and innate racial characteristics in European immigrants and blacks. His explanation for the adjustment problems of Poles—individual demoralization—was structural rather than pathological. His syncretic description of Polish-American communities was well before its time, emphasizing immigrants' difficulties in reconstructing an adequate social organization in the midst of the decay of old social rules (disorganization). But his status quo orientation is exposed in his proposed solution to the "inability" of individual Poles to develop "appropriate morality." Systematic Americanization—the exposure of Poles to "dominant white culture and society" represented an effective control over these peasant immigrants.[16]

Commentators on the history of the sociology of race relations have claimed that before World War I American sociologists paid little attention to the empirical conditions of blacks. These claims are based largely on examination of the major works of Albion Small, George Vincent, William Sumner, Franklin

Giddings, William I. Thomas, Charles Cooley, and other prominent sociologists active in the earliest years of American sociology. These historians have excluded early, influential sociologists of blacks who where employed either in Southern academic institutions or in nonacademic institutions. W.E.B. DuBois of Atlanta University and, to a lesser extent, Robert E. Park of Tuskegee Institute are the only "marginal" early sociologists of blacks whose works have been evaluated. Others, such as Alfred Stone, the Mississippi planter; Thomas J. Jones of Hampton Institute and the Phelps-Stoke Fund; Howard W. Odum, graduate of the University of Mississippi and Columbia University; and Willis D. Weatherford of the Southern Young Men's Christian Association, have been ignored completely or have had only later stages of their careers evaluated. (This was particularly true of Robert Park. Only Park and Odum eventually became prominent race scholars in the organized profession and have had their professional careers extensively evaluated.)

The exclusion of these early researchers from conventional histories of the sociology of race relations resulted from changes in the definition of professional sociology in the years between the wars. In the effort to develop a scientific approach to the study of blacks and of race in general, E. Franklin Frazier, Charles S. Johnson, Gunnar Myrdal, and other prominent scholars of the period critiqued the ideas of researchers prior to World War I. Such criticisms attempted to move away from the perspectives of the early scholars (excepting DuBois, Thomas, and Cooley), rather than to clarify the influence that early sociologists of blacks had in their era.[17]

Consideration of early sociologists who studied blacks is important, since many of their works had a profound impact on federal and foundation policies as well as sociological thought about race. During the earliest years of the twentieth century, sociologists who advocated industrial education for blacks, encouraged the confinement of blacks to the South, or statistically demonstrated innate inferiority of blacks were highly praised. Critical assessments of the status of blacks in society were ignored or ridiculed, since most, with the significant exception of Franz Boas, were conducted by black researchers in black institutions and published in black periodicals and newspapers.

THE LACK OF INTEREST IN THE EMPIRICAL STUDY OF BLACKS IN THE INSTITUTIONAL NEXUS OF PRE–WORLD WAR I SOCIOLOGY

Before World War I major sociologists occasionally offered theoretical or rhetorical statements either defending or critiquing prevalent ideas about the innate inferiority of blacks and other nonwhite races. These tended to be either passing comments made in their larger, systematic sociologies or brief journal articles with no further elaboration. Charles Cooley and William I. Thomas were the only major sociologists attempting to develop significant environmental and caste explanations about the origins and persistence of racial differences. But their ideas on race, like those of Franz Boas, were ignored until the period between the wars.[18]

The stark neglect of the Negro problem among prominent sociologists was significantly apparent in the writings of Lester F. Ward. Ward, the first president of the American Sociological Society, was the foremost professional sociologist of the Gilded Age. A staunch environmentalist and a vehement opponent of laissez-faire social evolution, he wrote radical critiques of class inequality, predicting the eventual uprising of the proletariat. But he believed that education, not revolt, was the dynamic of an uprising. He opposed, and often reversed, arguments about the genetic superiority of the rich and the inferiority of the lower classes. But in his numerous books and articles about inequality, he stressed class and, to a lesser extent, women. In his discussion of blacks, Ward lashed out against popular biological claims of Anglo-Saxon superiority and advocated education as the means of black development. But like his colleagues, he remained silent on the possibility of amalgamation in white/black relations. He did not address the concept of desegregation as a means of resolving the Negro problem. Ward advanced only well-worn liberal solutions, such as education.

The lack of interest in empirical inquiry into conditions of blacks can be attributed to social Darwinism and Anglo-Saxon ideologies which influenced American social thought about race relations, and to the regional orientation of professional sociology.

SOCIAL DARWINISM AND ANGLO-SAXONISM

In the early years of the organized profession of sociology, prevalent beliefs in the superiority of the "Anglo-Saxon race" were crystallized in the writings of the eminent economist Walter Wilcox of Cornell University, who was the only prominent member of the young American Sociological Society to complete extensive empirical research into the socioeconomic conditions of blacks. An abstract empiricist, he was confident that his statistical demographies of the Negro problem were objective interpretations owing nothing to his negative personal views of blacks. But his selection and manipulation of data about the social and economic conditions of blacks for the United States Census Bureau illustrates how an analysis of census data can be used to legitimate racially biased ideas. Wilcox's accounts of conditions among blacks were pseudo-scientific rituals that reinforced conventional wisdoms—social Darwinism.[19]

The prevailing opinion among sociologists was that the innate inferiority of blacks made them irrelevant as subjects of inquiry. Why study the obvious? More important, why make an aggressive effort to examine inferior racial groups who could not possibly better the qualities of the Anglo-Saxon race? Many sociologists supported or were sympathetic to formal Anglo-Saxon causes. Those who opposed social Darwinism either did not extend their liberalism to the race question or created racially biased arguments by assuming that races were inherently unequal and by using biological analogies. The latter was Lester Ward's dilemma in his critique of European race-conflict theorists.

Many early writers of sociology textbooks, such as Albion Small and George Vincent, who were also liberal Anglo-Saxonists, assumed that even though blacks were not biologically inferior, they were culturally inferior and thus doomed to permanent servitude.

The race question is full of interest to the sociologist. Are differences of race so fundamental that it is impossible to combine all of them into organic unity, is the problem which confronts many nations, especially the United States. The Union is to be the laboratory where the combining possibilities of races will be tested. The experiment will decide whether widely different races can be amalgamated in a single civilization. The possibilities are threefold: (1) destruction of the weaker elements in the struggle for existence, (2) the reduction of these elements to a state of servitude, (3) elevation of the now inferior elements to actual equality of hereditary right in the civilization. Many fear the first possibility for the Indians; the second fate is often predicted for the Negroes; while the third is anticipated for the Chinese and other Eastern peoples.[20]

Other authors referred broadly to the physical basis of society or to the cultural evolution of the races or presumed that racial capabilities could be explained through normal curves of intelligence tests. A few writers of popular textbooks, such as James Q. Dealy, were militant Anglo-Saxonists who spoke of the dangers of black/white amalgamation to the "vigorous Anglo-Saxon race."[21]

The widespread belief that blacks and other nonwhite races had nothing positive to offer Anglo-Saxons made sociology prior to World War I a lily-white profession. W.E.B. DuBois, George Haynes, Richard Wright, and other black sociologists were completely excluded from professional affairs. Leaders in the Academy of the Political and Social Sciences and the American Sociological Society refused DuBois's requests for the development of race research centers in prominent white universities.[22] Early articles and book reviews on the condition of blacks published in the *American Journal of Sociology* also displayed disdain—if not hostility—for blacks and their presence in society.[23] The assumption among professional sociologists that nothing black could be good was revealed in an editorial footnote on the first page of Mary Blauvelt's 1901 article in the *American Journal of Sociology*. The article was a positive assessment of a black women's social club. The footnote read, "The writer of this paper has no Negro blood. She is a graduate of Wellesley and has done two years of graduate study in Oxford, England."[24] The editors felt that their readers assumed that only blacks had positive things to say about blacks which represented "propaganda" to them.

At first glance it might seem that mainstream sociologists prior to World War I ignored blacks due to the infancy of empirical methodologies. But this neglect actually resulted from racially biased ideas prevalent in the sociological community, which led to a lack of professional interest in blacks. This argument becomes especially convincing when the contributions of researchers marginal to the institutional nexus of mainstream sociology who did significant empirical sociological studies of blacks are acknowledged.

THE REGIONAL ORIGINS AND THE INSTITUTIONAL NEXUS OF PROFESSIONAL SOCIOLOGY

Before World War I, sociologists rarely inquired into black life mainly because they assumed that blacks were the South's problem. This attitude was easily defended because the redistribution of the black population from South to North was yet to begin, and professional sociology still was very much a midwestern and eastern discipline. Sociology in the South and West did not begin to professionalize until the years between the wars.[25]

This assumption was reaffirmed when in 1908, Alfred Stone, a southern planter, published his *Studies in the American Race Problem*.[26] This was the first sociologically oriented text on black people to gain widespread popularity in the sociological community. The reviewer in *The American Journal of Sociology* stated: "With due respect to some other valuable presentations on the same subject, the book as it appears represents the most valuable contribution yet appearing on the race problems of the United States."[27]

During the formative years of sociology, articles and books on race relations often supported their statements by citing Stone's text. His analysis of racial friction was even incorporated in the sociological bible, *Introduction to the Science of Sociology*, by Robert E. Park and Ernest Burgess. Acceptance of this attitude was made explicit in the closing paragraph of a review of Stone's text that appeared in the *American Journal of Sociology* in 1909:

. . . the people of the south are best situated to understand the negro and his problem, and can and will do more for him in a practical way than theorists who live at a distance. It is a national burden which the whole nation must sympathetically bear, but the people of the South represent the direct remedial agent.[28]

Only a few northern-based sociologists dissented from the established point of view and insisted that the Negro problem was also a northern problem. The pros and cons of this argument were spelled out in discussions generated around a paper read by Stone at the 1907 annual meeting of the American Sociological Society and published in the 1908 volume of *The American Journal of Sociology*, under the title "Is Race Friction Between Blacks and Whites in the United States Growing and Inevitable?" This article contained many assumptions about racial differences which were held by the professional sociological community until the early 1920s.[29]

Stone argued that race friction was based upon racial antipathy, which he defined as an "abstract mental quality" resulting in a "natural contrariety, repugnancy of qualities, or incompatibility between individuals or groups which are sufficiently differentiated to constitute what, for want of a more exact term, we call races." "Repugnant feeling" between racial groups was an instinctive dislike for which "sometimes no good reason can be given." Stone defined friction as primarily a "lack of harmony," or a "mutual irritation," and remarked that due to antipathy it increased in the case of racial groups. This observation led him to say, "We do not have to depend on race riots or other acts of violence as a measure of the growth of race friction. Its existence may be manifested by a look or a gesture as well as by a word or by an act." Racial friction, the concrete expression of racial antipathy, varied according to the form of contact between two racial groups.

A primary cause of friction between whites and other racial groups, Stone asserted, came from "the vague . . . but wholly real feeling of 'pressure' which comes to the white man instinctively in the presence of a mass of people of a different race." He referred to the example of the Chinese on the Pacific Coast, where "there is a direct relation between the mollified attitude of the people of the Pacific Coast and the fact that the Chinese population decreased between 1890 and 1900." Stone believed that numerical pressure was the primary cause for race friction. But he also thought that race friction, and the violence that results from it, were contingent not only upon numbers, "but also other influences, e.g., each group feeling superior to each other." In the postbellum period, according to Stone, race problems derived from black demands for equality and from the refusal of whites to acquiesce. In the antebellum period, racial antipathy was held in check by a relationship (slavery) which minimized race contact and race association (two concepts he considered crucially different) in a mutually accepted unequal intergroup relationship and thereby reduced the chances of race friction.

This conclusion created a paradox in Stone's argument. Since he believed that there was something inherent in race which made interracial contact repugnant, he contended that "good intergroup relationships" such as Southern slavery and the "more tolerant" attitude of white northerners, were artificial. The human behavior he was trying to explain was epiphenomenal. This became particularly clear when later in the article he noted that the extent to which racial antipathy triggered race friction was contingent upon local conditions. But he then reversed his argument by stating that "racial antipathy is a present, latent force in all of us." Thus, local conditions were also treated as epiphenomena.

Stone made it clear that the crux of the problem resided in race association, not race contact. He warned that Emancipation would lead to increased interracial association, which would result from social equality. He thought whites could not tolerate this because of their "instinctive mental impulse" or "instincts of self-preservation." They would be forced, when confronted with a sufficient number of blacks (which would create, according to Stone, a feeling of political danger or unrest), to do any number of things to keep black people in their place and thus maintain white dominance.

In essence, Stone perceived the Negro problem as a question of political control over a potentially dangerous and naturally repugnant racial group. Race friction occurred in proportion to the numerical strength of blacks and was aggravated by their demands for social equality. Since certain blacks with "white blood" (that is, mulattoes) were vying for social equality, Stone predicted that race friction would increase.

Stone's article was discussed at length by several social observers, most of whom were employed in northern academic institutions.[30] They wondered whether general racial friction was inevitable or whether the Negro problem was only a Southern problem. Several of the academicians predicted the expansion of the Negro problem by pointing out instances of crime and other "immoralities" which occurred as blacks migrated to northern urban areas. Their assessments were based on the conventional wisdom that blacks were better controlled in the rural South. This assumption paralleled Booker T. Washington's claim that blacks should remain in the South and be taught industrial skills.

To limit black people to menial, rural occupations was an effective strategy of social control. It prevented them from competing with whites economically, kept them politically impotent, and more importantly prevented them from migrating to the North. The fear was that if blacks migrated to northern cities, their "natural Negroness" would not be controllable. Therefore, to most of the discussants, the Negro problem revolved around a possible increase of immorality as the numerical proportion of blacks increased. To southerners, the Negro problem necessitated the maintenance of political dominance by whites.

W.E.B. DuBois of Atlanta University was the only discussant who took issue with Stone in several critical areas. First, DuBois disagreed that race consciousness was an event occurring only among the black elite, most of whom were mulattoes. Second, he dismissed the racial antipathy argument as only another variant of Anglo-Saxon social philosophy. Third, he argued that there was a desperate need for scientific study of the race problem. (Unfortunately, such efforts were only taking place in Atlanta.) Sociologists turned deaf ears to his plea for at least eighteen years, even though Stone did not offer any empirical evidence to support his stand, while two of the discussants (both of whom were of southern birth) defended their stance on the Negro problem from personal experience. DuBois foresaw that racial segregation could not be maintained in a world becoming smaller and more economically interrelated. But sociologists continued to use Stone's arguments in their own articles and books about blacks until the early 1920s; this was evidence that DuBois's criticisms were not taken seriously. Until the end of World War I, most writers on the Negro problem in *The American Journal of Sociology* continued to discuss the mental limitations of blacks, the natural repugnance between the white and dark races, and the qualities of "black immorality."

THE SOUTHERN ROOTS AND PREMISES OF THE SOCIOLOGY OF BLACKS PRIOR TO WORLD WAR I

As seen by the influence of Alfred Stone's works on race, pre–World War I empirical inquiries into the conditions of blacks were the province of southerners or researchers employed in southern-based institutions. The extent of the southern monopoly on the sociological analysis of blacks becomes even clearer when contrasted with the works and influences of numerous other researchers, for example: W.E.B. DuBois of Atlanta University, Kelly Miller of Howard University, George Haynes of Fisk University, Thomas J. Jones of Hampton Institute, T. P. Bailey of the University of Mississippi, Howard Odum, Willis D. Weatherford of the Southern YMCA, and Robert E. Park of Tuskegee Institute.[31]

The institutionalization of the southern perspective in the sociology of blacks was reinforced through the establishment, in 1912, of the Phelps-Stokes Fund Fellowship Program for southern white scholars. The purpose of the program was to encourage graduate students attending major southern universities to study blacks scientifically through empirical analyses never before encouraged in white academia.[32]

The program's greatest accomplishment was the sponsorship of its first fellow, Thomas J. Woofter, Jr., a graduate student at the University of Georgia in 1912. Woofter enjoyed a long and profitable career as a race scholar and contributed immensely to the work of the Phelps-Stokes Fund, the Commission on Interracial Cooperation, the University of North Carolina Department of Sociology, and New Deal reform programs. He helped to write some of the first government reports on the origins and impact of the migration of blacks, wrote the first American college textbook on race relations, and published one of the first accounts on the urbanization of the black population.[33]

Prior to World War I, most of the more popular sociological analyses of blacks were concerned, in part, with the problems of adjustment black people had experienced from the end of the Civil War through the first decades of the twentieth century. This approach to the Negro problem was part of a larger search for order in the midst of a rapidly changing America. Although all early writers on race discussed the moral development of blacks, most of the white writers also stressed the ex-slaves' "need" to be under white control.[34]

THOMAS J. JONES'S SOCIOLOGY OF BLACK EDUCATION

The interest of these researchers in the moral development of blacks was most apparent in their appraisals of the value of industrial education for blacks. This educational emphasis arose from the desire of capitalists and their representatives on foundation boards to shape blacks into efficient marginal workers in the evolving corporate state in the rural South and later in the urban North. Thus the well-known debate between W.E.B. DuBois and Booker T. Washington on "proper" education for blacks took on political and economic as well as intellectual ramifications. Thomas J. Jones's sociology of black education clarifies the political and economic function that industrial education took on.

Jones's perspective illustrates the racially biased use of empiricism in early sociological studies of black conditions. Jones, like Howard Odum, was an early student of the eminent Columbia sociologist Franklin Giddings. Jones, a Welshman, taught sociology at Hampton Institute from 1902 to 1909 before moving to the federal Bureau of Education and to the Phelps-Stokes Fund as its director of education in 1910. Since Caroline Stokes's major purpose in establishing the Phelps-Stokes Fund was to support education for blacks in the American South and in Africa, Jones was able to play a central role in shaping education for black people on both sides of the Atlantic.[35]

Like Booker T. Washington and General Samuel Armstrong of Hampton Institute, Jones was an enthusiastic supporter of industrial education for blacks, since he believed it enabled them to adapt to their "natural" environment—the rural South—and since it was suited to their supposed mental limitations. Soon after joining the Phelps-Stokes Fund, Jones was able to spread his ideas on "proper" education for blacks to a wide audience when he was commissioned by the federal Bureau of Education to make an extensive survey and evaluation of black schools in the United States.[36]

The idea of this nationwide assessment developed when Anson Stokes of the Phelps-Stokes Fund asked his friend Booker T. Washington how $5,000 to $10,000 could best be spent. Washington suggested a survey of black schools, to help determine which ones were weak in industrial education. The study could also benefit foundations, which were planning for unprecedented intervention in education for blacks in the South. Although Washington wanted Robert E. Park, one of his chief advisors, to make this nationwide study, Jones managed to get himself appointed to the task. He considered it a great opportunity to nationalize the Tuskegee idea of education for blacks.[37]

It took Jones three years to complete the survey, which was published in two volumes as *Negro Education: A Study of the Private and Higher Schools for Colored People in the United States*. The study became the base for nationalization of the Tuskegee model of education and a source of inspiration for the adoption of the model in the British African colonies in the period between the wars.[38]

Even though Jones claimed that the study was an objective evaluation which showed a "national" need for sound industrial schools for black students, it is obvious through his selection and interpretation of data that he used empiricism to justify his personal views. His total reliance on 1910 census reports created a static picture of blacks. His "finding" that most of them lived in the rural South allowed him to make interpretations and recommendations about "congruent adaptations" in communities, that is, rural industrial training. Jones's interpretation had an anti-urban bias and, more important, produced the fatalistic impression that blacks were doomed to remain in the rural South.[39] The North, as a supplier of teachers and philanthropic funds, could contribute to the alleviation of the South's Negro problem but, supposedly, did not have a Negro problem of its own.[40]

If Jones had been more concerned about an impartial assessment of education for blacks than with crusading for the nationalization of the Tuskegee idea of education, he would have considered the implications of the migration patterns of blacks between 1865 and 1910, which clearly predicted the future urbanization and redistribution of the black population. This urbanization made rural industrial skills only marginally important, if not obsolete.

Jones's use of empiricism to legitimize his racial biases is also evident in his discussion of the failure of many traditional black schools. He attributed their shortcomings to moral inadequacies rather than to the socioeconomic pressures that forced conformity with the white educational system. Industrial education, he maintained, was needed to provide adaptable skills and character for blacks but was not intended to give them the economic and social mobility to move into significant positions in society.

Jones's sociology of black education influenced the direction and ideology of foundation support of black education for several years.

WORLD WAR I AND AFTER

World War I had a profound impact on American race relations and radically altered foundation sponsorship of sociological research on the black experience. The economic opportunities of the war accelerated the black migration to the city, which in turn dramatically swelled urban black communities and caused frequent clashes with whites as well as conflict between established and migrant black families. In the South, lynchings and other forms of racial violence increased as whites anticipated the return of black soldiers. The white elite concern for the impact of migrants and the growing racial tension both in the North and in the South is apparent in the great number of articles discussing these issues in popular and professional periodicals and newspapers between 1917 and 1923.[41]

This immense flow of articles was symptomatic of the culture shock white elite groups experienced as it became apparent that blacks could no longer be considered the South's problem. In the late 1910s and early 1920s, elite groups within and outside the social sciences began to expand the image of black status from a regional to a national base. It was no longer realistic to view blacks as a minority group fixed in the rural South. Rather, they were increasingly viewed as a competitive national minority in an urban context. While midwestern and eastern sociologists began to discuss the social control implications of urban black adjustment and "disturbance problems," southern sociologists began to warn about how black migration to the industrial North was a strike against the South's faltering rural economy. Midwestern, eastern, and southern sociological interpretations of the black experience were interrelated in the growing awareness and concern over the dramatic demographic redistribution of the black population.[42]

While perceptions about black status began to change among American sociologists, the absence of viable theories and reliable empirical data through which to redefine the Negro problem became painfully obvious. Under these circumstances, the importance of Robert E. Park's entry into professional sociology and foundation financing of race relations social science research became clear.

Park's move from Tuskegee Institute to the University of Chicago in 1913 could not have been timed better.[43] Within a few years, the black migration north, race riots, and the assertive demands of the National Association for the Advancement of Colored People and more radical organizations eroded the premises of biological and cultural Anglo-Saxonism in social thought and brought rural industrial education as a method of social control increasingly into question. Park's ideas about racial attitudes and interaction between racial groups were accepted readily in professional sociology and political circles, since they explained changing race relations in a society presumed to be permanently segregated. Park's acceptance of industrial education while at Tuskegee was transformed into sociological theory at Chicago by denying the validity of biological racial differences and explaining patterns of racial segregation in social terms, as a product of sentiments and attitudes. In this way, Park turned social Darwinism on its side. Park's replacement of Anglo-Saxonism with "horizontal social Darwinism" became the major theoretical foundation of the Chicago school of race relations.

The Park race cycle framework and E. Franklin Frazier's application of Ernest Burgess's concentric zone model (another example of horizontal social Darwinism) to family organization, mobility, and community of the urban blacks were the major manifestations of the paradigm of horizontal social Darwinism in the 1920s and early 1930s. Both were acceptable in the profession and among civic leaders, since they explained social change in a biracial society without tampering with the political-economic structure of racial caste.

Horizontal social Darwinism eroded, but did not destroy, the question of biological differences between races.[44] Sociologists continued to study sociobiological issues through the mid–1930s, as is evident in the large number of book reviews devoted to sociobiology published in the *American Journal of Sociology* and *Social Forces* in the 1920s, and the numerous sociobiological articles in *Social Forces* in the 1930s. The selection of sociobiologist Frank Hankins as the first book review editor of *Social Forces* in the 1920s and as the first editor of the *American Sociological Review* in 1935 indicates that biological explanations of human differences were still respected alternative paradigms in the interwar years.[45] There lurked a belief that sentiments advocating racial separatism might be biologically based. As Benjamin Bowser has noted, many prominent interwar sociologists were uncomfortable with explanations of racial differences which emphasized *only* social conditioning.[46] Such thoughts were incongruent with the ontology of an apartheid society.

We now turn to a closer look at Park, since he, more than anyone else, professionalized research on the Negro problem and made way for foundation sponsorship of it between the World Wars.

NOTES

1. E. Digby Baltzell, *The Protestant Establishment: Aristocracy and Caste in America* (New York: Random House, 1964); Richard Hofstader, *Social Darwinism in American Thought* (Philadelphia: University of Pennsylvania Press, 1944); John Higham, *Strangers in the Land* (New York: Atheneum, 1963); Barbara M. Solomon, *Ancestors and Immigrants* (Cambridge, Mass.: Harvard University Press, 1956); Forrest G. Wood, *Black Scare: The Racist Response to Emancipation and Reconstruction* (Berkeley, Calif.: University of California Press, 1968).

2. Ferdinand Lundberg, *America's 60 Families* (New York: Vanguard Press, 1938); Robert H. Wiebe, *The Search for Order* (New York: Hill and Wang, 1967). Historian Peter T. Hall claims that the search for a new order began among American businessmen years before the emergence of professionalization among middle-class occupational groups. Peter T. Hall, "Corporate Philanthropy, 1860–1960: An Overview" (Presented at the Program for Not for Profit Organizations Seminar Series, Yale University, February 16, 1984).

3. Winthrop D. Jordan, *White Over Black: American Attitudes Toward the Negro, 1550–1812* (Chapel Hill, N.C.: University of North Carolina Press, 1968); Ronald Takaki, *Iron Cages: Race and Culture in Nineteenth Century America* (Seattle, Wash.: University of Washington Press, 1979); Wood, *Black Scare*; Gunnar Myrdal, *An American Dilemma: The Negro Problem and Modern Democracy* (New York: Harper & Row, 1944), Chapters 1, 2; Ulysses G. Weatherley, "The Racial Element in Social Assimilation," *Publications of the American Sociological Society* 5 (1910).

4. Harmamus Hoetink, *Slavery and Race Relations in the Americas: Comparative Notes on Their Nature and Nexus* (New York: Harper Torchbooks, 1973).

5. Wiebe, *Search for Order*.

6. Recent major studies of the American Social Science Association fail to address in a significant way the organization's role in resolving the racial and ethnic dimensions of the "crisis" in authority which occurred in the last quarter of the nineteenth century and the first decades of the twentieth century. See Mary O. Furner, *Advocacy and Objectivity: A Crisis in the Professionalization of American Social Science, 1865–1905* (Lexington, Ky.: University Press of Kentucky, 1975); and Thomas L. Haskell, *The Emergence of Professional Social Science: The American Social Science Association and the Nineteenth-Century Crisis of Authority* (Urbana, Ill.: University of Illinois Press, 1977).

7. F. B. Sanborn, "Socialism and Social Science," *Journal of Social Science* 31 (1894): 40–49.

8. See, for example, Friedrick Kapp, "Immigration," *Journal of Social Science: Containing the Transactions of the American Social Science Association*, no. 2 (1870): 1–30. See also T. M. Logan, "The Opposition in the South to the Free School System" *Journal of Social Science*, no. 9 (1878): 92–100; C. A. Gardiner, "The Race Problem in the United States," *Journal of Social Science*, no. 18 (1883): 266–275; H. L. Wayland, "Higher Education for Colored People," *Journal of Social Science*, no. 34 (1896): 68–78.

9. Weatherly, "The Racial Element"; Myrdal, *An American Dilemma*, pp. 57–58, 586–587, 589, 590–591, 603.

10. Emile Durkheim, *The Division in Labor in Society* (New York: Free Press, 1938); George Fitzhugh, *Sociology for the South: or The Failure of Free Society* (New York: Burt Franklin, 1854).

11. Albion W. Small, "The Era of Sociology," *American Journal of Sociology* 1 (July 1895): 1–15; Albion W. Small, "A Decade of Sociology and Editorial," *American Journal of Sociology* 9 (July 1905): 1–10; and C.W.A. Veditz, "The American Sociological Society," *American Journal of Sociology* 11 (March 1906): 681–682. For an insightful analysis of the incomplete institutionalization and professionalization of sociology, see Henrika Kuklick, "Boundary Maintenance in American Sociology: Limitations to Academic 'Professionalization,' " *Journal of the History of the Behavioral Sciences* 16 (July 1980). An excellent examination of Albion Small's professional world view is found in Ernest Becker, *The Lost Science of Man* (New York: G. Braziller, 1971), pp. 3–70.

12. Julia and Herman Schwendinger, *The Sociologists of the Chair* (New York: Basic Books, 1974).

13. For a discussion of the regional basis of early urban sociology, see J. Graham Morgan, "Preparation for the Advent: The Establishment of Sociology as a Discipline in American Universities in the Late Nineteenth Century," *Minerva* 20 (Spring-Summer 1982): 41–42; and S. J. Diner, "Department and Discipline: The Department of Sociology at the University of Chicago, 1892–1920," *Minerva* 12 (Winter 1975).

14. For example, L. L. Bernard, Review of *Social Heredity and Social Evolution* by Herbert W. Conn, *American Journal of Sociology* 21 (March 1916): 706–708; L. L. Bernard, Review of *Naval Officers, Their Heredity and Development* by Charles B. Davenport, *American Journal of Sociology* 25 (September 1919): 241–242; L. L. Bernard, Review of *Inbreeding and Outbreeding* by Edwin M. East, *American Journal of Sociology* 26 (September 1920): 251–252; C. R. Henderson, Review of *Race Culture, or Race Suicide?* by Robert Reid Rentoul, *American Journal of Sociology* 13 (July 1907): 120–121; Fayette A. McKenzie, Review of *Immigration: A World Movement and Its American Significance* by Henry P. Fairchild, *American Journal of Sociology* 19 (March 1914): 679–681; E.B. Woods, Review of *The Contributions of Demography to Eugenics* by Corrado Gini, *American Journal of Sociology* 19 (November 1913): 383–384; Scott Nearing, Review of *Race Improvement* by Helen L. Baker *American Journal of Sociology* 18 (May 1913): 846; Robert M. Yerkes, Review of *Heredity in Relation to Eugenics* by Charles B. Davenport, *American Journal of Sociology* 18 (July 1912): 115–120.

15. William I. Thomas and Florian Znaniecki, *The Polish Peasant in Europe and America* (New York: Knopf, 1927; 1958).

16. Ibid.

17. Floyd H. House, *The Development of Sociology* (New York: McGraw-Hill, 1936), pp. 345–355; Gunnar Myrdal, *An American Dilemma*, vol. 1, pp. 83–123; E. Franklin Frazier, "Sociological Theory and Race Relations," *American Sociological Review* 12 (June 1947): 265–267, reprinted in G. Franklin Edwards, *E. Franklin Frazier on Race Relations* (Chicago: University of Chicago Press, 1968); Howard W. Odum, *American Sociology* (New York: Longman, Green, 1951), pp. 322–343; Thomas Pettigrew, *The Sociology of Race Relations* (New York, 1980).

18. Boas's major work usually cited in discussions such as this one is *The Mind of Primitive Man* (New York: Macmillan Company, 1911). It should be remembered, however, that although Boas held positive opinions about Africans, he had traditional beliefs about the mental and cultural "underdevelopment" of Afro-Americans. See Franz Boas, "The Outlook for the American Negro," Commencement Address at Atlanta University, May 31, 1906, Atlanta University Leaflet, No. 19; "Changing the Racial

Attitudes of White Americans," letter from Boas to Andrew Carnegie, November 30, 1906; and "Race Problems in America," address as vice-president of Section H, American Association for the Advancement of Science, Baltimore, 1908, as published in *Science* 29 (1909): 839–849, reprinted in George W. Stocking, ed., *The Shaping of American Anthropology, 1883–1911: A Franz Boas Reader* (New York: Basic Books, 1974), respectively, pp. 310–316, 316–318, 318–330.

19. See Walter Wilcox's Contributions in Alfred H. Stone's *Studies in the American Race Problem* (New York: Doubleday, Page & Company, 1908), pp. 493–529. Mark Aldrich, "Progressive Economics and Scientific Racism: Walter Wilcox and Black Americans, 1895–1910," *Phylon* 40 (Spring 1979): 1–14.

20. Albion W. Small and George Vincent, *An Introduction to the Study of Society* (New York: American Book Company, 1894), p. 179.

21. James Q. Dealey, *Sociology: Its Development and Applications* (New York: D. Appleton, 1909, 1920), pp. 378, 440.

22. William E. B. DuBois, Comment on Alfred H. Stone, "Is Race Friction Between Blacks and Whites in the United States Growing and Inevitable?" *American Journal of Sociology* 13 (July 1908): 839–840; Schwendinger, *Sociologists of the Chair*, pp. 503–508.

23. Paul S. Reinsch, "The Negro Race and European Civilization," *American Journal of Sociology* 11 (July 1905): 145–167; Stone, *Studies in the American Race Problem*, pp. 676–697; Charlotte P. Gilman, "A Suggestion on the Negro Problem," *American Journal of Sociology* 13 (July 1903): 78–86; Alzada P. Comstock, "Chicago Housing Conditions: The Problem of the Negro" *American Journal of Sociology* 18 (July 1912): 241–257; Charles Ellwood, a future president of the American Sociological Society, was especially vicious in his comments about blacks as the *American Journal of Sociology*'s chief reviewer of race relations books in the early 1900s; Charles Ellwood, Review of *The Negro* by Thomas N. Page, *American Journal of Sociology* 11 (March 1906): 698–699; Charles Ellwood, Reivew of *The Negro and the Nction: A History of American Slavery and Enfranchisement* by George S. Merriam, *American Journal of Sociology* 12 (September 1906): 274–275; Charles Ellwood, Review of *Races and Immigrants in America* by John R. Commons, *American Journal of Sociology* 13 (January 1908): 561–562; Charles Ellwood, Review of *The Negro Races* by Jerome Dowd, *American Journal of Sociology* 13 (May 1908): 855–858; Charles Ellwood, Review of *Following the Color Line* by Ray S. Baker, *American Journal of Sociology* 15 (July 1909): 119–120; Charles A. Ellwood, Review of *The Color Line* by William B. Smith, *American Journal of Sociology* 11 (January 1906): 570–575.

24. Mary T. Blauvelt, "The Race Problem," *American Journal of Sociology* 6 (July 1901): 662–672.

25. Dewey W. Grantham, *The Regional Imagination: The South and Recent American History* (Nashville: Vanderbilt University Press, 1979); Michael O'Brien; *The Idea of the American South 1920–1941* (Baltimore, Md.: Johns Hopkins University Press, 1979); and David J. Singal, *The War Within: From Victorian to Modernist Thought in the South, 1914–1945* (Chapel Hill, N.C.: University of North Carolina Press, 1982). We have no comprehensive analyses of the development of regional social science in the West.

26. Stone, *Studies in the American Race Problem*.

27. Frank W. Blackman, Review of *Studies in the American Race Problem* by Alfred H. Stone, *American Journal of Sociology* 14 (July 1909): 837.

28. Ibid. p. 837; see also Robert E. Park and Ernest W. Burgess, *Introduction to the Science of Sociology* (Chicago: University of Chicago Press, 1921; 1969 edition), pp. 634–640. The pro-southern sympathies of pre–World War I sociologists were apparent in published articles and book reviews in *The American Journal of Sociology*. For instance, see: Albion W. Small, Review of *Civil War History of the Confederate States* by Albert B. Currier, *American Journal of Sociology* (May 1901): 847–849; Albion W. Small, Review of *Reconstruction in Mississippi* by James W. Garner, *American Journal of Sociology* 7 (September 1902): 285–286; A. B. Wolfe, Review of *The Southern South* by Albert B. Hart, *American Journal of Sociology* 17 (November 1911): 411–412. Additionally, C. Vann Woodward in *The Strange Career of Jim Crow* cites the role of Sumner and Giddings' sociology in giving strength to southern segregation arguments. *The Strange Career of Jim Crow* (New York: Oxford University Press, 1957), pp. 88–89.

29. Alfred H. Stone, "Is Race Friction Between Blacks and Whites Growing and Inevitable?" *American Journal of Sociology* 13 (July 1908): 839–840. The following analysis through note 31 is drawn from the Stone article.

30. The following persons were the discussants: William E. B. DuBois (Atlanta University), Edwin L. Earp (Syracuse), John J. Halsey (Lake Forest), Edwin S. Todd (Miami University of Ohio), U. G. Weatherly (University of Indiana), and Walter L. Wilcox (Cornell).

31. William E. B. DuBois, *The Philadelphia Negro* (Philadelphia: University of Pennsylvania Press, 1899); *The Souls of Black Folk* (Chicago: A. C. McClung, 1903); *Atlanta University Publications* (New York, 1968); Kelley Miller, *Radicals and Conservatives* (1908; repr. New York: Schocken Books, 1963); George Haynes, *The Negro at Work in New York City* (New York: Columbia University Press, 1912); Thomas J. Jones, *Negro Education: A Study of the Private and Higher Schools for Colored People in the United States* (Washington, D.C., 1917); Howard Odum, *Social and Mental Traits of the Negro* (New York: Columbia University Press, 1910); Willis D. Weatherford, *Negro Life in the South* (New York: YMCA Press, 1910); Willis D. Weatherford, *Present Forces in Negro Progress* (New York: Association Press, 1912); Robert E. Park, "Negro Home Life and Standards of Living," *The Annals: The American Academy of Politican and Social Science* 49 (September 1913): 147–163; Thomas P. Bailey, *Race—Orthodoxy in the South and Other Aspects of the Negro Question* (New York: Neale, 1914).

32. Anson Phelps Stokes, *Negro Status and Race Relations in the United States, 1911–1946: The Thirty-Five Year Report of the Phelps-Stokes Fund* (New York: Anson Phelps-Stokes Fund, 1948), pp. 17–18.

33. Thomas J. Woofter, Jr., *The Basis of Racial Adjustment* (New York: Books for Library Press, 1925); *Negro Problems in Cities* (New York: Doubleday, Doran, 1928; 1969 edition); *Black Yeomanry: Life on St. Helena Island* (New York: H. Holt, 1930); *Southern Race Progress; The Wavering Color Line* (Washington, D.C.: Public Affairs Press, 1957); Thomas J. Woofter, Jr., *Negro Immigration in 1916–1917* (Washington, D.C., 1919).

34. See works cited in note 31, especially those by Bailey, Odum, Park, Stone, and Weatherford.

35. Stokes, *Negro Status and Race Relations in the United States*.

36. Kenneth J. King, *Pan-Africanism and Education* (London: Oxford University Press, 1971), pp. 21–58.

37. Ibid.

38. Thomas J. Jones, *Negro Education*.

39. Ibid., pp. 22–24.

40. Ibid., p. 1.

41. For example, W. H. Baldwin, III, "Negro Labor Migration," *New York Evening Post Saturday Magazine*, 3 (February 1917): 6–7; J. M. Boddy, "Getting at the True Causes of Migration of Negro Labor from the South," *Economic World* 18 (March 1918); Adelene Moffat, "New Problems Caused by the Importation of Colored Labor into the North," *Proceedings of the National Federation of Settlements* (1918): 18–20; T. B. Moroney, "Americanization of the Negro," *Catholic World* 113 (August 1921): 577–584; "New York State Probe of Bolshevism Asked: Union League Club Committee Declares Facts Warrant Full Inquiry Especially as to Those Who Seek to Stir Negroes: Formenting Discord Among Negroes," *National Civic Federation Review* 4 (March 25, 1919): 12–13, 20; W. J. Schieffelin, "Harmful Rush of Negro Workers to the North," *New York Times Magazine* (June 3, 1917): 7; W. O. Scroggs, "Interstate Migration of Negro Population," *Journal of Political Economy* 25 (December 1917): 1034–1043; "Will Negroes Stay in Industry?" *Survey* (December 14, 1918): 348–349; A. W. Taylor, "When the Negro Comes North," *Christian Century*, 40 (May 31, 1923): 691–692; "Exodus in America," *New Statesman* 9 (July 28, 1917): 393–395.

42. Ernest W. Burgess, Review of *The Color Line in Ohio* by Frank U. Quillin, *American Journal of Sociology* 19 (March 1914): 695–696; Ernest W. Burgess, "The Growth of the City," reprinted from Robert E. Park, Ernest W. Burgess, and Roderick D. McKenzie, *The City*, in *Ernest W. Burgess: On Community, Family and Delinquency* (Chicago: University of Chicago Press, 1973), p. 29; Guy B. Johnson, "Newspaper Advertisements and Negro Culture," *Social Forces* (May 1925): 706–709; Guy B. Johnson, Review of *The Negro's Struggle for Survival* by Samuel J. Holmes, *Social Forces* 17 (May 1939): 583–584; R. D. McKenzie, Review of *The Neighborhood: A Study of Local Life in the City of Columbus, Ohio*, *American Journal of Sociology* 27 (January 1922): 486–509; Gustavus Adolphus Stewart, "The New Negro Hokum," *Social Forces* 6 (March 1928): 438–445; Ulysses G. Weatherly, "In Freedom's Birthplace," by John Daniels, *American Journal of Sociology* 29 (1915): 290–304; Ulysses G. Weatherly, Review of *Industrial Conditions Among Negroes in St. Louis* by William A. Crossland, *American Journal of Sociology* 21 (July 1915): 114–115; Thomas J. Woofter, Jr., "Negro and Industrial Peace," *Survey* 45 (December 18, 1918): 420–421; Thomas J. Woofter, Jr., "The Negro on a Strike," *Social Forces* 2 (1923): 84–88; Thomas J. Woofter, Jr., "The Negro and the Farm Crisis," *Social Forces* 6 (1928): 615–620.

43. E. Franklin Frazier, "Sociological Theory and Race Relations," *American Sociological Review* 12 (June 1947): 37.

44. The interwar years were also a period of continued negative commentaries about other racial minorities. See Emory S. Bogardus, Review of *The Japanese Problem in the United States* by H. A. Millis, *The American Journal of Sociology* 22 (July 1926): 106–108; Jessie F. Steiner, Review of *Oriental Exclusion* by R. D. McKenzie, *American Journal of Sociology* 34 (1929): 732; Max Sylvus, Review of *Mexican Immigration to the United States* by Manuel Gamio, *American Journal of Sociology* 36 (November 1930): 485–486.

45. See the following book reviews and articles for a sense of the diverse survival of sociobiology during interwar years: F. Stuart Chapin, Review of *Studies in Evolution and Eugenics* by Samuel J. Homes, *American Journal of Sociology* 3 (November 1924):

357–358; N. M. Grier, Review of *The Genetical Theory of Natural Selection* by R. A. Fisher, *Social Forces* 9 (December 1930): 295–296; Frank H. Hankins, "Social Biology" (Book Review Essay), *Social Forces* 12 (1933): 242; Samuel J. Holmes, "The Increasing Growth-Rate of the Negro Population," *American Journal of Sociology* 2 (1936): 202–214; Floyd N. House, Review of *The Factors of Social Evolution* by Theodore DeLaguna, *American Journal of Sociology* 32 (November 1926): 510–511; Floyd M. House, Review of *The Essential Factors of Social Evolution* by Thomas N. Carver, *American Journal of Sociology* 41 (November 1935): 373; Edward B. Reuter, Review of *Prometheus, or Biology and the Advancement of Man* by H. S. Jennings, *American Journal of Sociology* 31 (March 1926): 692; Edward B. Reuter, Review of *Heredity and the Social Problem Group* by E. J. Lidbetter, *American Journal of Sociology* 40 (September 1934): 284; Edward B. Reuter, Review of *Heredity and Environment* by R. S. Woodworth, *American Journal of Sociology* 42 (1942): 780.

46. Benjamin P. Bowser, "The Contributions of Blacks to Sociological Knowledge: A Problem of Theory and Role to 1950," *Phylon* 42 (1981): 180–193.

3

Robert E. Park of Tuskegee and Chicago

Robert Ezra Park was the father of modern research on the Negro problem in American sociology. Before Park arrived on the scene in the mid–1910s, there was no well-respected sociologist specializing in race relations. Walter Wilcox was an economist; Alfred H. Stone was a planter; Charles H. Cooley was a social psychologist; William I. Thomas and Edward Ross concentrated on European immigrants; and William E. B. DuBois was black and too radical. Park played a central role in legitimating race-relations research in American sociology. His students, Charles S. Johnson in particular, carried out his ideas through foundation sponsorship.

BOOKER T. AND ROBERT E.: POPULAR MYTHS

Booker T. Washington, through his sponsorship of Robert E. Park, was a founder of the Chicago school of race relations. But the facts of their relationship have been distorted. Biographers of Park who mention his Tuskegee days simply discuss briefly how Booker T. Washington sensitized him to southern race relations. Another popular version of the relationship between Washington and Park suggests that Park, as Tuskegee's chief public relations officer for several years, was the ghostwriter of numerous books and articles bearing Washington's name. This second interpretation portrays Park as an intelligent, prolific, white journalist who helped to build and sustain the career of a black leader who lacked a writer's skill.[1]

Some accounts about Booker T. Washington do not even mention Robert E. Park. This oversight is not due to lack of data—the Booker T. Washington and Robert E. Park Papers are full of materials on the relationship between the two men.[2] But those scholars who have done the most extensive work on Washington have been historians more interested in Washington's racial philosophy, his impact on black education, and to a lesser extent the political economy of black underdevelopment, than on his influence on the careers of the men and women he employed. Historians may also have been embarrassed by the unusual situation of Park, a white man working for a black, and by his dependency on Washington, revealed in the archival materials.

Those historians of sociology who have described Park's Tuskegee days most extensively have been his students.[3] However, these accounts provide no comprehensive discussion of how Park's Tuskegee experiences—let alone his complex relationship with Washington—influenced his work in Chicago. Their rosy eulogies about their mentor mitigate discussion about the central role of the Washington-Park relationship in developing what would eventually be called the Chicago school of race relations.

A probable argument would claim that it is not necessary to consider Washington's impact on Park's career, since Washington was not a sociologist. This hypothetical argument entertains a questionable standard in the traditional historiography of sociological thought. Given the necessity of funding for intellectual activity, patrons outside the social sciences have inevitably played an important part in the production of social scientific knowledge. The world views and values of patrons are as crucial as the beliefs and research interests of their clients in shaping such knowledge. Additionally, it is imperative to explore shifts in scholars' interpretations of reality and those of their patrons.

Park was born in Red Wing, Minnesota, in 1864. His biographers portray Park's pre-Chicago days as the glamorous and exciting story of a man who enjoyed employment and education, graduate study here and abroad, newspaper reporting, reform work, and public relations activities. Actually, until Park arrived at Chicago in 1913, he was financially insecure and did not know what to do with himself, except to find ways to make money. He represented in the flesh the sociological concept he coined—the marginal man. Thus, although it is true that Park was a great admirer of Booker T. Washington's work, it was his financial insecurity which led him to accept employment from Washington and entangle himself in investment schemes which fostered racial accommodation.[4]

Information about Park's financial condition during the first thirty-six years of his life, which concluded with his stint as a reporter for a midwestern newspaper, is scanty. The available data reveal Park's insecurity and restlessness, which generated much anxiety in his life. His wife, Clara, exerted tremendous influence over her husband's journalism career and was an important sounding board during his Chicago years. A brilliant writer, Clara maintained contact with prospective writers and gave Park numerous ideas for articles. The following advice Clara gave her husband soon after he arrived at the University of Chicago exemplifies her concern over the future of his career:

I suppose one of the reasons you have more students this year is that the subject of your lectures is more alluring. Hardly anyone seems to study the Negro, but almost everyone is more or less interested in crowds even if in trying to escape from them. I think if you put lots of ginger into what you have to say that you will make yourself famous, and your newspaper training helps you there, to make what you have to say, "get across." After all, it is very nice to know that you have made your niche, and that you fit there, and can go to work from this added advantage of a recognized standpoint.[5]

Clara Park's family, which was financially secure, also had a great influence in directing Park's career and giving him financial advice.[6]

Park's interest in race relations predated his involvement with the New York Colonialization Society and the Tuskegee Institute. In a sketchy diary he kept in the 1880s or 1890s, he refers to race-related issues in the course of his involvement with the Republican party.[7]

Park came to Booker T. Washington's attention through his involvement with the Congo Reform Association and accepted Washington's offer of a job in public relations not only because he agreed with the Tuskegee conception of black education and race relations, but, more importantly, because he needed money. Working on the Tuskegee job as well as for several news media, Park attempted to become financially solvent. But it was still not enough. His wife had to work, and he was dependent upon relatives on both sides to pay his house mortgage. Washington often agreed to pay him in cash advances. When Park's father became seriously ill in Minnesota, Washington paid his fare to Florida for recovery and gave him a house complete with servants. Thus, even though relatives and friends could not understand why Park continued to work in the South, for "niggers" as they put it, it was clearly a matter of survival.[8] Park's love for the facts and human feature stories had their origins in his journalism background. But Washington and his machine were also influential in developing these elements of Park's sociological thinking about race relations. Because Washington needed accurate figures to support his arguments, Park had to familiarize himself with data sources yielding statistical information on black conditions. But given the general audiences Washington addressed, life histories were also needed to balance statistical presentations.

While working for Washington, Park invested in real estate and in enterprises sponsored by the Negro Business League. The league, founded by Booker T. Washington and financed by Julius Rosenwald, was an effort to demonstrate the feasibility of black business development in a formally segregated society as a source for black self-help. In his work for Washington, which included encouraging accommodative black economic activity, Park was a great supporter of the league and attempted to reap financial benefits from its activities. Park's interest in making a profit from the Negro Business League ventures is just as revealing about his conformity to racial accommodation and formal segregation as was his devotion to the philosophy of black industrial education.[9]

Park made three intellectual contributions to the elaboration of the ideologies of racial accommodation during his Tuskegee years—his ghostwriting for Washington and his secretary Emmett Scott; his own speeches and articles; and the Negro Encyclopedia Project.[10] In all three, Park displayed a sociological perspective which was to be the basis of his future professional posture.

Park's work for Washington and Scott involved planning and writing letters to influential newspaper editors, particularly just before the launching of a major Tuskegee campaign in a certain city or country. He also wrote and edited many of Washington's and Scott's speeches, articles, and books. Park never wrote anything for his superiors without their input and control. Correspondence between Park and his superiors contain editorial remarks by Washington and Scott and their final stamp of approval or rejection. Park was a public relations man, not the chief Tuskegee ideologue. Scott's and Washington's correspondence to him, which often had a condescending tone, suggests his unquestionably subordinate position.

Park's capacity to give Washington and his assistants what they wanted was due to his deep admiration for the Tuskegee ideology. Articles and conference papers bearing his name showed his belief in "racial" uplift and Washington's accommodative black industrial education. His enthusiasm for black industrial education was indicated also in his successful attempt to persuade Washington to extend the Tuskegee idea to British colonial Africa. Through this move, Park sowed the seeds of the career of another European-descent sociologist: Thomas J. Jones, who, as the Phelps-Stokes Fund's director of Negro education, activated the extension of the Tuskegee model to British colonial Africa.[11]

Park's attempt to draw parallels between the educational needs of native Africans and those of Southern blacks created a contradiction which represents the complexity of his race consciousness. Between 1904 and 1913, Park published radical exposés of King Leopold II in the Congo. Soon after George Edmond Pierre Achille Morel-de-Ville (E. D. Morel), the British spearheader of the Congo Reform Association movement, visited the United States in 1904, Park organized the American chapter through the Massachusetts Commission of Justice.

Morel was a radical reformer, "one of Britain's most powerful pamphleteers,"[12] who was determined to expose Belgian King Leopold II for exploiting natural resources and natives for personal gain. The major problem Morel faced was Leopold II's masterful manipulation of European and American public opinion to make himself appear as a generous benefactor of the Congo and its peoples. He planted agents in Great Britain, France, Germany, and the United States who wrote flattering books and newspaper articles about his Congo activities. The joining of Park's American chapter to the Morel effort to bring Leopold II's tyranny to public view strengthened the movement, since it helped to solidify European public opinion against the king—it could no longer be claimed that the effort merely grew from British dislike of Belgium.

Park joined Morel's organization and staged a brief public relations campaign against Leopold because he agreed personally with the Englishman's radical views about the race problem in Africa, the Congo in particular.[13] In his assault on King Leopold II he displayed a profound awareness of how elites create and control the production of knowledge.[14]

Park maintained a radical posture on the Congo throughout his affiliation with Tuskegee Institute. But at the same time, he offered a routine accommodative defense of Tuskegee and its work in the South, stressing its masses uplift function.[15] He stressed the value of industrial and manual education, which would give its subjects a guaranteed, albeit limited, function in society. He did not totally dismiss academic education, but insisted that it was best rooted in occupational preparation.[16] Park also emphasized that the sociopolitical control function of Tuskegee would assure the constructiveness of its alumni.[17]

Thus, although Park was very aware and concerned about exploitation and control of indigenous African peoples by Europeans, this concern was transformed into an apologetic position when the issue was African Americans in the South. He did not see this contradiction, however, and in fact highly recommended the extension of the Tuskegee model to Africa.[18] Interestingly enough, although he described at length the adaptive function of Tuskegee and similar institutions in developing the black masses, he was silent about how the model could be applied in Africa without inflicting the very kind of imposition and control he criticized.

There were, however, some consistencies in Park's views about Africans and African Americans. Nowhere in Park's radical expose of King Leopold II, for example, did he advocate a free African state in the Congo. He criticized the way European intervention in the Congo was handled, but did not imply that European colonialism was wrong. Like Morel, Park was a radical reformer but not a revolutionary. In his writings on Tuskegee and in his later publications on race relations, he criticized the means by which whites in America exploited and abused blacks and other minorities, but he never called into question the legitimacy of white domination.[19]

Park's enthusiasm for white-dominated industrial education and his avid investment in racial accommodation explain why he began to feel estranged from Tuskegee in 1912. The 1912 International Conference on the Negro, sponsored by Tuskegee, represented the beginning of the end of Washington's unshakable support of industrial education and racial accommodation. That year, Park began to express concern over Washington's and Scott's growing reluctance to support completely the Tuskegee idea. Washington and Scott were critical of his concern.[20] Park was also unsuccessful in getting Washington to support seriously the organization of a research center.[21]

Meeting William I. Thomas at the 1912 conference marked a turning point in Park's career. Thomas offered not only intellectual stimulation (Park introduced Thomas to the Negro and Thomas gave Park social psychological insight), but eventually an offer from Chicago that gave Park, near fifty, a security he had never had before. No longer would he have to moonlight and get involved in investment schemes. He did, however, continue his hack work—he wrote or finished at least one paper and one book involving W. I. Thomas.[22] As Park's professional eminence increased and Thomas's decreased, hack work was no longer a necessity. But Park learned the benefits of being a hack—he used his students to promote his own career by writing introductions for their books and sponsoring those who popularized his ideas.

This is not to suggest that Park purposely exploited his students, but to point out that habits learned in an early stage of adult development do not necessarily disappear in later stages. In some instances, they eventually become subconscious. By the time Park began to train students extensively in the 1920s, he did not see anything wrong either with insisting on the devout emulation of his ideas or with putting his hand on the work of each student.

ROBERT E. PARK'S PROFESSIONAL VIEWS ON RACE, CULTURE, AND CIVILIZATION

Park's anti-activism was connected with his support of laissez-faire policies regarding American racial minorities. So was his concept of "natural history." He was dedicated to a biracial society which should advocate racial justice, but not racial equality. An analysis of his professional work at Chicago is in order.

Park never formulated a systematic sociological theory of race relations. The so-called Parkian theories of race relations, particularly the "race cycle theory" are his students' creations. Park presented most of his statements as conjectures, personal impressions, and "frames of references," while his students refined and empirically tested his ideas. However, many of Park's impressions on race, particularly regarding blacks and Asians, profoundly influenced sociological thought on race between the wars and were congruent with the world views of philanthropists and foundation administrators concerned about the Negro problem.

In developing his arguments about race relations, Park drew from comparative historical cases. His favorite comments centered on the similarity between the plight of Afro-American ex-slaves and European peasants:

There is a striking similarity in the sentiments and mental attitudes of peasant peoples in all parts of the world, although the external differences are often great . . . a German, Russian, or Negro peasant of the southern states, different as each is in some respects, are all very much alike in certain habitual attitudes and sentiments.[23]

In his writings, he offered numerous illustrations of the similarity between the rise of European nationalism and Afro-American ex-slave race consciousness. In a 1923 *American Review* article on the emergence of the literature of race consciousness, Park commented:

So much for the general social conditions, under which the new Negro poetry, and the new vision which inspires it, have come into existence. These, however, are the same conditions under which new literary movements have sprung up, within a period of a hundred years, among all the disinherited races of Europe . . . . The struggle of these racial and cultural minorities to maintain their historical traditions and lift their folk speech to the dignity of literary language has, one might almost say, made the history of Europe during the last seventy-five years . . . all naturalist struggles in Europe and elsewhere, seem to have had a history not unlike that which has been described as the negro renaissance.[24]

What made the assimilation of Africans and Asians in America more problematic than that of peasants in Europe was their skin color. Park argued continually that skin color was a negative symbol that made nonwhite races targets of race prejudice or racial antagonism.

. . . the chief obstacle to the assimilation of the Negro and the Oriental are not mental but physical traits. It is not because the Negro and the Japanese are so differently constituted that they do not assimilate. If they were given an opportunity the Japanese are quite as capable as the Italians, the Armenians, or the Slave of acquiring our culture and sharing our national ideals. The trouble is not with the Japanese mind but with the Japanese skin. The "Jap" is not the right color.[25]

The Oriental in America experiences a profound transfiguration in sentiment and attitude, but he cannot change his physical characteristics, he is still constrained to wear his racial uniform; he cannot, much as he may sometimes like to do so, cast aside the racial mask. The physical masks of race, in so far as they increase the racial visibility, inevitably segregate the races, set them apart, and so prolong and intensify the racial conflict.[26]

Even though Park did not attempt to develop a systematic theory of race relations, he did present and describe concepts which were meant to have universal implications. This was particularly apparent in his conceptions of human migration, civilization, culture, and race relations. Park stated, "When the existing economic and social order is disturbed, migration and population movements take place in an effort to achieve a new equilibrium."[27] Park attributed the inevitable migration trend to the emerging machine age and mass communications.[28]

Park carefully distinguished culture from civilization.

Culture is the sort of order existing in a society which has a cult or a religion. It preserves morale and enables the group to act collectively. . . . If we could use the word *culture* to refer to society that has a moral order and *Civilization* to refer to the order that applies to a territorial group, we could bring out the important distinction more clearly.[29]

The culture produced in society is composed of habits which include individual folkways, art, science, philosophy, formal law, and technology. These are passed down from generation to generation, and become a "communal possession" once they have become conventionalized. The transmission of culture allows people in a society to act collectively and to control effectively large numbers of persons.

Park related culture to massive human migration through the concept of cultural diffusion:

when people of widely different cultures come into contact and conflict . . . certain elements of the invading or borrowed cultures are assimilated first, while others are incorporated in the complex of the invaded culture only after a considerable period of time, if at all.[30]

Using a botanical analogy, Park described the process of cultural diffusion as in some instances being "analogous to that which, in a plant community, an existing 'formation' is broken up by the invasion of alien species." He further argued that "this plant formation, like the cultural complex, is a highly complex structure in which the interruption of one function tends to throw the whole into confusion."[31]

Related to cultural diffusion is the concept of spontaneous culture borrowing, about which Park said:

Diffusion does not always take place by a process that can be described as invasion nor by the imposition of one culture upon another. It sometimes takes place by what Wissler describes as "spontaneous borrowing." Individuals and peoples borrow from the cultures of their neighbors, particularly from the peoples with whom they are in competition and conflict, and more particularly, from the people by which they have been subjected and reduced to a status of conscious inferiority.[32]

Park had an asymmetrical conception of cultural diffusion and related phenomena, particularly assimilation. The migration of Europeans into non-European societies and the ready native acceptance of the "superior" culture allowed cultural diffusion on a world scale. He criticized anthropologists who tried to preserve non-European cultures from the destructive affects of contacts with traders and missionaries, stating, "The greatest enemy of the whole experiment (native culture preservation) is the native himself."[33]

So, according to Park, the diffusion of "superior" European culture, through advances in technology and communication, was inevitable. Park's more refined descriptions of culture are found in his article "Culture and Cultural Trends," which appeared in the 1915 *Publications of the American Sociological Society*. In this paper he elaborated upon W. H. Rivers's distinction between the form and content of culture. Forms of culture—external and tangible objects—are easily transmitted and diffused while contents of culture—ideas, norms, and memories—are not. Park claimed,

The most striking illustration of the sudden and successful adoption of an alien culture is Japan. And yet those observers who have had an opportunity to know Japan intimately assure us that as yet European culture has merely changed the exterior of Japanese life. Japan has taken over the science, the technique, and many of the external forms of European culture, but is, perhaps, less disposed today than it was sixty years ago to adopt the mores of the occidental world.[34]

In this case, externalities changed first and more rapidly than "the Japanese ethos, rooted in temperament and reinforced by tradition."

Park further noted that though Rivers described horizontal cultural transmission (group to group), vertical cultural transmission (generation to generation) was also crucial. This conjecture can be found throughout his works and other Chicago school products. Park suggested that Old World culture is completely lost by the third generation, because

Children seem to take over intuitively and without resistance just those elements of a foreign culture which an adult alien finds most difficult to understand and assimilate . . . when children of immigrants grow up in the country of their adoption they inevitably take over all the events, the local cultural idioms of the native population.[35]

For Park, the major task was applying the dichotomy of cultural form and content to the problem of cross-generational cultural fusion as it related to "the study of conflicts and fusions of racial and national cultures in our cosmopolitan and contemporary life."

The significance of cultural form and content to the blending of cultures was that "form and content tend to fall apart, and gain each a more or less independent existence." Park called these independent processes "cultural trends." But, like his conception of cultural differences, his discussion on cultural forms and contents promotes an asymmetrical process. After discussing the expansion of European cultural hegemony in the guise of civilization ("generalized, rationalized, and intelligible culture"), Park proceeded to explain the disorganization of dissimilar cultural groups as "evidence of conflict or incongruity between the group mind and the instrumentalities through which the mind acts." Although he admitted that discrepancies between material and ideal culture affected everyone in society, he believed that the problem was more serious when it came to dissimilar racial and cultural groups who had to assimilate themselves into the host society to survive and prosper.

Park implied here that when dissimilar racial and cultural groups enter a host society, the form and content of their cultures must completely disintegrate in order to be successfully absorbed into society. Park's notions were based on the assumption that European culture was superior and that the disintegration of immigrant cultures was inevitable in the face of this competition.[36] This asymmetrical assertion about cultural diffusion and "cultural blending" does not allow consideration of the impact of immigrant contributions to a host society, nor does it even allow for the possibility of transformation of a host's society cultural forms and contents by immigrants. Thus, through his asymmetrical ideas about cultural fusion, Park was a major progenitor of that sociological school of thought which described immigrant experiences in terms of pathology.

Though Park applied the form-content to the cultural assimilation problems of immigrants, hobos, and the always vague "everyone else," he did not apply it to the experiences of African Americans. Park did not view the Old World culture of European immigrants as savage. At most, he assumed it was inadequate for modern industrial life and thus had to be replaced with the culture of the host society. His views about Africa and Africans were starkly different. Park may have been interested in studying Africans for better understanding of their characteristics, and he opposed their exploitation, but he assumed that they were cultural savages. Following are some excerpts from Park's unpublished notes:

We have no . . . adequate picture of Africa and African life as a whole. We have: 1) Travellers' Tales, 2) Descriptions of the strange and barbarous customs, pictures of strange nosed people, a considerable collection of their folklore, some investigation of their arts and crafts, their social organization and their barbarism.[37]

Illustrating the Negro's method with the white man. The way the primitive mind shows in the Negro, he will watch your face. He will not take what you say literally. He will frequently answer something in your mind before you speak; he will say yes, sir when he means no [sic]. *He will approach a subject* (steadfastly); not . . . circle *around* it, like an animal stalking its prey. He has no conception of knowledge for its own sake.[38]

In Park's earliest professional writings on blacks and cultural fusion, he discussed at great length how the dispersion of ethnically related Africans and the harshness of the slavery experience destroyed African culture. He addressed this topic through conjectures and personal impressions rather than through presentations of empirical evidence:

There was less opportunity in the United States than in the West Indies for a slave to meet one of his own people, because the plantations were considerably smaller, more widely scattered, and especially, because as soon as they were landed in this country, slaves were immediately divided and shipped in small numbers frequently no more than one or two at a time to different plantations. This was the procedure with the very first Negroes brought to this country. It was found easier to deal with slaves, if they were thrown together with slaves who had already forgotten or dimly remembered their life in Africa.[39]

Park's own perspective on the dichotomy between cultural form and content, as outlined in his article, would describe the experiences of Africans in America very differently. This point of view would suggest that while the *formal* aspects of African cultures were quickly destroyed and reshaped by white powers in America, the *contents* of African cultures were not destroyed as rapidly and some not at all. Paradoxically, in Park's view, slavery and the dispersion of African tribes easily destroyed both the forms and contents of African cultures. Thus Park avoided the uncomfortable thought that certain aspects of African cultures might transform the culture of white society. This question was considered briefly in reference to white immigrants, but not when it came to

Africans. To Park and others of his age, African cultures—forms and contents—were too savage to survive in and contribute to white America.[40] Any African contributions, they believed, depended more on racial temperament than cultural uniqueness. For example, Park claimed, in arguing against the possibility of the survival of African culture in plantation hymns,

So far as I know (emphasis added) there are, among the plantation hymns, no such remains of ancient ritual, mystical words whose meanings are unknown, no traces whatever of African tradition. If there is anything that is African about the Negroes' christianity it is not African tradition but the African temperament which has contributed it. *I assume* (emphasis added), therefore, that what we find in the most primitive form of Negro Christianity is not the revival of an older and more barbaric religion but the inception of a new and original form of Christianity.[41]

Park's distinction between culture and civilization closely parallels Emile Durkheim's mechanical/organic solidarity dichotomy. Culture was a characteristic of familial societies which enjoyed ethnic solidarity, exhibited clearly defined moral orders, and were expressive societies. Familial societies inhibited individual liberty through valuing the traditional above the rational and the collective above the individual. On the other hand, civilization was a territorial phenomenon which was "built up by the absorption of foreign ethnic groups . . . and by secularizing their culture and sacred order." The secularization of unique ethnic characteristics of dissimilar groups in a civilizing process freed the individual, created an impersonal moral order, and replaced sentiment with rationality as the basis of relationships. Because the impetus of civilization was urbanization, the city became a central attribute in Park's thought. Park helped to popularize the now classical view of the city as representing liberation, impersonalization, progress, and economic vitality while rural areas represented social and cultural restraint, "folk" social relations, regression, and economic underdevelopment.[42] Since his views were sociocultural rather than structural and political, he was unable to see how northern urban areas underdeveloped the countryside as a way of gradually institutionalizing the dominance of urban-based power elites. His descriptions of the secularization of ethnic characteristics as a means of describing the power of northwestern European descent culture in contact with dissimilar ethnic and racial groups overlooked the persistence of unique ethnic and racial communities. "Ethnic persistence," in Park's terminology, represented temporary aberrations in an overall pattern of eventual integration and assimilation, or pathological deviations from the "mainstream."

This explains why Park considered the integration and assimilation of dissimilar ethnic groups as the major problem of civilization. He believed that the process of civilization required the dominance of one cultural group over another to assure the liberation of the individual and the development of an appropriate moral and political order. Throughout his writings, sometimes explicitly, but mostly implicitly, Park saw this ethnic dominance as a privilege belonging to those of European descent. To Park, civilization *was* northwestern European culture. In any country, be it the Soviet Union, South Africa, Australia, or the United States, extending European economic, political, and moral orders to dissimilar groups, particularly nonwhites, was extremely problematic.[43]

Park presumed that racially similar ethnic groups would eventually assimilate culturally and physically. Indeed, this is what enabled the civilization processes to proceed all the more smoothly.[44] Ideally, race mixing created vast melting pots of races which "loosened local bonds, destroyed the cultures of the tribe and folk, and substituted for the local loyalties the freedom of the cities; for the sacred order of tribal custom, the rational organization which we call civilization." But Park was quite aware that successful race mixing was rooted in the premise that races where physically as well as culturally similar. (In seeing this dilemma, Park tended to use the terms race and ethnicity interchangeably and thus to convolute the sociological meanings of both terms.) "Race problems" in the otherwise progressive, liberating process of civilization emerged when physically different populations came into contact, since divergent physical markers deter cultural assimilation—"particularly where peoples who come together are of divergent cultures and widely different racial stocks, assimilation and amalgamation do not take place at all, or take place very slowly."[45]

There are no doubt periods of transition and crisis in the lives of most people that are comparable to those which the immigrant experiences when he leaves home to seek his fortunes in a strange country. But in the case of the marginal man the period of crisis is relatively permanent. . . . Ordinarily the marginal man is a mixed blood, like the Mulatto in the United States or the Eurasian in Asia . . . who lives in two worlds, in both of which he is more or less a stranger.[46]

In application to mulattoes in the United States, Park's conception of cultural hybrids became distorted. Park developed his thought on this problem from the experiences of Jews. Confusing ethnicity with race, he assumed that Jews were a race with a unique culture which became problematic in European societies dominated by gentiles. In general, he saw marginal people, like Jews, as adherents to an outmoded cultural past and not quite incorporated into the culture of the host society. But according to Park's own arguments, this could not apply to mulattoes, because, in Park's view, African culture had been completely destroyed in America. Thus, there were no two cultural worlds between which mulattoes could be caught. But still, Park and his students Edward Reuter, Everett V. Stonequist, and E. Franklin Frazier ignored this conceptual contradiction and proceeded to make the mulatto, as a marginal person, a central theme in Chicago race-relations sociology.[47]

A major result of the emancipation of slaves and their forced confinement in segregated communities was a mode of solidarity—race consciousness maintained through white prejudice.

One of the effects of the mobilization of the Negro has been to bring him into closer and more intimate contact with his own people. Common interests have drawn the blacks together, and caste sentiment has kept the black and white apart. The separation of the races, which began as a spontaneous movement on the part of both, has been fostered by the policy of the dominant race.[48]

Race consciousness as an ecological phenomenon tended to be regional, most predominant in the South:

This sense of solidarity has grown up gradually with the organization of the Negro people. It is stronger in the South, where segregation is more complete, than it is in the North where, twenty years ago, it would be safe to say it did not exist.[49]

It is interesting that Park believed race consciousness to be a product of segregation. Since Park presumed the assimilation of physically dissimilar groups was problematic yet inevitable, it followed that segregated black communities were necessarily temporary, and, therefore, that race consciousness was also temporary. Because Park viewed race consciousness as a temporary response to oppression, he did not consider the normality of race consciousness in dominant as well as in subordinant populations. In sum, he ushered into sociological literature an a-cultural and an a-sociological conception of race consciousness. He did not consider race consciousness a normal aspect of learning and identity formation in a rigidly multiracial society. This set the stage for succeeding generations of sociologists to view black race consciousness negatively as a product of antagonistic relations with whites, which materialized through conscious white racism and the formation of ghettos. The idea that whites and blacks develop race consciousness as a normal aspect of human development in a multiracial society has not traditionally been considered in sociological thought.

RACIAL DIFFERENCES AND RACE RELATIONS

Historians of Chicago sociology claim that Robert E. Park played the central role in ushering into organized sociology environmental explanations of racial differences.[50] He fought vigorously against the eugenic and biological arguments about racial differences prevalent in his day. But at least through the late 1920s, Park did not totally reject biological explanations, nor did he totally accept environmental ones. Biological determinism was apparent in his concept of "racial temperaments," which he believed, was the true factor behind so-called cultural uniqueness among blacks.

Park's biological determinism has been overlooked easily, however, since from the late 1920s to his death in 1944, he moved from discussing the sources of racial differences to their consequences. His focus on sources of racial differences appeared in his writings which attempt to define culture, civilization, and migration, while his focus on their effects can be found in his writings about cultural hybrids, personality, attitudes, and opinions. His writings on race prejudice and race consciousness included discussions of both the sources and effects of race consciousness.[51] His earliest professional writings often fell back on biological deterministic arguments by giving preeminence to the influence of racial temperament and racial sentiments.

During Park's Tuskegee days, his observations of political, economic, and social conditions in the South and the nation as a whole led him to develop explanations about white/black relations centered around the function of race sentiments. Sentiments were biologically grounded feelings and attitudes. No matter how many laws were passed to eradicate racial inequality, they would not work if they were the antithesis of white sentiments. Specifically, white sentiments were opposed to such events as significant black mobility, black political activity, and public race mixing, especially open miscegenation. While describing the regionally and nationally declining conditions of blacks in 1913, Park commented on how race reform legislation succeeded or failed depending upon its relation to white sentiments. In a paper entitled ''Southern Sentiments and Southern Policy Toward the Negro,'' Park stated:

One thing which law cannot control is sentiment. If there is prejudice against the Negro, law cannot remove it. On the other hand an unjust law, no matter against whom it is directed will in the long run work injury to the whole community and the sentiments of the community will not support it.[52]

Park, then, agreed with Alfred H. Stone's explanation of racial conflict. In the Park and Burgess classic, Stone's conception of interracial conflict was used to explain the inevitable results of contact between physically dissimilar groups, particularly whites and blacks.[53] This biological perspective assumed that a harmonious racial caste system was the natural order of things. Racial problems occurred when subordinate groups were not incorporated effectively into such multiracial societies. Throughout his early professional writings on the history of southern race relations, Park emphasized the virtues of the old plantation South. He felt that the unfortunate consequences of the Civil War and Reconstruction had deeply injured paternal ties between the races.

Where conditions of slavery brought the two races . . . into close and intimate contact there grew up a mutual sympathy and understanding which frequently withstood not only the shock of the Civil War, but the political agitation which followed it in the southern states.[54]

In a book about Tuskegee Institute (never completed), Park attempted to explain how Booker T. Washington's philosophy of industrial education was the most constructive solution to the political threat of emancipated African slaves in a society dominated by whites[55] and the key to restoring the harmonious southern racial caste order characteristic of that region prior to the Civil War. It was through his admiration of Booker T. Washington's and Tuskegee's functions as stabilizers of the reconstructed southern racial caste order that Park developed the concept of accommodation which was to appear later in his race cycle perspective. Park assumed that accommodation was the settling down of a natural, harmonious racial caste system after a period of disturbing flux. While this was Park's early explanation of the stabilizing effect of Washington's educational institution in the disorganized postbellum period, accommodation later came to represent, on a more abstract level, an element of a race-relations cycle with supposedly universal applications.

Both racial conflict and racial accommodation preoccupied Park during his Tuskegee period and his early Chicago days. At that time he was concerned with the causes of different modes of white/black relations. These concepts also had biological implications, since they alluded to the different temperaments of the two races. Whites and blacks were inevitably in conflict due to their divergent biological inclinations. Accommodation was natural for both whites, who had the temperament to be rational and intellectual rulers, and blacks, who had the sunny dispositions needed to submit to their low caste status. His ideas about competition and assimilation, the two other elements of his race cycle frame of reference, were also grounded in assumptions about racial temperament. Competition between the races inevitably led to white dominance over blacks.[56]

Park's shift of emphasis from the causes to the effects of racial differences in the 1920s was influenced greatly by his involvement in three research enterprises undoubtedly more interested in the effects of racial differences than causes: the Pacific Race Relations Survey, the Chicago Race Relations Commission, and the University of Chicago Local Community Research Institute. The Pacific study, involved in exploration of the conditions and effects of Asian communities on the West Coast, served as the major impetus behind Park's ideas about racial attitudes, racial opinions, and multistage race-relations processes. Most of the race-relations ideas Park became known for developed through his observations of relations between whites and Asians. These ideas have been taken out of context and applied to Afro-Americans in efforts to demonstrate the universality of race cycle stages.[57]

At the University of Chicago's Local Community Research Institute, Park trained students to carry out studies that empirically demonstrated his ideas about urban life. In the aftermath of the Chicago riot of 1919, Park was commissioned to investigate the civil disorder. With his research assistant, Charles S. Johnson, Park set forth to develop an explanation of the riot based on public attitudes and opinions. This study greatly influenced Park's shift from the cause to effect of racial differences. From the publication of *The Negro in Chicago* in 1923 until his last articles, Park explored the effects of racial differences in domestic and international affairs.

In sum, Park's race-cycle frame of reference represents the presentation of the race-relations ideas he developed under various conditions prior to his arrival at Chicago. Its purpose was to clarify for policy makers (specifically in Chicago and on the West Coast) why and how nonwhites conflicted with whites and to offer an optimistic interracial relations explanation in an era (World War I and the 1920s) in which negative opinions about Asians and blacks were prev-

alent. Park's positive conclusions assured that after interracial contact and subsequent conflict, competition, accommodation, and assimilation, America would
still be dominated by whites. Such a view appealed to conventional public views
supporting permanent racial separation and white domination.

PARK'S SOUTHERN COMPOSURE

Robert E. Park was one of many northern-bred intellectuals who was in sympathy with the southern perspective on white/black relations. First, he believed
that Reconstruction was a mistake, since it disrupted an intimate antebellum
South characterized by friendly relations between the races. Second, he assumed blacks were docile beings who were as they appeared to whites and who
trusted whites more than members of their own race. Their accommodative behavior was, in Park's view, very similar to the behavior of women toward men.
"Man has got what he wanted by tackling things; going at them directly. The
negro and the woman have got them by manipulating the individual in control.
Women and Negroes have required the machinery of rapid and delicate adjustment to the words and temper of men."[58] The elements of contact, conflict,
competition, accommodation, and assimilation found in his race-cycle perspective were derived from his personal observations of the breakdown of the southern slave regime and the reassertion of a new racial caste order in the years
following the Civil War. Although these elements took on different ideological
and empirical meanings and even different sequences in other parts of the country and world, Park and his students did not make appropriate conceptual adjustments. They treated this race-cycle pattern as a universal, inevitable phenomenon which could be applied to cities, islands, and other diverse multiracial
areas.

Park did not attempt seriously to study northern race relations because he
believed that the black population in the North was insignificant. His writings
consistently denied the historical heritage of blacks in the North. Furthermore,
he assumed that the few blacks who did live in the North lacked race consciousness.

The southern composure of Park's ideas on race relations became apparent
in the work of his students. Those who studied blacks were principally concerned about plantation race relations and declining black folk culture. Park's
students studied urban race relations in the North only to determine the effects
of the civilizing process in disorganizing and reorganizing the folk culture of
southern migrants. This focus, which was exemplified in E. Franklin Frazier's
writings on the black family, failed to develop an isomorphic and coherent conceptual scheme of the origins and evolution of northern race relations, particularly in the city.[59]

PARK, BLACK STUDENTS, AND PHILANTHROPY

Robert E. Park was more of a mentor than a scholar. His ideas were in large
part developed by his students and lived on through them. He wrote prefaces

for their books, sponsored their publications by the University of Chicago Press and in the *American Journal of Sociology*, and supported their mobility in the American Sociological Society. Park's students also acted as ghostwriters for him.[60]

Caught up in the radical race-relations changes of the 1920s, Park was concerned about the poverty of scientific facts on black conditions. The best race-relations literature of the 1920s was poetry and fiction. Park reviewed some of this literature, particularly that produced by Harlem Renaissance figures, not only to celebrate the arrival of the new Negro, but also to point the underdevelopment of "scientific facts" about blacks.[61]

There were specific reasons why the 1920s was an era of little empirical race-relations study. Through World War I only blacks had been interested in documenting empirically black conditions. William E. B. DuBois, Kelly Miller, George Haynes, Carter G. Woodson, and Richard Wright, Jr., expressed interest in impartial studies of black experience. However, they were too marginal to have much of an impact on associational history and sociology. Indeed, except for Carter G. Woodson, these men had ceased publishing significant sociological studies about blacks by the 1920s.

By the early 1920s, there was a noticeable void in the production of quality scholarship on the black experience relative to that done between the 1890s and 1910s. At most, with the arrival of Howard W. Odum at the University of North Carolina—Chapel Hill in 1921 came an institutionalized white southern interest in black folklore and black chain gangs.

Thus, Robert E. Park as well as Charles S. Johnson and E. Franklin Frazier, both students of Park, were creators of their times as well as respondents to them. Charles S. Johnson arrived at Chicago as a student in sociology in the late 1910s. Soon after, Park discovered Johnson's extraordinary methodological skills. Park was president of the Chicago Urban League, and he hired Johnson as research director. Later, Johnson joined Park on the Chicago Race Relations Commission. Johnson was the organizing force and wrote most of the report under Park's supervision (see chapter 6).

Johnson was the outstanding race-relations social scientist of the 1920s. The foundations as well as Park realized this. While officers of the Laura Spelman Rockefeller Memorial had ambivalent feelings about Park and Burgess, they admired Charles S. Johnson. Neither Park nor Burgess was invited to the memorial's Negro Problems Conference, which influenced the direction of race-relations policy in the foundation sector for many years.[62] Foundation administrators recognized Johnson's skill in collecting and presenting "the facts."

Park supplied Johnson with the concepts and techniques needed to become a credible sociologist, and he and other Chicago faculty gave Johnson access to the University of Chicago Press, the *American Journal of Sociology*, and the American Sociological Society. But Johnson's broad professional career was a product of philanthropic interests. Julius Rosenwald, who was impressed with Johnson's work with the Chicago Race Relations Commission, was later a central influence behind Johnson's move from the National Urban League to Fisk University in 1930. Johnson was the only Chicago-trained social scientist at the memorial-sponsored Negro Problems Conference and was also research secretary of the National Interracial Conference, also sponsored by the memorial. Through the latter conference, Johnson collected the materials for his first book, *The Negro in American Civilization*. In the 1930s and 1940s, Johnson's professional career was further enhanced through extensive ties in the American Missionary Association, the General Education Board, and especially the Julius Rosenwald Fund. Johnson's attractiveness to philanthropists and foundations can be attributed to the Parkian ideas he espoused, which emphasized race relations in a (supposed) permanent biracial society. This was Park's most significant influence in the foundation sector. Johnson's career will be considered further in Chapter 6.

E. Franklin Frazier arrived in Chicago from the Atlanta School of Social Work, where he had served as director. When applying for a memorial fellowship for his graduate work, Frazier presented a well-conceived research strategy for studying the black family which changed very little during his professional career. Frazier used the ideas of Park, Thomas, and Burgess to organize and interpret his data on the black family in terms acceptable to the discipline's establishment. From Park, he borrowed the concept of assimilation in examining empirically the different degrees to which white norms and values were internalized by urban black families in association with black class differentiation. Park also influenced Frazier's crusade against the idea of the survival of African culture in black communities and his assumptions about the urbanization of black southern migrants as they came into contact with the dominant European-influenced urban culture. From Thomas, through Park and Burgess, Frazier used the organization-disorganization-reorganization framework to explain the process of adjustment and incorporation which took place among blacks who migrated to northern cities. Frazier used Burgess's concentric zone model to explain black class differentiation. Throughout most of his career, Frazier closely adhered to these ideas borrowed from his Chicago mentors, although he modified them and applied them to different empirical questions. Only toward the end of his life did he begin to break away in disillusionment from these assumptions.[63]

Unlike Johnson, Frazier became a prominent sociologist in associational affairs through the support of Park and other Chicago sociologists. Although Johnson was also involved in such affairs, his sphere of activity was wider and more independent of organized sociology. But during the interwar years Frazier was unable to obtain foundation support, not only because of his critical attitude, but also because his view was too narrow, that is, too much that of a professional sociologist whose only major intellectual contribution was correlating ecological and class variables in black family research.[64]

Because he was the black representative of Parkian sociology in professional affairs, Frazier's creativity was stifled. But, unlike Johnson, he did become dei-

fied as the best black sociologist ever, due to his devoted professional commitment. In contrast, Johnson, who was more creative but was not a professional
celebrity, has been gravely misunderstood, labeled as a competent administrator who had too much undeserved power. More of this will be discussed in a
later chapter. For now, the question is, why were foundation administrators interested in Park's and Johnson's race-relations ideas to begin with?

NOTES

1. Robert E. Park, *Race and Culture* (Glencoe, Ill.: University of Ilinois Press, 1950),
pp. v–ix; Louis R. Harlan and Raymond W. Smock, eds., *The Booker T. Washington
Papers*, 12 vols. (Urbana: University of Illinois Press, 1979), 8:203–204; August Meier,
Negro Thought in America, 1880–1915 (Ann Arbor: University of Michigan Press, 1963),
p. 271; Everett Hughes, "Robert E. Park," in *The Sociological Eye* (Chicago: Aldine-
Atherton, 1971), reprinted from *New Society*, December 31, 1964, pp. 543–549; Winfred
Raushenbush, *Robert E. Park: Biography of a Sociologist* (Durham: Duke University
Press, 1979), pp. 43–63, 76; R. Fred Wacker, *Ethnicity, Pluralism, and Race: Race
Relations Theory in America Before Myrdal* (Westport, Conn.: Greenwood, 1983), pp.
41–59; and the most critical interpretations, Fred H. Matthews, *Quest for an American
Sociology: Robert E. Park and the Chicago School* (Montreal: McGill-Queen's Univer-
sity Press, 1977), pp. 57–84, and St. Clair Drake, "The Tuskegee Connection: Booker
T. Washington and Robert E. Park," *Society* (May/June 1983): 82–92.

2. See especially Meier, *Negro Thought in America*.

3. For example, Hughes, "Robert E. Park"; and Raushenbush, *Robert E. Park*.

4. There is evidence throughout the Booker T. Washington Papers (1905–1914) about
Park's financial and in some cases, personal dependency on Washington. Booker T.
Washington Papers, Library of Congress.

5. Clara Park to Robert E. Park, June 23, 1914, Addendum to the Robert E. Park
Papers, University of Chicago.

6. Letters in the Addendum to the Robert E. Park Papers are replete with correspondence attesting to Clara Park's writing skills and her influence on her husband's
pre-Chicago career. In this collection are also letters between Park and relatives (a brother
and a brother-in-law) alluding to real estate activities in which Park was involved to
generate cash. There is also much correspondence about Park's dire financial condition
and family assistance with his home mortgage payments. Examples of these points are
found in: Capital Savings and Loan Association to Clara Park, December 21, 1909; Herb
A. Park to Clara Park, December 11 [no year]; Clara Park to Robert E. Park, August
30, 1906; Robert E. Park to Judge Cauhill, May 24, 1910; Herb Park to Robert E. Park,
April 5, 1911; and Herb Park to Robert E. Park, May 14, 1911. Addendum to the *Robert E. Park Papers*, University of Chicago.

Also, Park did not hesitate to defend his work at Tuskegee. For instance in a lengthy
letter to his father-in-law, a Judge, Park explained why he had to be away from home
so much while working for Tuskegee and why his family was poor but still faring well.
In part, he said:

Clara has told you no doubt that I will go abroad this summer. I am sorry that I have to be away
from home so much of the time and do not intend to spend as much time from home in the future
as I have in the past. I wish none of you get the idea, however, that I am doing this work at

Tuskegee merely for fun or for philanthropy. I have looked over the field and there is nothing that I can do that would keep me at home more, that would earn me money or that I could do so well in. The fact is Judge . . . I am doing good work at Tuskegee, valuable, original first hand work. I am not getting any great reputation out of it but I am doing the work. [Robert E. Park to Judge Cauhill, May 24, 1910]

7. Miscellaneous diaries, Robert E. Park Papers.

8. Especially see 1910 Booker T. Washington and Robert E. Park correspondence in the Booker T. Washington Papers about Park's father. See correspondence between Robert E. Park, his brother, brother-in-law, and close friends in the Addendum to the Robert E. Park Papers which reveals the displeasure some had about his work for Washington and Tuskegee Institute.

9. There is particularly extensive correspondence about Park's interest in the activities of the Mississippi's Negro Business League. See the Robert E. Park to Charles Bank correspondence, Addendum to Robert E. Park Papers.

10. For a brief period of time (1907–1908), Washington and Park attempted to organize a Negro Encyclopedia Project through the Singer Company Publishers. The encyclopedia was to be "scientific," offer practical stress on black Americans rather than Africans, and emphasize history more than ethnology. Washington and anthropologist Franz Boas were to be editors-in-chief. The project never materialized because Washington could not find funds for it. He was led to assume, incorrectly, that Singer Company Publishers would finance the encyclopedia. The Robert E. Park–Isadore Singer correspondence gives an especially interesting preview to Park's later approach to the study of blacks. See Washington–Isadore Singer correspondence; Park–Isadore Singer correspondence; and Park to Washington, January 29, 1909; Addendum to Robert E. Park Papers.

11. The Booker T. Washington Papers are replete with correspondence about Robert E. Park's ghostwriter role. Park's "Education by Cultural Groups," which he presented at the 1912 Tuskegee Institute International Conference on the Negro (where he first met William I. Thomas), is quite revealing about his views about industrial education for black Americans and Africans. For more information on Robert E. Park's and Thomas J. Jones's industrial education philosophies, see Kenneth J. King, *Pan-Africanism and Education* (New York: Oxford University Press, 1971), p. 31. Park, it should be mentioned, also played an important role in developing curriculum at Tuskegee, offering courses, and editing the student newspaper (Booker T. Washington Papers).

12. Edmund Dene Morel, *History of the Congo Reform Movement*, with supplementary chapters by William Roger Louis and Jean Stengers (New York: Oxford University Press, 1968), p. ix.

13. Ibid.

14. Robert E. Park, "A King in Business: Leopold II of Belgium, Autocrat of the Congo and International Broker," *Everybody's Magazine* 15 (November 1906): 624–633; Park, "The Terrible Story of the Congo," ibid., 15 (December 1906): 763–772; Park, "The Blood Money of the Congo," ibid., 16 (January 1907): 60–70. Park kept this critical perspective through the last phase of his career. See Robert E. Park, "News as a Form of Knowledge: A Chapter in the Sociology of Knowledge," *American Journal of Sociology* 45 (March 1940): 669–686.

15. Robert E. Park, "Education by Cultural Groups," 1912 Tuskegee Institute International Conference on the Negro, Robert E. Park Papers.

16. Ibid.

17. Ibid.

18. Ibid.

19. Oliver C. Cox, "Introduction" to Nathan Hare, *Black Anglo Saxons* (London, 1965).

20. For example, Emmett Scott to Robert E. Park, February 29, 1912; Robert E. Park to Emmett Scott, June 25, 1912, Booker T. Washington Papers.

21. At least throughout 1912, Robert E. Park attempted to leave Tuskegee. When he was about to resign at one point, he wrote to Washington in part:

I want to say, now that I am leaving here, that I have never been so happy in my life as I have since I have been associated with you in this work. Some of the best friends I have in the world are at Tuskegee. I have and shall always feel that I belong, in a sort of way to the Negro race and shall continue to share, through good and evil, all its joys and sorrows. [Park to Washington, April 10, 1912, Booker T. Washington Papers]

22. In Robert E. Park to Datyschen [Park?], February 23, 1916 (Addendum to Robert E. Park Papers), Park mentions "digging away" at a paper for Thomas. After Thomas left the University of Chicago in disgrace, Park finished and published a book manuscript he had begun: *Old World Traits Transplanted*, published with Herbert A. Miller (New York: Harper and Brothers, 1921). I should also mention that for at least one year after arriving at Chicago, Park remained on the Tuskegee payroll. Washington attempted to exploit that fact. Louis Harlan and Raymond W. Smock, eds., The *Booker T. Washington Papers*, p. 230.

23. Robert E. Park, "Racial Assimilation in Secondary Groups: With Particular Reference to the Negro," *Publications of the American Sociological Society* 18 (1913):67–68.

24. Robert E. Park, "Negro Race Consciousness as Reflected in Race Literature," *American Review I* (September–October 1923):514–515.

25. Robert E. Park, "Racial Assimilation in Secondary Groups," *Publications of the American Sociological Society* 8 (1913):70–71.

26. Robert E. Park, "Behind Our Masks," *Survey Graphic* 46 (May 1926), reprinted in idem, *Race and Culture* (New York, 1950), p. 252.

27. Robert E. Park, "The Problem of Cultural Differences," Preliminary paper prepared for the Institute of Pacific Relations, Hangchow, China (New York, 1931), reprinted in idem, *Race and Culture*, p. 10.

28. Ibid., p. 10.

29. Robert E. Park, "Culture and Civilization," unpublished paper, no date (probably written in the 1920s), published in idem, *Race and Culture*, p. 10.

30. Park, "The Problem of Cultural Differences," p. 5.

31. Ibid., p. 6.

32. Ibid.

33. Ibid.

34. Robert E. Park, "Culture and Cultural Trends," *Publications of the American Sociological Society* 19 (December 1925), reprinted in idem, *Race and Culture*, p. 25.

35. Ibid., p. 27.

36. Robert E. Park, "Our Racial Frontier on the Pacific," *Survey Graphic* 9 (May 1926), reprinted in idem, *Race and Culture* (New York, 1950), p. 148.

37. See his notes on Africa (no date), Robert E. Park Papers.

38. Ibid.

39. Robert E. Park, "Culture and Cultural Trends," p. 25.

40. John F. Szwed, "An American Anthropological Dilemma: The Politics of Afro-American Culture," in Dell Hymes, ed., *Reinventing Anthropology* (New York: Pantheon, 1974), pp. 158–159.

41. Robert E. Park, "Education in Its Relation to the Conflict and Fusion of Cultures: With Special Reference to the Problems of the Immigrant, the Negro, and Missions," *Publications of the American Sociological Society* 13 (1918): 52; see also p. 45.

42. Robert E. Park, Ernest Burgess, and R. D. McKenzie, *The City* (Chicago: University of Chicago Press, 1925).

43. Park, "Culture and Civilization," p. 16.

44. Ibid., p. 17.

45. Robert E. Park, "Human Migration and the Marginal Man," *American Journal of Sociology* 33 (May 1928):890.

46. Ibid., p. 893.

47. See Everett V. Stonequist, *The Marginal Man: A Study in Personality and Culture Conflict* (1937; repr. New York: Russell & Russell, 1961).

48. Robert E. Park, "Racial Assimilation in Secondary Groups: With Particular Reference to the Negro," *Publications of the American Sociological Society* 8 (1913):77.

49. Ibid., p. 214.

50. For example, Robert E. Lee Faris, *Chicago Sociology, 1920–1932* (San Francisco: Chandler Publishing Co., 1967); Lewis A. Coser, *Masters of Sociological Thought: Ideas in Historical and Social Contexts* (New York: Harcourt Brace Jovanovich, 1971), Robert E. Park Chapter.

51. See, for instance, articles reprinted in Park, *Race and Culture*, especially numbers 6, 16, 17, 18, 19, 21, and 22.

52. Notes on "Southern Sentiments and Southern Policy Toward the Negro," 1913. Robert E. Park Papers.

53. Robert E. Park and Ernest W. Burgess, *Introduction to the Science of Sociology* (1921; repr. Chicago: University of Chicago Press, 1959), pp. 634–640.

54. Unpublished notes on the Negro, Robert E. Park Papers.

55. Robert E. Park, "Tuskegee and Its Problem: A Study in Racial Education," Robert E. Park Papers.

56. Unpublished notes on the Negro, Robert E. Park Papers.

57. Park's attempt to develop a universal race-cycle frame of reference from his observations on the Pacific Coast is quite explicit in his "Our Racial Frontier on the Pacific," pp. 192–196.

58. Unpublished notes on the Negro, Robert E. Park Papers.

59. Park's a-historical comments on northern race relations can be found throughout his articles on culture, civilization, and blacks published in the late 1910s and 1920s. The southern composure of Park students was found either in regional focus (Charles S. Johnson, Bertram Doyle, and Edgar Thompson) or in southern migrant adjustment problems in the urbanization process (E. Franklin Frazier).

60. Charles S. Johnson wrote over half of the Chicago Race Relations Commission study although Park has been given most credit for its authorship (see chapter 6). Winifred Raushenbush wrote much of *The Immigrant Press and Its Control* (New York:

Harper & Brothers, 1922). See Fred H. Matthews, *Quest for an American Sociology: Robert E. Park and the Chicago School* (Montreal: McGill-Queen's University Press, 1977), p. 118.

61. Robert E. Park, Review of *Negro Yearbook, Seventh Edition, 1925–26* by Monroe N. Work, *American Journal of Sociology* 31 (March 1926):696; Robert E. Park, Review of *The Melting Pot Mistake* by Henry P. Fairchild, *American Journal of Sociology* 32 (September 1926):300–303; Robert E. Park, Review of *The New Negro: An Interpretation* by Alaine Locke and Winold Reiss, *American Journal of Sociology* 32 (May 1936):821–824; Robert E. Park, Review of *The Negro and His Songs* by Howard W. Odum and Guy B. Johnson, *American Journal of Sociology* 31 (May 1926):821–824; Robert E. Park, Review of *On the Trail of Negro Folk Songs* by Dorothy Scarborough, *American Journal of Sociology* 31 (May 1926):821–824; Robert E. Park, Review of *Temperament and Race* by S. D. Porteus, *American Journal of Sociology* 32 (September 1926):300–303; Robert E. Park, Review of *Religious Folk-Songs of the Negro, as Sung at Hampton Institute* by R. Nathaniel Dett, ed., *American Journal of Sociology* 33 (1928):98; Robert E. Park, Review of *Folk Beliefs of the Southern Negro* by Newbell N. Puckett, *American Journal of Sociology* 33 (1928):988.

62. Negro Problem Conference folders, Laura Spelman Rockefeller Memorial Archives.

63. Grace E. Harris, *The Life and Works of E. Franklin Frazier* (Ph.D. dissertation, University of Virginia, 1975); Nathan Hare, Epilogue in *Black Anglo Saxons* (London, 1965); E. Franklin Frazier, "The Negro Intellectual," reprinted in G. Franklin Edwards, *E. Franklin Frazier on Race Relations* (Chicago: University of Chicago Press, 1968). Also see the proposed doctoral research plans on the black family Frazier submitted to the memorial, Frazier Folder, Laura Spelman Rockefeller Memorial Archives.

64. E. Franklin Frazier, "The Changing Status of the Negro Family," *Social Forces* 9 (1931):386–393; E. Franklin Frazier, "Some Aspects of Family Disorganization Among Negroes," *Opportunity* 9 (1931); E. Franklin Frazier, "Certain Aspects of Conflict in the Negro Family," *Social Forces* (1931):76–84; E. Franklin Frazier, *The Negro Family in Chicago* (Chicago: University of Chicago Press, 1932); E. Franklin Frazier, "The Impact of Urban Civilization Upon Negro Family Life," *American Sociological Review* 2 (1937):609–618; E. Franklin Frazier, *The Negro Family in the United States* (Chicago: University of Chicago Press, 1939); E. Franklin Frazier, *Negro Youth at the Crossways* (Washington D.C.: American Council on Education, 1940); E. Franklin Frazier, "The Negro Family in Bahia, Brazil," *American Sociological Review* 7 (1942):456–478; E. Franklin Frazier, "Rejoinder to the Negro in Bahia, Brazil: A Problem in Method," *American Sociological Journal* 3 (1943):402–404; E. Franklin Frazier, "Problems and Needs of Negro Children and Youth Resulting from Family Disorganization," *The Journal of Negro Education* 19 (1950):269–277; E. Franklin Frazier and Eleanor H. Bernert, "Children and Income in Negro Families," *Social Forces* 25 (1946):178–182. During the 1950s, though, Frazier became one of the first scholars the Ford Foundation used for developing African Studies programs. Ford Foundation Folders, E. Franklin Frazier Papers, Howard University.

4

The Laura Spelman Rockefeller Memorial

The Laura Spelman Rockefeller Memorial did more to finance the institutional development of American and northwestern European social science during the 1920s than any other foundation or state agency. By the time the memorial was absorbed into the Rockefeller Foundation in 1929, its officers had spent more than $25 million on social science programs, child development research, social work, and race-relations research. The innovative activites of the memorial, especially its sponsorship of race-relations research, can be traced to the efforts of three men—Beardsley Ruml, Leonard Outhwaite, and to a lesser extent, James R. Angell. The roles these men played in the memorial, especially in the foundation's activities concerning the Negro problem, are the subject of this chapter.

THE CHIEF

Mentors exert their influence by selecting and grooming charges endowed with thought processes, philosophies, and personalities similar to their own. The similarities between mentor and charge create an intimate bond which possesses features of the most wholesome parent-child relationships. The mentor guides, promotes, praises, and rebukes his charge and offers him comfort in the hours of uncertainty typical in the early stages of any career. In turn, the charge returns to his mentor unshakable loyalty while continuing to ask for advice and assistance. These relationships sometimes sour as the charge spurs on to an independent course while the mentor ages and becomes part of an outmoded generation. But more often than not, the bond strengthens through the years.[1] This picture aptly describes the relationship between mentor James R. Angell and his charge Beardsley Ruml.

Angell was the son of James B. Angell, president of the University of Vermont and later of the University of Michigan. The younger Angell attended undergraduate school at the University of Michigan and graduate school at Harvard University. In the course of his career Angell became a well-published materialistic psycholgist, but he was most recognized as a man of ideas and an excellent administrator. At the unusually early age of thirty-seven he was elected president of the American Psychological Association. Angell's keen ambition kept him moving from institution to institution in order to avoid becoming locked into an unsatisfying position. At Chicago, he rapidly moved up the professorial ranks and soon was appointed dean of the faculty, second in command to the president. He subsequently became acting president, but soon grew restive when he began to realize that he could not become president of the university. (Only Baptists could be elected president, and Angell was Congregationalist.)

In the summer of 1917, Angell traveled to Washington, D.C. to work for the Committee on Classification of Personnel. He later joined the Committee on Education and Special Training. While in Washington, he played a major part in convincing the National Research Council to use psychological and anthropological knowledge in the war effort. In 1919, when President Woodrow Wilson signed an executive order giving the National Research Council permanent status, Angell was appointed its chairman. In 1920, he was elected president of the Carnegie Corporation of New York. He stayed for two years, until conflicts with the powers there forced him to leave.

During the competition for the Yale University presidency in 1922, two Yale men (Anson Phleps Stokes and Fred Towsley Murphy) deadlocked, and the trustees decided to select an outsider to break the tie. They chose Angell, who was the first non-Yale graduate to become president of the university. At least one biographer of Angell has claimed that his midwestern, non-Yale background retarded the effectiveness of his administration. But Angell did accomplish a number of things which had lasting positive effects on the university. He effected its physical expansion, upgraded the curriculum, and, most important here, developed the most dynamic center of psychological research in New England. From World War I until his retirement in 1937, Angell stimulated the growth of institutional social sciences, particularly psychology. The internationally known Yale Institute of Psychology and the Institute on Human Relations owe their existence and success to Angell's administration.[2]

Apparently, Angell was attracted to people who, like himself, were promoters of ideas. His star student and lifetime friend Beardsley Ruml was born in Iowa in 1894. He received his undergraduate degree from Dartmouth College and attended graduate school in psychology at the University of Chicago between 1914 and 1917. Ruml, Angell's student at the University of Chicago, adopted his teacher's materialistic perspective. He finished his doctoral dissertation at age twenty-three. In 1922, Angell had this to say about Ruml's abilities in a reference letter:

Of all the young men who passed under my hand, I regard him as, on the whole, the most brilliant. . . . He is a man of boundless intellectual and physical energy; he has more ideas in an hour than most men in a week; he has the power to put his ideas into practical form and the industry and energy to carry them through to a conclusion. I regard him as quite the ablest man of his age that I know. He is a fellow of the finest character and of thoroughly agreeable personality.[3]

Angell's admiration for Ruml was unfailing. Ruml accompanied him when he went to Washington to work for the war effort. When Angell became president of the Carnegie Corporation, Ruml followed. When Angell realized he could not get along with guiding personalities in the Carnegie Corporation and decided to accept the offer from Yale, he advised Ruml to leave, too. He made arrangements through connections at the Rockefeller Foundation and General Education Board to have his charge join the recently formed Laura Spelman Rockefeller Memorial, but also wished that he would take an administrative post at Yale.

I ventured some fortnight ago to intimate to both Vincent and Flexner that, owing to my conflicts with the ''powers that be'' in the Corporation, you might wish to migrate in the near future to some other coast. . . . I think if the Spelman people make you any sort of a reasonable offer, you had better take it. It will at least be a comfortable horizontal transfer and may lead to very important opportunities. . . . I should bring you up here in an instant . . . if there were any available jobs . . . the only possibility now, i.e. a sort of personal assistant to me, would not pay you enough to warrant you considering it. I could certainly keep you busy, however, as there are at least half a dozen important pieces of work that need to be done immediately and I have as yet failed to lay hands on anybody satisfactory to me to undertake the job.[4]

Ruml took a position at the memorial and stayed there for seven years. After the memorial closed its doors in 1929, Angell again tried to lure Ruml to Yale and was disappointed when he decided to accept instead the University of Chicago deanship of the School of Social Science.[5]

Ruml reciprocated Angell's devotion, often calling his mentor "Chief." When Angell was about to depart from the Carnegie Corporation, Ruml wrote to him about his plans to join the memorial and his admiration for his mentor:

As [Raymond] Fosdick describes it [the Memorial], it seems a most unusual opportunity and I should like very much to make connections with it. I do not know that I can do more at the present time than wait. From my experience this summer, I am afraid there may be a tendency to delay decision—due to the pressure of other things—and it may be necessary for me to work up some other opportunity so that I will have a legitimate basis for asking for a decision. This I feel reasonably sure of, Fosdick personally would like to have me; but just what influence he has or how rapidly things may develop I have no way of knowing. Next to the above, I would rather be your man Friday than anything I can think of; but of course I understand how important it is that you have a Yale man on the job. I have not excluded strictly academic work from the horizon, but I am more or less saving that as a last resort. I have pretty much decided against any straight business job.[6]

While Ruml remained at Carnegie waiting to hear from the Rockefeller people, he took orders from Angell and kept him abreast of the foundation's activities. When Ruml became executive director of the memorial, he often called on his chief for advice, especially when it came to psychology, social science policy, and proposals from the University of Chicago.[7]

RUML THE IDEALIST

Beardsley Ruml can be described as an ideas man who was best at high-level brainstorming behind closed doors and who seldom aired his views publicly.[8] He was a member of an emerging intellectual elite which believed that science could find cures for critical societal and natural ills. In the 1920s he corresponded with fellow enthusiasts about the promise of popularizing science for the masses. Ruml's idealism was also displayed in his views on liberal education and capitalistic enterprises. In a 1936 paper, "Confusion and Compromise in Education," Ruml expressed great disdain for the conventionality of institutions of higher learning which emphasized student assimilation into prevailing norms, values, and mythologies at the expense of genuine intellectual development. He called for a university which stressed intellectual power (over and beyond the mere lip service universities gave to intellectualism), while realizing the financial and social barriers to the establishment of such an institution.[9] His book, *Tomorrow's Business*,[10] offers deeper insights into his ideas about how capitalism can benefit from using the skills of the talented.

Like most idealists, Ruml became increasingly disillusioned as his ideas clashed with unyielding empirical realities. Shortly after leaving the memorial, he expressed to psychologist Robert Yerkes a dilemma which he had had a role in creating: an empirical trend in experimental psychology which made it more "scientific" but distracted from synthesis and "gross observations."

The whole situation makes me concerned as to the present state of education and training of persons who may go into psychology. It should be possible to give training in scientific method without destroying capacity for gross observation and synthesis. Perhaps it is not the training that is at fault but the differential regard which the profession has for a painstaking bit of experimental investigation as compared with what must necessarily be the less exact natural history observation. I suspect that psychology became experimental too soon, or perhaps I should say over-emphasized experimentation at too early a date in its development.[11]

His deepest disillusionment was over foundations which, as he slowly and painfully learned, displayed the rhetoric of innovation but offered no great progressive substance. They were, most fundamentally, conservative institutions using the surplus capital of the rich to protect the status quo. Ruml was attracted to the memorial because he felt it would give him a great deal of freedom in determining expenditures.

From the very beginning, the memorial was a controversial experiment in the Rockefeller conglomerate. Some Rockefeller officers feared bad publicity; others did not believe the social sciences were really scientific and did all they could to destroy the memorial. Still others, part of the old guard of the Rockefeller conglomerate, began to experience "status panic" as they neared retirement age and therefore were opposed to anything new. The opposition was finally victorious in its push for a reorganization of the Rockefeller Foundation. A few of the memorial's projects were absorbed into the Rockefeller Foundation in 1929. Although Ruml left on good terms and directed another Rockefeller foundation in the 1930s, the politics of the memorial's demise did not sit well with him.

While Ruml served as dean of the University of Chicago School of Social Sciences, he became one of the most influential trustees of the newly reorganized Julius Rosenwald Fund. He outlined the Rosenwald Fund's agenda for inquiry into black economic conditions and wrote a letter concerning this which was sent to President Herbert Hoover over Julius Rosenwald's signature. His proposal laid the groundwork for the Rosenwald Fund's race-reform activities of the 1930s.

While serving on the Macy's Board of Trustees, Ruml also directed the Rockefeller Spelman Fund, a small foundation which attempted to stimulate the professionalization of public administration sciences. The directorship of the Spelman Fund was Ruml's last direct foundation tie, but he remained an influential personality in the foundation sector, especially in the Carnegie Corporation, for many years.

In the late 1930s and 1940s, Ruml became increasingly dissatisfied with the growing complacency of the big foundations. He criticized the reluctance of the Rockefeller foundations and Carnegie Corporation to support the peace movements of the 1940s. These foundations turned down his proposal for a pro-peace organization.[12] His disillusionment with the stagnation of big foundations led him in the late 1940s to agree to write a popular article with Edwin Embree attacking the complacency of the foundations. But when Embree asked Ruml to sign the draft he had completed, Ruml balked. Thus, when *Harper's* magazine published "Timid Billions" in 1948, it bore only Embree's name.[13]

RUML'S SOCIAL SCIENCE POLICY AND PROGRAM

John D. Rockefeller, Sr., established the Laura Spelman Rockefeller Memorial in 1918 in memory of his wife. The memorial was to make contributions primarily to social and child welfare organizations. By 1922, major memorial appropriations supported emergency relief activities to the Soviet Union and China, Baptist organizations, and large institutions for social work such as the Y.M.C.A., the Y.W.C.A., the Boy Scouts, the Girl Scouts, and the Salvation Army. When Ruml joined the memorial in 1922, the foundation had capital funds totaling nearly $74 million and an annual income of over $4 million.[14]

He was given extraordinary leeway in determining how the funds were to be spent.

Approximately six months after taking office, Ruml asked Angell for his advice on "a memorandum on the Memorial's policy for the future that I have been working on." [15] Ruml's forty-page report was a remarkable document outlining the memorial's resource income, past appropriations, and future programs.[16] Its greatest significance lay in Ruml's justification for what was to become the foundation's major funding activity for the remainder of its life: a program financing the social sciences.

Ruml recommended the curtailment of appropriations to social welfare organizations and public health agencies. He recommended that the memorial's funds should be spent according to a ten-year plan which would disperse a projected income of $2 million per year. Ruml proposed that the memorial's programs address fundamental issues and produce immediate results. He felt that the expanded memorial program should supplement traditional appropriations. Ruml recommended extensive financing of social science research to tie in with the memorial's traditional emphasis on social welfare.

He argued, quite persuasively, that most who worked toward social welfare were "embarrassed by the lack of that knowledge which the social sciences must provide." [17] One might as well ask engineers to do without adequate development in chemistry and physics or physicians to do without biology. "The direction of work in the social field," Ruml lamented, "is largely controlled by tradition, inspiration, and expediency, a natural condition in view of our ignorance of individual and social forces." [18]

Ruml assumed that the absence of an empirical base for social sciences was due to the condition of academic social science. The academic social sciences were very young. Most of them—experimental psychology, economics, sociology, and anthropology—were less than fifty years old, especially in the United States. Specialized social science associations were also quite young. More important, university facilities were inadequate for the development of scientific social research. It was clear to Ruml that the development of academic social sciences would be beneficial to business, industry, and government as well as to social welfare organizations. Thus Ruml emphasized the need for development of empirical social sciences, which could help resolve pressing social problems, rather than the more theoretical and philosophical social sciences.

In outlining his social science program, Ruml focused on four issues. First, he wanted to define the social science field and identify empirical problems to be addressed. Second, he emphasized the need to give social scientists engaged in empirical social research access to adequate facilities for data collection and evaluation. Third, he mentioned the need to recruit and train social scientists in empirical research. Fourth, he pointed out the need for dissemination of social scientific knowledge. The first three of these issues became the pillars of Ruml's program.

Problems to be addressed in Ruml's program were those of immediate concern such as issues of child life, leisure time and recreation problems, vocational concerns, immigrant and race problems, age and poverty problems, and neighborhood perplexities. On the other hand, Ruml felt that "peoples of remote times or of remote places would scarcely be of major interest,"[19] and "The general fields of education and public health may be set aside because of the agencies already at work here."[20]

Creating possibilities for research meant developing organizations and providing facilities. Ruml believed that the university provided the best setting for research, because "the stability of the organization, the presence of a wide range of professional opinion, the existence of scholarly and scientific standards of work, recognized and reasonably effective channels of inter-university communication, all make for a favorable environment of investigation."[21]

In order for social scientists to gain access to data, it was necessary to facilitate closer contact between social scientists and community settings. Ruml therefore required social scientists to use social welfare and law enforcement agencies as research settings and to provide feedback to these institutions. This encouraged practical social research. Ruml also advocated interdisciplinary research, pointing out that the professional distinctions among the social sciences were misleading. Thus the memorial financed only research institutes and organizations which included representatives from the various social sciences.

Ruml felt that it was necessary "to avoid creating a situation in which the Memorial is itself actually carrying on social investigations. The Memorial cannot assume responsibility for the outcome of any specific piece of research or for the opinion of any single scientist."[22] This was meant to encourage the separation of social research from its sources of funding to promote the concept of "value-free" empirical social research.

Ruml believed that "social research should be conducted by permanent organizations, not by councils, committees, and staffs that are brought together for the study of a particular question and that disperse after the publication of a report." The most effective form of collaborative research involved a permanent institution which continued "interest in a group of related problems indefinitely." This attitude, of course, insured that only the most elite white male universities and private organizations would be worthy of significant funding, because only these institutions were considered "permanent" enough.[23]

Ruml recommended that "social research should ordinarily be associated with opportunities for graduate and undergraduate instruction . . . the opportunity for presenting students with fresh material and for discovering research talent among graduate students is too great to be neglected."[24] Prior to the 1920s, social science undergraduate and graduate programs did not have a significant empirical thrust. The memorial sponsorship of academic social research encouraged widespread use of fieldwork in graduate training and brought into being the practice in which professors employ teams of graduate students to collect and analyze data.

Ruml was concerned about the social sciences' lack of commercial value, in contrast to the physical sciences and the arts. He felt that a stronger empirical base would make the social sciences more marketable. He also discussed the need to disseminate social science literature for popular and professional consumption. He suggested use of popular and professional periodicals, creation of new periodicals, assistance in publishing social scientific books, and financial assistance to museums.

WHAT THE MEMORIAL DID

Ruml's program ideas were adopted by the memorial trustees almost to the letter. By 1924, the foundation's funding priorities were the creation of academic social science research institutes in America and Europe, assistance to isolated research programs, establishment of private social research organizations, and sponsorship of an international fellowship program. Only Ruml's ideas for the popularization of social sciences were not fully realized.[25]

The first funding priority was the support of social science research in elite white male institutions and in interdisciplinary social research organizations. Ruml's success in expanding academic social sciences was in large part due to the cooperation of university administrators enthusiastic about the potential of the social sciences. Memorial officers had close ties with the presidents of the University of Chicago, the University of North Carolina at Chapel Hill, Yale University, and Fisk University. Through Ruml, the National Research Council under the direction of Robert Yerkes received major grants for research in eugenics and psychobiology in the early 1920s. This research, which was the primary emphasis of the National Research Council's new Division of Psychology and Anthropology, paralleled the psychological perspectives of Beardsley Ruml and his chief, James Angell.

The Social Science Research Council was the major nonacademic social research organization supported by the memorial. Ruml and officers from other foundations created the organization in the mid–1920s. By selecting researchers representative of the "new social sciences" and by endorsing policy-related research, Ruml and the other foundation officers were able to nationalize the concept of social science they had previously supported only in local academic institutes. The Social Science Research Council, the symbol of abstract empirical social science, institutionalized the separation of social science from its humanistic, ethical and epistemological roots.[26]

In his 1922 report, Ruml had originally proposed to help about ten universities to develop interdisciplinary social science research institutes. Actually, the University of Chicago received most of the funds, because Ruml was very concerned about how the social sciences, particularly psychology, developed at his alma mater. The inclusion of Chicago political scientist Charles Merriam in the memorial's inner circle and his appointment as the first chairman of the Social Science Research Council exemplified the tie between the memorial and the University of Chicago. Chapel Hill, Fisk, and the London School of Economics were also favored by the memorial.

The amount of monetary support given to each institution cannot be seen as a direct measure of that institution's importance in the memorial's plans. Many important projects received relatively little funding—the National Research Council for example. Some, such as the Association for Negro Life, were outside mainstream social science. The central importance of Yale, the University of North Carolina, and Fisk in the memorial's plans for institutional social science are not reflected in the comparatively small appropriations these institutions received. Likewise, figures do not reveal the biases some memorial officers held against particular social sciences. Though Ruml was interested in promoting interdisciplinary research, he attempted to emphasize psychological and psychobiological research whenever possible as seen in the memorial-sponsored Hanover Conferences on Psychology, his concern over the weakness of psychology at the University of Chicago, and the foundation's support of the National Research Council and Yale University. Memorial officers also emphasized financing research institutions which were staffed by well-known economists and political scientists.

Contrary to recent accounts of the memorial, Ruml was not very impressed with sociology and supported sociologists only when one of the more prominent social scientists (for example, Charles Merriam of Chicago) or a sociologist with great visibility and interdisciplinary goals (Howard Odum of Chapel Hill and Charles S. Johnson of Fisk) was the primary memorial contact.[27]

Although Chicago, Fisk, and Chapel Hill sociology flourished through memorial financing, this was not the result of a conscious attempt on the part of memorial officers to develop the discipline. Thus, the institutionalization of sociology in the 1920s through memorial financing was a side effect of the effort to strengthen other more established social sciences.

In the early 1920s the memorial trustees developed a twelve-point policy plan to guide social science funding priorities. This plan was drawn up in 1924 in response to pressure from Rockefeller executives. It helps explain why empirical social science developed in such a conservative fashion and why the memorial trustees did not use the studies they sponsored for political purposes.[28]

THE MEMORIAL'S WHITE SOCIAL SCIENCE PROGRAM

Ruml's social science program laid the ideological and institutional groundwork for the expansion of European-descent social science in the United States and northwestern Europe. It was taken for granted in the phenomenological context of an apartheid society that only white men had the capacity to be trained to do the research in search of generalizable knowledge. The creation, reproduction, and distribution of mainstream social science revolved around the experiences of Anglo-Saxon males occupying elite positions in academia, professional associations, and funding organizations. When Ruml and his staff discussed "good" social science research, they were envisioning formalized white conceptions of empirical "realities." This was understandable, since social sciences were the invention of middle-class professionals of European descent who used their own experiences to formalize what they saw as universal principles of human individuality and personal behavior.

The white male bias of mainstream social sciences is quite apparent when one examines which institutions the memorial officers chose to receive funding and in noting what sorts of people the memorial considered able social scientists. As previously mentioned, the memorial supported research activities of scholars in the most elite white male universities in America and northwestern Europe. Women's colleges and black colleges, however, were not considered appropriate settings for social science research attempting to generate universal laws governing the causes, effects, and substance of human nature. The experiences of blacks and women did not count in a rigid order rooted in presumptions about the universal application of white male experience.

One might argue that the memorial did not finance mainstream social science in female and black colleges because they did not have the resources. Metaphorically speaking, this puts the cart before the horse. The memorial officers could and did create social science research centers wherever they wanted to. The University of North Carolina at Chapel Hill was not a wealthy institution, but the memorial and other foundations made it into the most prestigious social science center in the South. Although Yale was certainly wealthy in the 1920s, social science research there was grossly underdeveloped at the time. Through the help of the memorial and, later, the Rockefeller Foundation, Angell was able to fulfill Yerkes's dream to establish the Institute on Human Relations, which absorbed the Institute of Psychology and the Yale Laboratories of Primate Biology. Yale itself had neither the resources nor the personnel to create such a research enterprise. The foundations, especially the memorial, enabled Angell to do so. In sum, the lack of "resources" argument ignores the fact that foundation administrators could patronize whomever and whatever they pleased.

Perhaps the clearest indicators of the foundations' attitudes about white male dominance of social science research can be found in the composition of the Social Science Research Council and the memorial's internal division of labor. The Social Science Research Council symbolized white male dominance of empirical social science. Black social scientists qualified to participate in the council were virtually nonexistent in the 1920s, but in subsequent years able black scholars were essentially excluded from the organization's decision-making process. Furthermore, during the 1920s, the council made no concerted effort to train black social scientists through their fellowship program. The council kept the empirical study of race relations dependent on white decision making and consequently white assumptions.

The closest the Social Science Research Council came to recognizing the existence of the black experience and black scholars in the 1920s was the establishment of the Advisory Committee on Problems Relating to the Negro of the Social Science Research Council in 1926. Present during the initial meeting of the Advisory Committee were Frank Ross (Chairman), Clark Wissler, Robert E. Park, Thomas J. Woofter, Jr., Melville Herskovits, and Sterling Spero.

Howard Odum, who apparently could not attend, had suggested that two or three blacks be invited who represented different fields. The meeting's minutes stated: "It was the general consensus of opinion of those present that we should later include Negroes in our group but that just now we are organizing and that at this time it does not seem opportune to include [persons] other than whites." Shortly after the Advisory Committee's procedures for evaluating black related projects were set, membership was extended to: Charles S. Johnson, Carter G. Woodson and Monroe N. Work.[29]

The memorial was a small, informal foundation. Its staff ranged in age from mid-twenties to early thirties. Each person was assigned a particular area. Ruml handled white social science programs, Snydor Walker's domain was social work, and Lawrence Frank was responsible for child development issues. Leonard Outhwaite was responsible for black social science programs plus everything else related to race—further evidence of the memorial officers' assumption that black social scientists and empirical inquiries into black conditions had little to do with mainstream white social science.

LEONARD OUTHWAITE

Leonard Outhwaite was recruited to direct the memorial's race-relations work in 1923. He was born in California in 1892, the son of a Cleveland industrialist who was an early associate of John D. Rockefeller, Sr. Independently wealthy, he was educated in several private schools in the U.S. and abroad and attended Yale University, the University of California, Columbia University, and the College of Physicians and Surgeons.[30] Outhwaite's was the classical well-traveled background of an anthropologist, while his high intelligence was more than apparent in the versatility of his educational and employment history.

At the University of California at Berkeley, Outhwaite was greatly influenced by Alfred Kroeber. In turn, Kroeber and his faculty were so impressed by Outhwaite that in 1916, they invited him to teach in the Anthropology Department, even though he had not yet obtained an advanced degree. In 1917, he decided to become a professional anthropologist. At that time acquiring a Ph.D. in anthropology required a grounding in physical as well as social anthropology. Thus, Outhwaite completed a premedical course at the Columbia University summer school in 1917 and in the fall entered the College of Physicians and Surgeons. Outhwaite intended to return to the University of California to complete his Ph.D., but before he could do so, America entered World War I, and Outhwaite was invited to join the Committee on Classification of Personnel in the United States Army. With the committee, Outhwaite applied the principles of personnel management to military manpower needs. This work "brought [him] into contact with the men who were then leaders in the field of psychology, including the field of educational psychology."[31] James R. Angell and Beardsley Ruml were undoubtedly among the well-known psychologists with whom Outhwaite worked for two years.

When the war ended, Outhwaite, Ruml, and others associated with the committee organized the Scott Company of Philadelphia which "provided labor selection and personnel administration services to industry." At the same time, he and several others reorganized the Bureau of Industrial Research, which also specialized in industrial personnel administration and labor relations. While working for the Industrial Research Bureau and the Scott Company, Outhwaite also conducted surveys in various industries and organized the personnel offices of the Philadelphia Company in Pittsburgh, which managed all the public utilities of that city.

Outhwaite also devoted much attention to the development of textbooks on personnel administration. He taught courses on personnel administration at Columbia University at the request of John J. Cross, dean of the Columbia Summer Session, who was a former member of the U.S. Army Personnel Classification Committee and was to become an influential liberal voice in the Julius Rosenwald Fund in the 1930s. About 1923, Outhwaite, Ruml, and others organized the Personnel Research Federation. As its director, Outhwaite founded and edited the *Journal of Personnel Research*.

Outhwaite's first Rockefeller commission led, in 1924, to his employment in the memorial under the direction of Beardsley Ruml. When the memorial was absorbed into the Rockefeller Foundation in 1929, Outhwaite spent a year as captain of his auxiliary schooner *Kinkajou* on a fourteen-thousand-mile cruise on the Atlantic Ocean. During the 1930s and 1940s, he worked for the federal government, for the Rockefeller Foundation as a consultant, and for Lawrence Rockefeller. He acted as administrator of the Minority Group Relations Office of the War Manpower Commission, a federal agency directed by Will W. Alexander and in the Farm Security Administration, an agency in which Alexander also played a significant part.

LEONARD OUTHWAITE'S RACIAL WORLD VIEW

On November 13, 1924, the memorial governing board formally announced their entry into the field of the Negro problem:

Resolved that it is the sense of the Board that the negro problem should receive serious consideration of this Board, and Resolved further that the officers of the Memorial be, and they hereby are, requested to study the possibility of a desirable approach in connection with this problem and to report back to a later meeting of the Board or of the Executive Committee.[32]

This resolution formalized groundwork that Beardsley Ruml and Leonard Outhwaite had laid for a serious inquiry into black conditions. The evolution of the program was a reflection of Outhwaite's racial world view. Like the other memorial program officers, Outhwaite was given extraordinary autonomy in determining the direction and substance of his assigned domain. All race-related matters fell to him. The small size of the foundation and the similarity in age of its officers created a tight-knit organization which facilitated an informal exchange of information.

Outhwaite spent a year talking with other foundation officers and traveling through the South before submitting a plan of action to Ruml and President Arthur Woods in the fall of 1925. During his travels, Outhwaite became a supporter of the southern liberal approach to the Negro problem, which urged that blacks be justly treated in a permanently segregated South. Southern liberals feared bloodshed if militant blacks became popular leaders or if conservative whites prevailed. They believed that racial tension could best be handled through the cooperation of the "better elements" of both races. "Interracial cooperation" became the catchword for racial accommodation in the new South.[33] On his first tour of the South in 1923, Outhwaite recorded the opinions of an observer of the interracial cooperation movement:

Professor Fisher was enthusiastic about the Interracial work. Speaking of the need for such work, he cited instances of the unrest among the negroes since the war. . . . He indicated that. . . he feared that some of the hot heads would precipitate some sort of general uprising. . . . He felt that the Commission was doing a fine work in removing some of these irritants, and in restoring confidence among the negroes in the Southern white people. . . . He called attention to the difficulty which a negro leader had in retaining the confidence of his own people, unless he was a radical. The man who follows the middle course was not acceptable either to the white or the colored people. He felt that one of the great uses of the Interracial Commission was making vocal this large group of fair minded people of both races. . . . Heretofore there has been no machinery through [which] the midway groups could work. . . . Through the agency of the Interracial Commission, the saner members are being brought in contact with each other and are encouraged to find that there are so many of their kind.[34]

Though some southern liberals privately supported integration, most did not dare to air these views in public, particularly those who advocated interracial cooperation.

It is not surprising that Outhwaite agreed with southern white liberals about race relations. Beardsley Ruml and other Rockefeller executives and trustees also supported the Southern white liberal world view. Southern-bred officers lobbied especially energetically for memorial support of southern white liberal concerns such as the Commission on Interracial Cooperation.[35] Outhwaite's correspondence reveals his opposition to the white conservatives' view of race, which suggested that blacks should be ignored or eliminated from American society. Outhwaite wished to stimulate the development of viable segregated institutions which would make it possible for the black "to get upon his feet and take care of his own needs in schools, health, etc. by his own support either through taxes or personal contributions."[36]

The fundamental liberal solution to the problem of the rapidly changing exslave population was the development of formal black education, which would assure the proper moral training of ex-slaves, teaching them how to adapt and prosper in a segregated society. Southern liberals were able to persuade the General Education Board, the Rockefeller Foundation, the Julius Rosenwald Fund, and other foundations that industrial education and limited higher education represented the best way to "help Negroes." Even though the memorial did not routinely sponsor education projects, Outhwaite supported education for blacks. He believed that it could make blacks "more sober, more industrious, more competent."[37]

Outhwaite and his superiors encouraged memorial support of conservative interracial and black organizations and conferences. The friendship between Outhwaite and Will Alexander, as well as the endorsement of high-level Rockefeller executives and trustees, helped make the Commission on Interracial Cooperation the civil rights organization most heavily financed by the memorial. Alexander was Outhwaite's major advisor on race matters, and he also greatly influenced the foundation officers' views on black leaders, the funding of black social work, schools, and organizations, and the selection of candidates for the memorial's Negro Social Science and Social Work Scholarship Program. The friendship tie between Outhwaite and Alexander allowed the Commission on Interracial Cooperation to receive funding even when its leaders failed to meet matching agreements.[38]

Outhwaite supported the activities of the National Urban League, the New York City Urban League, and Negro Boy Scouts because they stressed social work and moral training for urban black populations. He endorsed the Negro Business League because it promoted accommodative black business development.[39] Outhwaite's faith in the concept of racial justice in a formally segregated society led him to admire conservative and moderate black leaders who were followers of Booker T. Washington's philosophy of racial accommodation. He and Will Alexander particularly respected Robert R. Moton, Booker T. Washington's successor at Tuskegee Institute.

Obviously, Outhwaite's admiration for Moton and other accommodative black leaders was in conformity with his assumption that asymmetrical race relations in America were permanent. He wished to promote the views of moderate and conservative black leaders in shaping foundation policy. In 1927 with recommendations from Will Alexander, he organized the Negro Problems Conference of white and black leaders who discussed the future of the race problem and the role of foundations in helping alleviate it. Most of the blacks selected to participate were older men not sympathetic to the radical view of younger leaders.

Although Ernest Just and A. Phillip Randolph were the most outspoken black leaders at the conference, their comments about the need for financially independent black education and black labor unions went unheard. The suggestions which were incorporated in the foundation policy of the next twenty years were those of the accommodative black participants and like-minded whites. These included the establishment of fellowship programs to train blacks to staff their own segregated academic institutions and greater foundation support of higher education for blacks.[40]

Living in New York City, Outhwaite became quite knowledgeable about prominent Harlem Renaissance figures such as Alaine L. Locke, James W. Johnson, and Charles S. Johnson. He admired the poet Langston Hughes as a "pleasant and capable youngster"[41] and liked Congolese art. His appreciation of black culture, while it did not override his conventional views about the place of blacks in society, helps explain his special effort to redefine the Negro problem. This effort is best seen in his sponsorship of social scientific inquiries about black conditions.

OUTHWAITE'S ADVOCACY OF THE SCIENTIFIC STUDY OF BLACKS

A process leading to radical redefinition of race relations began in the late 1910s and early 1920s with the dramatic black migration to northern urban areas. Outhwaite was determined to use memorial resources to understand these changes and to remedy the lack of scientific information about blacks.

New economic and social pressures are developing and migration continues as a symptomatic phenomenon. In particular the mores and social customs which served an older generation as methods of control and of adjustment are breaking up or are no longer adequate. It seems, therefore, that demands for study and assistance in this field are likely to increase rather than to diminish and it may be well to call attention to some of the ways in which it may be approached.[42]

From the end of the Civil War to the 1920s, most research on blacks was theoretical and rooted in the premises of social Darwinism. The scanty empirical studies were done almost exclusively by scholars marginal to or outside institutional social science. Hence, when federal policy makers wished to commission researchers to investigate the earliest waves of black migration to the North and consequences of migration such as the race riots of 1917 and 1919, they had to look outside mainstream academia.[43] Thus, Robert E. Park's and Charles S. Johnson's assessment of the 1919 Chicago race riot gained fame not only for its theory and interpretation of data, but also because it was the first interwar effort by mainstream sociologists to analyze racial changes empirically.[44]

In "The Negro in America," Outhwaite laid out an extensive plan for research on black conditions.[45] He criticized previous research for its excessive generalization about a vague Negro problem. Such generalizations, he warned, were "inadvisable not only as being subject to an undue amount of scientific error and confused statement but also as being irritating and dangerous."[46] They focused on "that aspect which is the least easy to deal with and arouses the greatest amount of controversy and emotion—the matter of color and physical dissimilarity."[47] Furthermore, Outhwaite argued, blacks resented such generalizations: "There is a considerable body of Negro people of intelligence and standing that will become irritated if continually referred to as 'problems.' "[48]

Outhwaite proposed to supplant generalized analysis of the Negro problem with empirical research. Differentiation of the Negro problem would reveal the complexity of black conditions through ecological, regional, and interracial comparisons. At the same time, however, Outhwaite cautioned against losing sight of the most fundamental issue, namely the social definitions and consequences of racial differences in American life.

The various special studies . . . should not obscure a recognition of the fact that we are faced, in the first place, with fundamental differences in pigmentation and structure of the two groups, which we characterize as racial differences; and in the second place, we are faced with the belief, and the behaviors growing out of the belief, that these physical differences are attended by differences in capacity and adjustment which demand, for one group, necessary specialized treatment.[49]

Outhwaite felt that through scientific study it would be possible to develop social mechanisms to assure the rational and harmonious management of intergroup relations.[50] The scientific study of black conditions was a tool to help incorporate blacks into post–World War I American society, which still demanded the segregation of blacks into low positions. Scientific inquiry was not meant to be charitable to blacks, but to expedite their "new accommodation," as Outhwaite implied in a 1927 staff conference:

We are dealing with a group of people incorporated in our country for better or worse; that they are handicapped in many respects. There seems to be no way of getting rid of them even if we desire to do so.

Our objective then, probably is to bring them as early as possible to a state where they can develop their own leadership, and where they can finance their own welfare. The sooner that is done, the sooner the burden will be taken off the general welfare and public administration of the rest of the country for their support.[51]

Outhwaite made frequent attempts to persuade social welfare agencies to use scientific data in developing programs to eradicate black adjustment problems. He also attempted to use black and interracial organizations such as the Negro Business League as research generators:

It does . . . seem to me that there are several projects, or rather possibilities for work, that are worthy of consideration. Among these possibilities I should mention: A study of Negro business conditions and credit facilities by Negroes themselves. It is possible that the Negro Business Men's League . . . might be induced to undertake a genuine study of this character.[52]

In 1928 Outhwaite sponsored the National Interracial Conference, which was attended by foundation representatives and delegates from social welfare and civil rights organizations. Charles S. Johnson was commissioned to write a summary of the conference and to analyze the existing literature on black social, economic, and health problems. The resulting book, entitled *The Negro in American Civilization*, was the most comprehensive survey of black conditions at the time of its publication in 1930.[53] Nevertheless, it had little impact on social work practice. Outhwaite's scientific solution to the adjustment problems of blacks was evidently thought to be impracticable.

FUNCTIONAL DIFFERENTIATION OF THE NEGRO PROBLEM AND COMMISSIONED SOCIAL RESEARCH

In "The Negro in America" Outhwaite recommended research in various areas, especially anthropometry, psychopathology, black crime, black business and credit, and black history. He sought and supported social scientists carrying out research in these areas. The memorial's policy, which forbade researchers to mention its support of their work, has created the impression that many race-related studies published in the 1920s were motivated entirely by scientific curiosity. But although the commissioned researchers were interested in working on the projects Outhwaite endorsed, his correspondence reveals his efforts to select congenial social scientists. He occasionally pressured them to conform to his expectations.

Outhwaite was disturbed by the lack of American work in African anthropology and Afro-American history (including West Indian history). He decided that black Americans should be supported to work in these areas, and proposed that the memorial should work through the Association for the Study of Negro Life. He urged its director, Carter G. Woodson, to de-emphasize "documentary history" in favor of training black scholars, literary figures, and musicians.

It seems to me that Carter Woodson's organization might be utilized as a medium through which studies could be made in Negro anthropology and contemporary Negro life. There is a good deal of misinformation and misinterpretation going about touching on the Negro's African background. It also seems that Woodson's Journal loses a good deal of its popular appeal and also of its value as a social service in confining itself strictly to documentary history. Woodson should be training some younger Negro scholars in history and in anthropology so that they might take up themselves the study of their own people on a somewhat wider and more vital basis. This organization might also be made the medium for inducing some of the younger Negro poets and musicians to undertake the study of their folk songs on a more extensive and scientific basis.[54]

Outhwaite attempted to stimulate American anthropological research in the Congo and Southern Africa, areas which were inhabited by rapidly vanishing tribal groups.

The primitive culture of the Bantus is being subjected to certain European influences. The race itself is rapidly disappearing under hardship and disease. An astronomer on the path of a total eclipse who neglected to take his observations would be guilty of a scientific crime—yet an eclipse is recurrent while the passage of a primitive people is a unique and irrecoverable phenomenon.[55]

But Outhwaite soon discovered that there were no American anthropologists who had field experience in black Africa. He interviewed Yale anthropologist and memorial contact Clark Wissler, who told him of the neglect of this area by American anthropologists and suggested how it might be remedied.

Prof. Wissler said that he knew of no American anthropologists that had an opportunity for field study in Africa. Some American scientists had visited Africa but their interests had been in Geology, Vertebrate Zoology, Entomology, hunting and what not. Some American anthropologists, such as Fay-Cooper Cole, Albert Kroeber, Waterman, and others, had some acquaintanceship with the African field, but it had been built on documentary studies and specimens of material culture. Prof. Wissler spoke favorably of Prof. Cole's work and said he had some promising anthropologists with him at Chicago. Prof. Wissler spoke of a young investigator named Melville J. Herskovits, who has held a fellowship from the National Research Council and who has been working on negro problems in America. Prof. Wissler said he had not had foreign field experience but that he had enthusiasm and interest and might make a good field worker.[56]

Outhwaite wanted to find an experienced sociologist interested in making an extensive study of Congolese tribal groups. Clark Wissler told him that Chicago sociologist Ellsworth Faris had attempted, unsuccessfully, to obtain support for such research from the National Research Council. Outhwaite wrote to R. S. Woodworth of the Council, consulted Clark Wissler, and went to Chicago to talk with Faris. After some delay, Faris agreed to do the research under memorial sponsorship.[57]

Outhwaite was critical of the abuses of anthropometry, the measurement of physical features. However, he supported the work of anthropologists such as Clark Wissler and Melville Herskovits, who eschewed the crude equation of racial traits and cultural behavior.

Since Outhwaite was interested in accommodative black economic development, he wanted to stimulate studies of black business and credit. He wanted to find out whether black economic problems were due to racial discrimination or to lack of ability and industry. To this end, he supported the activities of the Negro Business League, the research of Chicago business economist L. C. Marshall and University of North Carolina sociologist Howard Odum.

The relationship between Leonard Outhwaite and Howard Odum's Chapel Hill Institute for Social Research was particularly fascinating. Ruml and Outhwaite selected the University of North Carolina at Chapel Hill as a field laboratory for memorial research interests in the South because of the liberal orientation of its President Howard Chase and its southern-bred faculty such as Odum. It was also ideal for collection of data on racial measurements, black crime, black credit, and black folklore. Odum's own interests led him to undertake studies on black folklore and crime, which the memorial financed, but he might not have pursued anthropometry and credit studies without Outhwaite's support.[58] Odum's eagerness to please his benefactors at the memorial bordered on obsequiousness, even though this was not really necessary for him to secure foundation support for his own pet projects. The memorial was particularly committed to funding race research at Chapel Hill.

Outhwaite used memorial-financed research organizations as well as university research institutes to realize his priorities. He periodically asked Chicago political scientist Charles Merriam and other officers of the Social Science Research Council to lobby for council approval of projects such as studies of intelligence testing, black crime, and even Mexican migration, while reminding other correspondents of the non-interference policies of his foundation.[59]

In sum, Outhwaite's attempts to usher in environmental perspectives on the Negro problem were virtually unceasing. Clark Wissler, Melville Herskovits, Howard W. Odum, Charles S. Johnson, and Ellsworth Faris all came into his orbit. Columbia sociologist Frank Ross, who at one point attempted to flatter Outhwaite by calling him his "mentor," undertook a forty-three-day tour of the South in 1925, giving the foundation officer abundant feedback about race relations.[60] Outhwaite also arranged for Bronislaw Malinowski, the eminent British anthropologist of primitive peoples, to tour the South while he took note of the visitor's observations on race relations.[61] But in spite of Outhwaite's activity, the obvious shortage, indeed virtual non-existence of black social scientists interested in researching the Negro problem eventually prodded Outhwaite to organize the Negro Social Science and Social Work Scholarship Program and to support the establishment of the Fisk University Social Science Department.

THE MEMORIAL'S NEGRO SOCIAL SCIENCE AND SOCIAL WORK SCHOLARSHIP PROGRAM AND FISK UNIVERSITY

Virtually every activity Outhwaite and his foundation sponsored on the Negro problem was geared toward developing new black leaders who could act as mediators in an era in which the black population was urbanizing rapidly and increasingly demanding civil rights. In order to understand Outhwaite's interest in training black social scientists, we must first realize the broader foundation interest in creating an accommodative enlightened black bourgeoisie through unprecedented financing of higher education for blacks.

In a 1927 special report on the status of black education, Jackson Davis of the General Education Board observed:

The education of the Negroes who constitute about one-third of the population of the South forms a necessary part of any plan of advancement and welfare of the South as a whole. . . . The development . . . has been mainly a rapid growth of institutions and of influences already at work, but under changing circumstances that have been in the main favorable. . . . The increase has not only been rapid for the entire period of eleven years, but it is still going on. It is a testimony of the ambition of the colored people, of their desire for higher education and of their capacity to receive it. It means that more of the race can supply its own leaders, its teachers, ministers, physicians, and business-men, and that in all the walks of Negro life a higher level of intelligence will prevail.[62]

This report and others convinced the governors of the General Education Board and the Julius Rosenwald Fund to de-emphasize funding of rural industrial ed-ucation in favor of black higher education beginning in the late 1910s.[63] Jack-son Davis and other race-relations experts in major foundations assumed that the best way to deal with the emerging "New Negro" was to develop an en-lightened black elite and to use science to solve the problems confronting blacks. With this goal in mind, foundations supported several Negro University Centers in the South (Howard, Fisk, Atlanta, Tuskegee, Hampton, and Dillard). This policy continued until the *Brown* Decision outlawed Jim Crow education in 1954.

A major goal of this policy was to develop functional differentiation among the Negro University Centers.[64] This policy of "differentiation" promoted un-even development of programs in Negro University Centers. Experts on blacks did not encourage black universities to develop in areas which were monopo-lized by its "sister institutions." For instance, since Tuskegee was earmarked for agriculture, Monroe Work's plea for funds to build up his social research program went unheard.[65] Atlanta University received Rockefeller funds to de-velop the only black school of social work but was not encouraged to develop a medical school. Also, black colleges which fell outside the Negro University Center circuit were unable to attract much attention from the Rockefeller foun-dations. Jackson Davis's diary indicates an intentional effort to steer projects to the appropriate black universities.

If the GEB [General Education Board] undertakes any work in this field, I should not choose West Virginia as the place for it. Fisk or Atlanta would be better, having more collateral resources on which to draw and being more in touch with the Negro popula-tion.[66]

THE SCHOLARSHIP PROGRAM

The memorial's white social science fellowship program, channeled through the Social Science Research Council, encouraged scholars to contribute to the quest for generalizable knowledge about human nature. In contrast, Outhwaite and his memorial colleagues saw the black social scientist as a "race leader." They also assumed that blacks could contribute only to knowledge about black issues, and consequently the memorial was willing to support Carter Wood-son's Association for the Study of Negro Life, which was a black institution studying black history. One of Woodson's white patrons wrote:

There are important portions of [black history] which cannot be so well elaborated by a white man as by a negro—fields in which a colored man can get, by "field work," facts and documents which a white man could not readily obtain. It is an unusual opportunity that is presented, when a colored man competently qualified, and who has the confidence of his race, is ready to embark upon this line of investigation.[67]

The memorial officers' assumptions about the convergence of leadership and black social science is especially apparent in the guidelines of their Negro Social Science and Social Work Scholarship Program, which operated between 1926 and 1929. This informal fellowship program was designed to offer a few blacks the opportunity to attend elite graduate schools. Outhwaite consulted Jackson Davis, Will Alexander, and other southerners in his recruitment decisions.[68] Most of the recipients of scholarships attended the University of Chicago; a few attended New York, Columbia, and Harvard Universities.

The scholarship program was meant to provide improved black leadership, since the foundation officers believed that "trained Negroes can reach the life of *their people* [my emphasis] in a manner to which no White man can hope to attain.[69] The "difference" in the aims of the Negro Scholarship Program is seen in the emphasis its candidates were expected to place on study of the Negro problem. The formal criteria of selection minimized the importance of academic ability. Contributions to social science were expected for white fellows only.

THE SCHOLARSHIP RECIPIENTS

Because of Outhwaite's interest in recruiting potential race leaders, most of the scholarship recipients were older men (thirty-three was the average age) who had administrative experience in a black college or university.[70] Most of the recipients had had previous graduate school experience. Outhwaite and his southern liberal advisors assumed that the South was still the "home region" of the black population—hence all the recipients but one (Albert Dunham) were born, educated, or employed in the South at the time of application (see Table 1).

The scholarship program was not meant to encourage recipients to pursue the Ph.D. degree. Recipients were selected according to their potential to "teach and lead their people," not their potential to become scholars. Most of those chosen desired to return South after one to three years of study and seek employment in a black institution. Rejected applications were not retained in the Memorial Archives, so investigation into the characteristics of persons who did not receive scholarships is impossible. But it is clear that most recipients were not chosen because they had coherent academic goals. The question "What are your plans after completing studies?" elicited vague responses such as "to continue work in the South under the auspices of____College," "to teach," "research in Negro education," and "carry out a research project in Negro Africa or return to the Southern section of the United States." Only four of those chosen, E. Franklin Frazier, Albert Beckman, A. Taylor, and Albert Dunham, had ambitious scholarly goals. These four scholarship recipients were the only ones who eventually obtained doctorate degrees.

Table 1
Selected Demographic Characteristics of Recipients of the Laura Spelman Rockefeller Memorial Scholarship Program for Negro Social Science and Social Work, 1927–1929

	Age*	Educational Background	Place of Birth (St. or Country)	Area of Interest	Last Occup. at time of Applic.
Beckman, A.	33	Linc. U. (A.B.) OH State U. (M.A.)	South Carolina	Psychology	Instructor at Howard U.
Blooah, C.	?	Taylor Wooster College	Liberia	Anthropology	None
Carrington, C.	24	Howard U. (A.B.)	Virginia	Anthropology	Instructor at Jarvis Col.
Chivers, W.	31	Morehouse Cl. (A.B.)	Georgia	Soc. & Ed. Admin.	Instructor at Morehouse Jr. Col.
Creswell, I.	25	Fisk U. (A.B.)	Mississippi	Econ., Bus. Adm. and Fin.	Bookkeeper at Fisk Univer.
Davis, R.	37	Fisk U.	?	Demogr. & Anthr.	Res. Asst. Tuskegee Institute
Dunham, A.	21	U. of Chic. (Ph.D)	Illinois	Ph.Soc. Sci.	Asst. Hotel Manag. Chicago, IL
Frazier, E.F.	33	Howard (A.B.) Clark U. (M.A.)	Maryland	Sociology	Dir. of Sch. of Soc. Work Atl. Univ.
Hubert, B.	43	N.Y.S. of Soc. Wk. Morehouse (A.B.) MA Agr.Cl.(B.S)	Georgia	Agr. Econ.	Pres., GA State Col.

Table 1—*Continued*

	Age*	Educational Background	Place of Birth (St. or Country)	Area of Interest	Last Occup. at time of Applic.
Taylor, A.	35	U. of Mich. (A.B.) Harvard U. (A.B.)	District of Columbia	History	Prof. Hist. & Dean of Men, Fisk Univ.
Whiting, J.	51	U. of Penn. (A.B.)	Virginia	Ed.	Inst. Tuskegee
Wilson, G.	?	?	?	Anthropology	?
King, L.	29	Howard U. (B.S.)	New York	Anthropology	Student, Howard Univ.

Source: Data from Scholarship application forms and Memorial
dockets respectively found in Negro Fellowship LSRM
series 3 subseries 8$_2$ and LSRM series 1, Box 4.

*At the time of application
?Information not available.

Most of the scholarship recipients were men who had been out of college for a while and who had rusty academic skills or heavy social responsibilities. Completing coursework was difficult for them, and doctoral study almost impossible. Benjamin Hubert, a member of a prominent black family in Georgia and president of Georgia State College, serves as an example of a typical fellowship recipient. Through Will Alexander, he received a scholarship to Harvard. He intended to work on his Ph.D. in agricultural economics, and presented grandiose plans of study to the memorial. Heavy responsibilities and illness forced him to apply for extensions which extended his scholarship from 1929 to 1937. Although he finally completed his coursework, he never obtained a doctorate.

Outhwaite's interest in black problems led him to exclude from consideration black social scientists who did not limit themselves to this area of study. His positivistic definition of social science also excluded those who emphasized a humanistic approach to social science. Thus Albert Dunham almost failed to receive a scholarship, even though he was probably the most brilliant of the recipients. Dunham planned to specialize in the philosophy of social science, emphasizing the theory of value. But Outhwaite questioned Dunham's eligibility for a scholarship for reasons outlined in the following letter from Outhwaite to Dunham's mentor at the University of Chicago, T. V. Smith

I note from your letter that Mr. Dunham's interests up to this time appear to have been primarily in the field of philosophy, and that even his interests in psychology appear to be of a philosophical-interpretive character. In the Memorial's interpretation, philosophy is not normally regarded as one of the social sciences. I am wondering to what extent Mr. Dunham's natural development will lead him into the fields of individual psychology, economics, sociology, etc.[71]

Smith succeeded in reassuring Outhwaite that Dunham's studies emphasized the social sciences as much as they did philosophy. In his letter, he spoke less of Dunham's work than of his "formal" affiliations and of the structure of the university's social science and philosophy departments.

Mr. Dunham's formal affiliations have been and are with the Department of Philosophy; his actual interests have been and are most likely to continue in the field you denominate as the social sciences. With us philosophy is formally and factually a social science. . . . This Chicago school of philosophy has almost completely, for better or worse, eschewed metaphysics and gone in for sociology and social psychology. Besides, Mr. Dunham has done and will continue to do something like half of his work formally in the social departments. Moreover, with his definitely empirical bent, he can be counted upon after graduate instruction is over to work in the broad field that you outline. He might as easily and as appropriately be formally in social psychology or sociology as in philosophy right now.[72]

The memorial gave scholarships only to blacks who were admitted into a graduate program in one of the social sciences. Once they were admitted, they were at the mercy of white social scientists, who used the scholarship program to get blacks to do their research, often "dropping" their students after they had ceased to be useful. This was almost a routine practice among well known anthropologists and their black students. For example, in the late 1920s and early 1930s, there was a faddish interest in African and Afro-American cultures among American anthropologists, which created a demand for fieldworkers to collect ethnographic data on these cultures. During this period a number of blacks were recruited into anthropology departments at Chicago, Columbia, and Harvard. But none of the memorial-sponsored black anthropology students finished their academic work, although most were competent researchers. Charles Blooah was particularly talented, and his case provides a good illustration of this practice.

Blooah was a Christianized native African from Liberia who came to the United States in 1911 through missionary sponsorship. He attended Taylor University in Indiana and Wooster College in Ohio before moving to Chicago in 1920. He applied to the University of Chicago's anthropology department in 1925, needing one year of courses to complete his A.B. degree. In the autobiography he submitted to the memorial, he credited anthropologists Edward Sapir and Fay-Cooper Cole for "picking him up out of a bowling alley and helping him get out of financial difficulties." He planned to return to Liberia as a missionary after obtaining the A.B. degree in anthropology.[73]

Fay-Cooper Cole and Edward Sapir were more interested in Blooah's potential skill as a fieldworker than in his academic career. They excitedly told the memorial about this "rare gem" they found in a bowling alley.[74] The Chicago anthropologists' obvious desire to exploit Blooah's skills made Outhwaite suspicious of the intent of their request for a scholarship for his "education."

Both from the material which you have transmitted and from the previous conversation we had in Chicago, I have no doubt of Mr. Blooah's abilities and usefulness. I should like, however, to recall to you the general purpose for which the scholarships for negroes were created. These scholarships were designed primarily to help in the technical and professional education of American negroes of unusual ability who seemed likely to become leaders of their race in professional or educational work. . . . Is he likely to develop a capacity either to write or to teach in such a way that his training and experience will be transmitted to other members of his race?[75]

Cole assured the memorial that they were definately concerned about Blooah's academic career. But actually Cole and Sapir had other plans for Blooah, evident in their support for his return to Liberia after completing his degree. In his letter to Outhwaite asking for a renewal of Blooah's scholarship, Fay-Cooper Cole wrote:

Blooah is not the all-around student that Gold Refined Wilson has shown himself to be, but in the linguistic field he is a rare find. He is also a valuable man for the gathering of ethnological material . . . it appears that if Blooah remains in school this summer and fall he can receive his degree at Christmas. I thought he could make it this summer but he works quite slowly.[76]

More bluntly (and in routinely contradictory fashion), Cole wrote to Outhwaite:

Personally I am not nearly so much interested in having him obtain a degree as to see that he has the proper equipment to do the work for which he is fitted. We think he is a good investment and hope that it will be possible for him to go on with his training.[77]

Blooah did return to Liberia for several years. Soon after his return to America in 1931, he asked the memorial about the possibility of receiving a two-year fellowship to further his academic career. Sapir now balked when asked about Blooah's potential for advanced study. Suddenly, the "rare gem" of an African did not have the ability to undertake independent research.

I am answering your letter of inquiry of January 31st in regard to Mr. Charles G. Blooah. I have been very much interested in him and have considered him a very valuable informant and assistant in a research program which we have been conducting at the University of Chicago. Owing to our interest in him, we have encouraged him to the extent of teaching him how to write his own language phonetically, giving him elementary instruction in anthropology, encouraging him, to the extent that opportunity offered, for the degree of bachelor of philosophy, and having him accompany Dr. George Herzog on a Liberian expedition, recently completed, as assistant and interpretor. All this does not mean that we consider Mr. Blooah a man who is capable of undertaking independent field researches in anthropology and linguistics. He has a very definite sphere of usefulness, from which we have profited and from which we should hope to profit in the future, but I think it would be giving an entirely mistaken idea of Mr. Blooah's potentialities to encourage him to work for a higher degree in anthropology. I should therefore not recommend that he be given a graduate fellowship on the understanding that he fit himself for an independent career as anthropological investigator.[78]

Yet, Sapir was still willing to help Blooah return to Liberia to be used as a fieldworker:

On the other hand, if something could be done to make him of maximum usefulness within the very singular range of possibilities open to him, I think it should be done. The ideal thing would be to have him return to Liberia and help in some way, presumably with the support of a mission, in the education of his fellow tribesmen. There are probably very few, if any, other individuals of his tribe who have quite the degree of knowledge and sophistication that Mr. Blooah possesses and who are at the same time, so intimately associated with the life of the natives. If he were residenced in Liberia, we of the Department should certainly be glad to make arrangements with him for a certain amount of field anthropology under our guidance.[79]

The memorial officers decided to send Blooah to Fisk where he could continue his contributions to African ethnography, both for Fisk and the University of Chicago. Thus it is clear that even though they did not consider Blooah scholarly enough to study and teach in a white university, they felt that he was good enough for a black one. Sapir persuaded the Rosenwald and Rockefeller foundations to award a one-year teaching fellowship to Fisk's Department of Social Sciences to defray Blooah's expenses. After the year was up, however, the foundations refused Sapir's and Charles S. Johnson's pleas to renew Blooah's fellowship, even though he was doing an impressive job at Fisk. Blooah's fate is unknown.[80]

Outhwaite and the other memorial officers were quite reluctant to award scholarships to blacks who they felt might be "troublemakers." When Will Alexander and John Hope told Outhwaite of E. Franklin Frazier's difficulties in getting along with others,[81] Outhwaite expressed reservations about awarding him a scholarship to do graduate study in sociology at Chicago:

The facts advanced in his behalf indicate that he may be useful as a research worker. On the other hand, his experiences indicate that he has found difficulty in working with people and that it may be difficult for him, even when his training is over to find suitable employment. It seems to me that it may be perfectly right for us to provide for his training but we should not like to do so with the feeling that we would be called upon at a later time also to find him occupation and an outlet for his talents.[82]

The memorial officers granted Frazier a scholarship only after Hope and Alexander backed down, describing his behavior as immaturity which would work itself out.[83]

FISK UNIVERSITY

Outhwaite's last major project before the memorial was absorbed into the Rockefeller Foundation in 1929 was the development of the Fisk University Social Science Department. The idea was pushed by Thomas Elsa Jones, the new white president of Fisk, in the late 1920s, but memorial officers had long been interested in developing Fisk.[84]

Jones was appointed president following student protest at Fisk. He planned to reorganize the university and to develop a social science program in the process. The memorial officers and administrators of other Rockefeller foundations were impressed with Jones's efforts to reorganize the university's academic programs and with his fund-raising activities. In 1927 the memorial Board of Trustees authorized almost $200,000 for recruitment of well-qualified social scientists and for administration of the social science program over a five-year period. Jones predicted that after five years Fisk University would be prepared to "support on the basis of high quality out of its regular budget all of the undergraduate work in the social science department."[85]

As the years went by, the Fisk University Social Science Department offered a program of wide exposure to the uses of social science. From the start Fisk's was a race-relations social science program for which Jones sought to recruit personnel who were of "excellent quality and capable of doing first rate work in teaching research whether viewed from colored or white standards." Fisk was expected to remedy the "dearth of materials" and general lack of "scientific method research" about black problems.

The aim of the Social Science department [was] . . . to produce original studies which would be of considerable value in understanding the Negro and his problems. It was proposed to realize these objectives by means of a program of teaching and research . . . that would not only acquaint the student with the facts of his social and economic background but inspire him to use these facts to benefit himself and his community.[86]

The Fisk University Social Science Department conformed to Jones's concept of the function of black universities:

The fourth responsibility confronting the Negro University is that of research in race relations. Both the white and colored races must be provided with information and point of view if proper development of American life and institutions is to take place. Facts regarding background, tradition, culture, attitude and achievements of all the races must be patiently assembled, classified, measured and interpreted.[87]

Curriculum and research at the Fisk University Social Science Department were restricted to race-relations issues throughout the 1930s and early 1940s. The significance of this restriction becomes clear when we compare the program at Fisk with the white social science programs the memorial financed. In this comparison are revealed the condescending attitudes and practices of foundation administrators toward Negro problem social science and black scientists. Traditionally, social scientists have warmly praised the contributions of the Fisk University Social Science Department to race-relations research.[88] Certainly, the contributions of the Department of Social Sciences were impressive and in many respects have yet to be surpassed, but to the foundations the department represented lower caste Jim Crow social science. The memorial officers did not use the same criteria that they used to develop white social science research institutes in establishing the Fisk Social Science Department. For example, the memorial's relationship with the University of Chicago's Local Community Research Institute serves as an example of their funding policies for elite white academic institutions. The institute was organized in 1923 through a memorial grant, and throughout the 1920s the memorial remained the major financier of the institute. Like other white social science institutes, the Local Community Research Institute was independent of academic departments at the University of Chicago. It was governed by an interdisciplinary group of senior social scientists who relied upon doctoral students to carry out their field work. The Local Community Research Institute used Chicago as a laboratory and collected and disseminated information on social problems such as juvenile delinquency, prostitution, and homeless men for social welfare and law enforcement agencies.[89] Most of those who received degrees from the institute became academic and nonacademic urban specialists. Robert E. Park, Ernest Burgess, and Charles Merriam were especially involved in public affairs.[90]

In studying the list of research projects in the Memorial Archives, one may notice the fact that race was not a central concern of the institute.[91] This is puzzling in light of Robert E. Park's involvement in the institute and the image the Chicago Sociology Department was trying to maintain as the progenitor of the sociological study of blacks and other racial minorities. Until the arrival of E. Franklin Frazier in 1927, most studies of black conditions were minor census analyses. Thus, Frazier's tenure at Chicago was significant because he completed both the first comprehensive study of the black family and the institute's only major sociological race study of the 1920s. Obviously, white social scientists at Chicago simply were not interested in extensive empirical race-relations studies.

At the University of North Carolina at Chapel Hill, memorial officers encouraged Howard Odum to develop a Southern research program, but they also allowed him to develop a range of research interests, including race relations. The Chapel Hill Institute for Social Research was also an independent unit governed by an interdisciplinary group of social scientists who used doctoral students to do fieldwork. Its personnel were encouraged to involve themselves in local social welfare agencies and organizations promoting interracial cooperation, especially the Commission on Interracial Cooperation. In the period between the wars, the Chapel Hill Institute for Social Research produced many highly credentialed leaders for the South.[92]

The character and development of the Fisk University Social Science Department contrasts sharply with these two examples of white institutions. The department combined teaching and research, and did not have a doctoral program. (Doctoral programs were not considered appropriate for black universities. Black students beyond level of the master's degree were expected to attend white graduate programs in the North to study black or Southern issues.)[93] Since the Fisk social science program was not separated into academic and research components, Fisk University social scientists were more heavily burdened than those at Chicago or Chapel Hill. Johnson had limited resources to attract and develop high-caliber graduate students. Consequently, he had to remain dependent upon white academia to provide staff and complete his students' training. This helps to explain why Johnson maintained close ties with the University of Chicago. Through his position on the Julius Rosenwald Fund's Fellowship Selection Committee he had access to funds to send many promising black graduate students to Chicago.

Since the Fisk Social Science Department focused on race, the program had little to offer students interested in other issues.[94] Nor was there a concerted effort, as there was in the white institutes, to stimulate a high level of community involvement. The Fisk program was apolitical, especially in racial matters, and it was insulated from the Nashville community.[95] Johnson's department did not enjoy the political and social influence among local policy-making circles that the major administrators of the Chicago and Chapel Hill institutes had given the etiquette of the racial caste system.[96]

There were also great differences in mobility between white and black graduate students. While the white graduates of Chicago and Chapel Hill could get jobs almost anywhere, including black colleges, blacks who received social science degrees from Fisk were forced to find academic employment in the few black institutions that could afford to hire them.[97] Long before white social scientist flight from academia began in the 1970s, many black social scientists were forced to find employment in non-academic settings or to change their occupational identities, since black academic institutions became overfilled much more quickly than white ones. This lack of opportunity for black scholars was due in large part to the attitudes of white foundation administrators and social scientists, who assumed, as discussed earlier, that black social scientists were useful only in the study of black problems. This became a longstanding conventional wisdom in American social science.

Fisk remained as the center of race relations social scientific research largely due to foundation support. The foundations played a major role in recruiting social scientists for the Fisk Department.[98] Jackson Davis even went so far as to channel social science projects proposed for other individuals and institutions to Johnson and Fisk.[99] The foundations legitimated Johnson's program by appointing him to their various "Negro study" committees. Edwin Embree, president of the Julius Rosenwald Fund, made Fisk into a field laboratory for the fund. Johnson was appointed to the Board of Directors of the Julius Rosenwald Fund in 1934 and along with Will Alexander became coordinator of its division of race relations. The decline of race relations social science at Fisk in the late 1940s was caused mainly by a shift in foundation funding priorities and a lack of foundation confidence in Johnson's successor.[100]

Contemporary criticism of Johnson and his foundation ties is inadequate because criticism has been directed toward Johnson, while the role of the foundations has been ignored.[101] When Johnson became director of the Fisk University Department of Social Science, he inherited the foundation's plan for black social science. His racial philosophy conformed with that of foundation experts, at least on the surface; thus foundations rewarded him because he carried out their plans to their satisfaction. But if Johnson had failed in this effort, he would have been replaceable.

NOTES

1. These works influenced my thinking about mentorship: Daniel J. Levinson, *The Seasons of a Man's Life* (New York: Alfred A. Knopf, 1978); Harriet Zuckerman, *Scientific Elites: Nobel Laureates in the United States* (New York: Free Press, 1977).

2. The analysis of Angell's life and career is based on: biography in James Rowland Angell Papers register, Yale University Manuscript and Archives Department; *The National Encyclopedia of American Biography* 40 (1955); *Dictionary of American Biography*, Supplement 4, 1946–1950.

3. James R. Angell to A. Lawrence Lowell, January 13, 1922, James R. Angell Papers.

4. Angell to Beardsley Ruml, December 3, 1921, Angell Papers.

5. Angell to Ruml, no date, Angell Papers.

6. Ruml to Angell, 1921, Angell Papers.

7. Angell-Ruml correspondence, Angell Papers.

8. Martin Bulmer and Joan Bulmer, "Philanthropy and Social Science in the 1920s: The Case of Beardsley Ruml and the Laura Spelman Rockefeller Memorial 1922–29," *Minerva* 19 (Autumn 1981): 347–407.

9. Beardsley Ruml, "Confusion and Compromise in Education," 1936, Angell Papers.

10. Beardsley Ruml, *Tomorrow's Business* (New York: Farrar & Rhinehart, Inc., 1945).

11. Ruml to Robert M. Yerkes, October 12, 1933, Robert M. Yerkes Papers. There was also great concern among Ruml's friends about the possibility of his becoming stale from being cut off from "current work." See Wesley C. Mitchell to James R. Angell, January 24, 1928 and Angell to Wesley C. Mitchell, January 15, 1928, Angell Papers.

12. Beardsley Ruml, "Prosperity and Peace," read at the Chestnut Street Association, Philadelphia, Pennsylvania, January 22, 1946, especially pp. 7–8. Julius Rosenwald Fund (hereafter, JRF) Archives.

13. Edwin R. Embree to Beardsley Ruml, December 5, 1947 and Ruml to Embree, December 8, 1947, JRF Archives.

14. Beardsley Ruml, "Memorial Policy in the Social Sciences," 1922, Laura Spelman Rockefeller Memorial (hereafter, LSRM) Archives.

15. Beardsley Ruml to James A. Angell, October 6, 1922, Angell Papers.

16. Ruml, "Memorial Policy in the Social Sciences," following paragraphs are based upon an analysis of this document.

17. Ibid.

18. Ibid.

19. Ibid.

20. Ibid.

21. Ibid.

22. Ibid.

23. See funding patterns in the Annual Reports of the Laura Spelman Rockefeller Memorial.

24. Ruml, "Memorial Policy in the Social Sciences."

25. See materials in the Policy folder, LSRM Archives.

26. John Higham, *Writing American History: Essays on Modern Scholarship* (Bloomington: Indiana University Press, 1979).

27. In 1926 Howard W. Odum asked Beardsley Ruml why he thought scoiologists were not well respected social analysts. Ruml replied, "The real case against sociology was probably made by a man at Hanover who remarked in a very small committee meeting, 'Unfortunately, we have no great men in sociology.' " Beardsley Ruml to Howard W. Odum, November 30, 1926, Howard W. Odum Papers. For a different perspective see Martin Bulmer, "Support for Sociology in the 1920s: The Laura Spelman Rockefeller Memorial and the Beginnings of Large-Scale, Sociological Research in the University," *American Sociologist* 17 (November 1982):185–192.

28. Especially points one, two, four, five, and six of this policy materialized this conservative funding policy: (1) Not to contribute to organizations whose purposes and activities are centered largely in the procurement of legislation. Examples: National Child Labor Committee, National Consumers League, National Woman's Party; (2) Not to attempt directly under the memorial to secure any social, economic, or political reform. Examples: more playgrounds, less unemployment, extension of the merit system in civil service; (4) Not to carry on investigations and research directly under the memorial, except for the guidance of the memorial: Examples: Handbook on Camping, Opportunities in Vocational Education of Women, Relations between Immigration and the Business Cycle; (5) Not to attempt to influence the findings or conclusions of research and investigations through the designation of either personnel, specific problems to be attacked, or methods of inquiry to be adopted; or through indirect influence in giving inadequate assurance of continuity of support; (6) Not to concentrate too narrowly on particular research institutions, incurring thereby the danger of institutional bias.

29. Meeting of the Advisory Committee on Problems Relating to the Negro of the Social Science Research Council, May 21, 1926. Charles E. Merriam Papers, University of Chicago.

30. The following analysis of Leonard Outhwaite's life and career is based on biographical materials in the Leonard Outhwaite Papers.

31. Autobiographical sketch, Leonard Outhwaite Papers.

32. Laura Spelman Rockefeller Docket, November 13, 1924, LSRM Archives.

33. For a similar view see Morton Sosna, *The Search for the Silent South* (New York: Columbia University Press, 1977).

34. Leonard Outhwaite memorandum, "Southern Trip," November 3–December 5, 1923, LSRM Archives.

35. Memos in Commission on Interracial Cooperation folder, LSRM Archives.

36. "Interview with Leonard Outhwaite," November 9, 1927, Edwin R. Embree diary excerpt, p. 149, Rockefeller Foundation Archives.

37. Leonard Outhwaite, "The Negro in America," 1925, LSRM Archives.

38. Memos in Commission on Interracial Cooperation Folder, LSRM Archives.

39. Correspondence in National Urban League, Negro Boy Scouts, and Negro Business League Folders, LSRM Archives.

40. Negro Problems Conference folders, LSRM Archives. See also Edwin R. Embree biographical information found in Box 140, Folder 30, of the Julius Rosenwald Fund Archives alludes to the policy impact of the Negro Problems Conference.

41. Leonard Outhwaite to Beardsley Ruml, March 20, 1926, LSRM Archives.

42. Outhwaite, "The Negro in America."

43. For example, Thomas J. Woofter, Jr., et al., of the Phelps-Stokes Fund's *Negro Immigration in 1916–1917* (Washington, D.C., 1919).

44. *The Negro in Chicago: A Study of Race Relations and a Race Riot: Report of the Chicago Commission on Race Relations* (Chicago, 1922).

45. Outhwaite, "The Negro in America."

46. Ibid.

47. Ibid.

48. Ibid.; Leonard Outhwaite, "Comments at the Dartmouth Conference," 1926, LSRM Archives.

49. Outhwaite, "Negro in America."

50. Ibid.

51. "Proceedings of a Staff Meeting of the Laura Spelman Rockefeller Foundation," August 24–27, 1927, LSRM Archives.

52. Outhwaite to Ruml, LSRM Archives.

53. Charles S. Johnson, *The Negro in American Civilization* (New York: H. Holt, 1930).

54. Leonard Outhwaite memorandum, "Negro History and Anthropology," to Beardsley Ruml, no date, LSRM Archives.

55. Ibid.

56. Leonard Outhwaite interview with Professor Clark Wissler, March 18, 1925, LSRM Archives.

57. Ellsworth Faris to Leonard Outhwaite, April 2, 1926, LSRM Archives. Faris did not actually go to Africa until 1932. I was unable to determine whether or not Rockefeller Foundation funds financed his trip.

58. See Howard W. Odum–Memorial officers correspondence in the Howard W. Odum Papers and LSRM Archives; Wayne Brazil, "Howard W. Odum, 1880–1930: The Building Years" (Ph.D. dissertation, Harvard University, 1975).

59. Leonard Outhwaite correspondence in Charles Merriam and Mexican Study folders, LSRM Archives.

60. Frank A. Ross folder, LSRM Archives.

61. Bronslaw Malinowski Folder, LSRM Archives.

62. Jackson Davis report on Negro education trends, 1927, LSRM Archives.

63. Raymond B. Fosdick, *Adventures in Giving: The Story of the General Education Board* (New York: Harper & Row, 1962). Edwin R. Embree and Julia Waxman, *Investment in People: The Story of the Julius Rosenwald Fund* (New York: Harper, 1949).

64. Numerous passages in Jackson Davis's diary discussed this arrangement, General Education Board Archives.

65. Anson Stokes–Monroe Work correspondence, Anson Stokes Papers.

66. Jackson Davis diary, General Education Board Archives.

67. J. F. Jameson to James R. Angell, October 9, 1920, LSRM Archives.

68. "Negro Scholarships" folders, LSRM Archives.

69. Leonard Outhwaite memorandum on the scholarship program, no date, LSRM Archives.

70. The analysis of scholarship recipients is based on correspondence in recipient folders, LSRM Archives.

71. Leonard Outhwaite to T. V. Smith, July 19, 1928, LSRM Archives.

72. Smith to Outhwaite, July 24, 1928, LSRM Archives.

73. Charles Blooah, "From Coconut Tree to College: A Digest," no date (about 1927), LSRM Archives.

74. "Digest Letter from Professor Edward Sapir to Dr. Fay-Cooper Cole," 1927, LSRM Archives.

75. Leonard Outhwaite to Fay-Cooper Cole, May 6, 1927. LSRM Archives.

76. Cole to Outhwaite, May 17, 1927, LSRM Archives.

77. Cole to Outhwaite, June 1, 1928, LSRM Archives.

78. Edward Sapir to Edmund Day, September 28, 1931, LSRM Archives.

79. Sapir to Syndor Walker, February 10, 1931, LSRM Archives.

80. Sapir to Walker, February 10, 1931; Sapir to Edmund Day, September 15, 1931; and M. D. McLean to Charles S. Johnson, August 22, 1931; Sapir to Johnson, May 6, 1932; Sapir to Day, May 18, 1932; Day to Sapir, June 14, 1932, LSRM Archives. Throughout the early 1930s, Johnson tried in vain to find Blooah employment in a missionary association or a black college. See Charles Blooah Folder, Charles S. Johnson Special Collection.

81. For example, Will Alexander to Leonard Outhwaite, May 12, 1927, LSRM Archives.

82. Leonard Outhwaite to John Hope, May 12, 1927, LSRM Archives.

83. Hope to Outhwaite, May 17, 1927; Will Alexander to Outhwaite, May 23, 1927; Outhwaite to E. Franklin Frazier, June 8, 1927. LSRM Archives.

84. L. H. Wood to Leonard Outhwaite, February 24, 1926; Outhwaite to Beardsley Ruml, March 12, 1926, LSRM Archives.

85. Ibid.

86. "Report of the Social Science Department of Fisk University," June 1930, LSRM Archives.

87. Thomas E. Jones. "Responsibilities of the Negro University," no date, LSRM Archives.

88. For example, Stanley H. Smith, "Sociological Research and Fisk University: A Case Study," in *Black Sociologists: Historical and Contemporary Perspectives*, ed. James Blackwell and Morris Janowitz (Chicago: University of Chicago Press, 1974).

89. "James T. Carey," *Sociology and Public Affairs* (Beverly Hills, Calif.: Sage Publications, 1975).

90. Chicago Local Community Research Institute folders, LSRM Archives. For example, projects sponsored by the Local Community Research Institute as of March 15, 1925 (taken from the Financial Statement, Burgess Papers) were:

A.1	Housing
A.2	Care of maternity
A.3	Truck garden
A.4	Dependent children adoption in Illinois
A.5	Child labor

A.6	Enforcement of laws
A.7	Public administration
A.8	Street trades
A.9	Adoption
A.10	Family welfare
A.11	Begging
A.12	Registration
A.13	Immigration
B.1	Density map
B.2	Community boundaries
B.3	Hotel study
B.4	Lower North Side
B.5	Old world cultural survivals
B.6	Primary group controls
B.7	The black belt
B.8	Mexicans in Chicago
B.9	The ghetto
B.10	Personality changes
B.11	The town of Pullman
B.12	The public dance hall
B.13	The growth of the city
B.14	Juvenile delinquency
B.15	The automobile
B.16	Suicide
B.17	Delinquent boys
B.18	Wieboldt project
C.1	Chicago vs. downstate
C.2	The Germans in Chicago
D.1	Relative valuation of chief interest
D.2	Changing ideals of life
E.1	Non-voting
E.2	Citizenship
E.3	City Hall
E.4	Municipal reporting
F.1	Type studies
G.1	Labor code
G.2	Chicago Federation
G.3	Special assessments
G.4	Ready made clothing
G.5	Ladies garment industry
G.6	Chicago strikes
G.7	Labor organization
G.8	Trust development
G.9	The R.R. Labor Board
G.10	Seasonality
H.1	Calumet preliminary survey
J.1	Standard of living
K.1	Census data
M.1	Migration and mobility

91. Chicago Local Community Research Institute folders, LSRM Archives.

92. See Guy B. Johnson and Guion Johnson, *Research in Services to Society: The*

First Fifty Years of the Institute for Research in Social Science at the University of North Carolina (Chapel Hill, N.C.: University of North Carolina Press, 1980).

93. See, for instance, Charles S. Johnson to Leo Favrot, September 22, 1937, General Education Board Archives.

94. For example, the following were research projects in the Fisk University Department of Social Science, 1929–1930:

African Origins (P. Radin)

Black Religious Conversion Experiences

A Study of 1,000 Negro Families in Nashville

Study of Differential Mortality

Comparative Abilities of White and Negro Children

Study of Interracial Attitudes

Study of the Negro Family

Vocational Opportunities for Negro High School Graduates

Social and Economic Background of Negro School Children in Reference to IQ Test Scores

[Data from ''Report of the Social Science Department of Fisk University,'' Thomas Jones to Edmund Day, June, 1930, LSRM]

95. The political paralysis of Fisk University faculty when it came to racial matters is one reason why the more outspoken E. Franklin Frazier left Fisk in the early 1930s. A Frazier biographer gave this example:

Frazier believed that Fisk was too ''respectably middle class'' in its outlook; and because of this attitude, the school tended to avoid facing certain important issues. He, therefore, considered it his duty to force these issues whenever possible. For example, when Juliette Derricotte, the Dean of Women at Fisk at the time, lost her life because a Southern white hospital refused her first aid after a car accident, the President of Fisk ordered his faculty not to discuss the incident. Frazier defied the order; not only did he discuss it in his classes but wrote strong letters to the press excoriating the inhumanity of the act. [Grace E. Harris, *The Life and Works of E. Franklin Frazier* (Ph.D. dissertation, University of Virginia, 1975), p. 40]

For other reasons why Frazier left Fisk, see note 22 in Chapter 6.

96. It was especially difficult for Johnson and his staff to have much policy-making power in nonracial areas. Consider the more broader career lines of Howard Odum, Louis Wirth, Robert E. Park, and Ernest Burgess, in public affairs who had policy influence in racial and other areas. Being a white social scientist meant one could be involved in a number of community activities, only one of them being race relations research and policy making.

97. Curricula stresses on religious training and on industrial/professional training in most pre–World War II black colleges stifled widespread growth of social science employment opportunities. About the negative impact of the denominational control of many black colleges on the development of social science programs, see S. P. Fullinwider, *The Mind and Mood of Black America* (Homewood, Ill.: Dorsey Press, 1969), pp. 92–100.

98. Leonard Outhwaite interview with E. Embree, Julius Rosenwald Fund, February 1927. See also correspondence between Thomas Jones and memorial officers about recruitment possibilities, LSRM Archives.

99. See passages in Jackson Davis diary, General Education Board Archives.

100. Robert Calkins Hoover, January 4, 1949; Hoover to Calkins, January 6, 1949; Calkins to Hoover, January 12, 1949; Hoover to Calkins, January 24, 1949, General Education Board Archives.

101. Butler A. Jones, "The Tradition of Sociology Teaching in Black Colleges: The Unheralded Professionals," in *Black Sociologists: Historical and Contemporary Perspectives*, ed. James E. Blackwell and Morris Janowitz (Chicago: University of Chicago Press, 1975); August Meier, "Black Sociologists in White America," *Social Forces* 56 (1977):259–270.

5

Edwin Rogers Embree and the Julius Rosenwald Fund

By the time of his sudden death in 1950, Edwin Rogers Embree had been transformed into an advocate of racial integration. His book *Peoples of the Earth*, published in 1948, and his numerous articles and letters to newspaper editors portray him as a bold racial integrationist. Although his foundation, the Julius Rosenwald Fund, spent most of its years servicing Jim Crow institutions and traditions, several years before Embree's death the fund had begun pushing for racial integration. In these years, the Julius Rosenwald Fund trustees organized their Division of Race Relations under the co-directorship of Charles S. Johnson and Will Alexander, and sponsored the organization of the American Council on Race Relations and the Fisk Institute on Race Relations. Most symbolic of the ideological shift was their last major project, a study which recommended banning Jim Crow in the nation's capital.

Embree became notorious after his death for his later views on race, although his earlier beliefs had been more influential. During the heat of the McCarthy era, the congressional Reeves Committee accused the Julius Rosenwald Fund of infiltration by Communists. Embree's *Peoples of the Earth* was condemned by parents in a local Chicago school district as a book inspired by Communists. Even in his grave, Embree continued to stir up controversy.[1]

JULIUS ROSENWALD

Julius Rosenwald, born in Illinois in 1862, came from a family of German Jewish clothing merchants. His parents had immigrated to the United States in the 1850s. Julius Rosenwald amassed his millions after moving to Chicago where he became a successful clothing merchant. After his company merged with Sears and Roebuck, Rosenwald became president and a major stockholder and continued to serve on its board of directors until his death in 1932.

Throughout his life, Rosenwald adhered to the tenets of Reform Judaism, a religious orientation which was amenable to the doctrines of racial uplift and racial accommodation—the dominant interpretation of proper white-black relations in the first decades of the twentieth century, the time when Rosenwald began his philanthropic activities. Thus, Rosenwald was susceptible to the Anglo-Saxons' dialectical idea of accommodation and assimilation in American life. In a speech he made at Hampton Institute in 1911 he said:

Not only does the record of nations demonstrate beyond the question of doubt the folly of race prejudice, but its pages are filled with evidence that indulgence of this pet vice is itself a prime factor in the decay of nations, and in modern times I believe Russia is a living example, of that theory. May our own country profit by Russia's example! In Russia the Jew is subject to a thousand infamous restrictions for no earthly reason except that he is a Jew and must be kept down. We Anglo-Saxons of course cry out against this as a barbarous outrage, and comment superiorly on the lowness of Russian civilization, and straightaway turn around and exhibit the same qualities in our treatment of the Negro, which today is little less barbarous than is the treatment of the Jew in Russia. . . .

No man or woman who encourages even the mildest phases of race prejudice can wholly escape responsibility for the horrors at which every decent individual shudders. . . . As an American and as a Jew, I appeal to all high-minded men and women to join in a relentless crusade against race prejudice, indulgence in which will result in the blotting out of the highest ideals of our proud nation.[2]

This speech reveals that by 1911, Rosenwald had fully accepted major aspects of American Anglo-Saxon ideology—the American democratic ethos and "the shame" of the mistreatment of blacks. Moreover, it clearly indicates that Rosenwald considered himself an Anglo-Saxon. Another aspect of Anglo-Saxon ideology that Rosenwald internalized was the idea that success was contingent more upon individual initiative than upon the power and resources available to his racial or religious group. This ideology of rugged individualism was endorsed by captains of industry and finance to justify their acquisition of wealth at the turn of the century.

In 1910 a friend sent Rosenwald a copy of a recently published biography of William H. Baldwin, Jr., a white trustee of Tuskegee Institute. Baldwin was a prominent advocate of industrial education for blacks. Rosenwald said later that the biography of William H. Baldwin, Jr., and Booker T. Washington's book *Up from Slavery* influenced him more than any of the other books he had read. Through them Rosenwald became concerned with the depressed conditions of black people. The individualistic and self-reliant rhetoric of Washington was especially appealing to him. "Both of them believed that it was better for individuals to start life without too many advantages, for neither of them had had too many himself."[3]

This point of view was the foundation of the doctrine of racial uplift. This concept suggested that, though blacks and whites were to remain separated, a small number of blacks, through extraordinary talent and initiative, could become upwardly mobile within their own group with the help of formal schooling. The doctrine of racial uplift was supported by whites because it encouraged the development of a black elite which nevertheless did not compete with white elites (or white working classes, for that matter). Rosenwald eventually conformed to the racial climate of the time and subsequently came to agree with Washington's philosophy of industrial education, racial accommodation, and biracial organization of society.[4]

Rosenwald demonstrated his interest in black industrial education through generous contributions to Tuskegee Institute. In 1912 he accepted a trusteeship for life on that institution's governing board. He also donated large sums of money for the building of rural schools for blacks in the South, stipulating that local black communities and state governments match his contributions. By the time of his death

he had contributed to the construction of 5,357 public schools, shops, and teachers' homes in 883 counties of fifteen southern states, at a total cost of $28,408,520, of which he had contributed $4,366,519 or 15 percent. Of the total cost $18,104,115, or 64 percent, had come from tax funds. The Negroes themselves had contributed $4,725,871 or 17 percent, in a flood of small contributions. Local white friends had contributed $1,211,975, or 4 percent.[5]

The construction of rural black schools constituted the major target of Rosenwald's philanthropic concern with the Negro problem through the mid–1930s. These schools were, in a sense, the structural expression of his endorsement of racial uplift and racial accommodation, as was his support of black health care institutions, which he presumed should be "for Negroes" but supervised by whites. Once, while discussing the sort of black hospital he would contribute to, he remarked:

My thought in connection with work of this kind is that I would only be interested in assisting a hospital for Negroes if it were tied up with a reputable white hospital, so that the white staff could supervise the work of the Colored and thereby secure a sympathetic cooperation.[6]

THE JULIUS ROSENWALD FUND

In 1917 Rosenwald organized his foundation under the incorporation laws for nonprofit organizations of the state of Illinois. The purpose of the Julius Rosenwald Fund was broadly defined as "the well being of mankind." Until 1928, its operations remained under Rosenwald's personal control, and the board of trustees was largely composed of family members. Between 1917 and 1927, the fund spent $4,049,974. In 1927, Rosenwald reorganized his foundation into a corporation to make it more efficient and effective.[7]

Perhaps the most unique characteristic of the reorganized fund was Rosenwald's novel stipulation that all of the foundation's funds should be used up within twenty-five years after his death. He did not support the tradition of a perpetual endowment, since he believed each generation in a society should deal with its own problems.

more good can be accomplished by expending funds as Trustees find opportunities for constructive work than by storing up large sums of money for long periods of time. By adopting a policy of using the Fund within this generation, we may avoid these tendencies toward the work which inevitably develop in organizations which prolong their existence indefinitely. Coming generations can be relied upon to provide for their own needs as they arise.[8]

This stipulation set a precedent that several other large-scale foundations were to follow. Due to this mandate, the decision makers of the Julius Rosenwald Fund were able to be more creative in defining funding priorities and practice than were those of other large foundations operating between 1928 and 1948. Perhaps this is why Embree said of the fund,

The trustees saw that any such agency must limit its work to a few definite programs if it hoped to make any substantial contribution to social progress. To give to all worthy causes could simply dissipate resources, leaving perhaps a pleasant philanthropic dew, but making no distinctive impress. . . . . Rather its unique opportunity was to mobilize all its resources—financial, intellectual, moral—for systematic attack on specific problems. It could cultivate fresh fields through studies, experiments, and demonstrations, leaving to society the support of new procedures and new institutions once their value was shown.[9]

The trustees of the Julius Rosenwald Fund decided to contribute to the alleviation of problems not already saturated with donations from other (larger) philanthropic foundations. They focused on black education, health, and fellowships as well as on race relations. Thus, the foundation's decision makers attempted to equalize opportunities for blacks in a segregated society. From 1928 to 1948 the Julius Rosenwald Fund was concerned with various facets of the race problem—health, education, interracial workshops, social studies, even the political activities of interracial cooperation organizations. This broad and exclusive interest in black social existence distinguished the Rosenwald Fund from other large philanthropic foundations of its time.[10]

Rosenwald chose Edwin Rogers Embree to preside over his reorganized foundation. As president of the Julius Rosenwald Fund from 1928 to 1948, Embree did more for black social scientists and the social science of race relations than did any other foundation administrator of this period. Although he was not a professional sociologist, he exhibited an extraordinary sociological imagination in his racial world view. Two years before his death in 1950, he identified himself in *Current Biography* as a sociologist.[11]

Edwin Embree's grandfather, John Gregg Fee, had a tremendous lifelong influence on his grandson, who consciously attempted to imitate major aspects of his ancestor's style of leadership and his racial philosophy. Embree's fervent effort to become a twentieth-century version of John Gregg Fee prodded him to develop a zeal for controversial race relations reform.

John Gregg Fee was born in Kentucky in 1816. His father was a slaveholder. Through adolescence, Fee viewed slave ownership as a normal part of life. But at age fourteen he became a devout fundamentalist Christian, a belief he retained for the rest of his life. A few years after his conversion, Fee entered Lane Seminary in Ohio. Lane had a tremendous impact on him, since it was a major institutional source of northern abolitionism. Fee had entered the seminary still adhering to slaveholding values but was soon confronted with the abolitionists' claim that slavery was sinful. Fee eventually made a spiritual decision to become an abolitionist. At age twenty-six, Fee prepared himself for a controversial life peppered with persecution and physical violence. He even carefully selected a wife who would be able to cope with a turbulent life.[12]

Fee accepted his family's and the church's rejection of his militant abolitionist stance. His acceptance made him even more persistent in his attempts to persuade them of the wrongs of slavery. Fee willingly exposed himself, his wife, and his children to frequent danger as he journeyed from town to town preaching against slavery. He was often mobbed, sometimes left for dead. But acts of violence against him did not bother Fee, since he assumed he was under God's protection and that those who persecuted him would be punished. He never carried a gun or any other weapon to defend himself.

Fee was such a bold and articulate orator against slavery and for racial equality that a doctoral dissertation has been done on his communication styles.[13] He was a master of cultivating public opinion in a controversial area through the medium of Christian theology. Fee's unusual ability to support successful stances against the stream of public thought was also apparent in the evolution of his theological beliefs. Like most other Presbyterian ministers of the time, Fee did not believe in immersion baptism until one day, when he was in his forties, a friend gave him a book on the matter. John Fee read the book and studied immersion baptism further. He finally decided immersion baptism was appropriate and devoted the rest of his life to advocating it.

Fee was a foe of organized religion, believing it a hindrance to genuine Christian teaching. He was an avid supporter of the American Missionary Association during its formative years, but as the association began to stress exclusively Congregational doctrine, Fee withdrew his support. By the mid–1850s Fee was an outspoken opponent of the American Missionary Association and denominationalism in general.

With the help of Henry Cassius Clay, in 1855 Fee established the Berea community, which became a refuge for northern and southern abolitionists. Occasionally, the community was attacked by mobs; during the Civil War, Fee and Berean families were forced to go into exile.

The Berea College charter included anti-slavery and anti-sectarian clauses. For many years after the Civil War, Berea College admitted both black and white students, although most of the students were black. However, during the William G. Frost administration (1892–1920) Berea became a college for white mountaineers. This was due in part to Frost's racial attitudes and in part to segregation laws passed in Kentucky in the early 1900s.[14]

The Berea College community supplied Fee with an independent power base for his unconventional ideas. The college guaranteed that Fee's ideas about racial issues, no matter how unpopular, would be passed on to succeeding generations. Without this base, Fee undoubtedly would have been forced to succumb to his opponents.

EDWIN ROGERS EMBREE

Edwin Rogers Embree was born in 1883 in Nebraska, the seventh child of William Norris Embree and Laura Fee Embree. William Embree, who came from an abolitionist family which settled in Berea, died in 1889, when Edwin was six. Laura shared many of her father's beliefs and consequently was exposed to severe persecution. When her husband died, she moved back into her father's house at Berea. Thus John Fee became the patriarch of the Embree family and had a lasting impact on his grandchildren, particularly Edwin and William.[15]

By the time Embree's family moved back to Berea in 1889, most of Fee's struggles were over. Edwin and his siblings were thrilled to hear stories about their grandfather's controversial and victorious life. Fee's successful struggles (especially his fight against slavery) were a source of inspiration for his grandson Edwin. Fee was even able to make friends later in life with those who tried to kill him in his earlier years. His cordiality to past enemies also influenced Edwin Embree.[16] Throughout his presidency at the Julius Rosenwald Fund, Embree often explained what he was trying to do in the context of his grandfather's motives.

In 1945 one of his southern trustees sent him an article opposing racial integration. In the article Virginus Dabney, a liberal-turned-conservative, blamed the death of the southern antebellum anti-slavery movement on northern abolitionists. Embree wrote:

Sending me the article by Virginus Dabney is a blow beneath the belt, since he starts off with a quotation from me! I have two or three comments on his argument.

I am sure he is wrong in saying that the anti-slavery movement in the antebellum South was "killed completely" by the assaults of the Northern Abolitionists. My grandfather was part of the purely Southern anti-slavery movement. He and his associates made great headway in Kentucky and were chiefly responsible for keeping that state from joining the Confederacy. The only complaint that he and his associates had vs. the North was that Northern agencies were not cooperative enough in furnishing support to the Southern movements. What I am suggesting is that the Fund give support to such Southern agencies as are on the progressive side in this fight. I am sure that you and Virginus Dabney greatly underrate the forces within the South that are working to mitigate and ultimately do away with segregation.[17]

Embree even saw his foundation activities as a crusade similar to Fee's campaign against slavery and racial inequality. Like his grandfather, Edwin Embree was known to be outspoken and occasionally extreme. He thrived on controversy, at times going out of his way to seek it. Embree was willing to be controversial not only because he had a well-fed ego but also because he did not believe in compromising his moral principles even if they were controversial. In the late 1940s Edgar Stern—Rosenwald's son-in-law and the fund's trustee in the deep South—protested to Embree about an *Ebony* story describing one of the foundation's famous interracial parties. Embree, however, boldly defended the event.[18] Embree occasionally became directly involved in controversial issues in order to raise eyebrows or make newspaper headlines.

Embree was an avid reader, and his views changed through gradual exposure to material that countered his personal opinions. He considered himself an intellectual and encouraged the foundation staff to write position papers and to review books about contemporary issues. His correspondence is filled with discussions of scholarly books. His intellectualism led him to insist that the board of directors be an active governing board rather than just a guardian of funds. The trustees were to be brainstormers.[19]

Embree wrote on contemporary issues, especially race relations, with no underlying attempt to be "professional." Professionalism, he claimed, stifled creativity. He once noted:

The professional educator, like the professional in any other field, likes to have statements made so guardedly and in such technical language that they carry little weight. . . . Kandel . . . says many of the things that Winsor advocates but he does it in so dull a style that no one is apt to read it or be impressed by it. I can imagine professional politicians saying that Lincoln's Gettysburg Address was naive and contained nothing new. True enough. But it said the old truths in a gripping fashion.[20]

Although Embree was attracted to "scientific facts," he wrote in a colorful fashion to avoid blandness. He often forewarned readers who he felt might be put off by his style.

Embree was a marginal figure in the foundation sector and in the liberal establishment because of his unconventional ideas about race relations.[21] But he was able to withstand persecution because his independent power base—the Julius Rosenwald Fund—was located outside the South. His powerful position in the Rosenwald Fund assured the promotion of his ideas which otherwise would have been lost.

Like his grandfather, Embree was anti-institutional and eventually became an outspoken critic of every institution in which he had participated both during and after World War I. Embree became involved in the Rockefeller Foundation in 1917, believing that it could become an instrument for innovative change. But he gradually became disillusioned by the Rockefeller Foundation and by foundations in general. His best criticisms of philanthropic foundations can be found in his article ''Timid Billions'' published in a 1948 issue of *Harper's*. Paradoxically, however, Fee and Embree were both founders of unconventional institutions of higher learning for the less affluent—Fee founded Berea College for mountain youth, and Embree helped to establish Chicago's Roosevelt University for working-class people.[22]

Embree began his race-relations work during World War I as secretary of the Rockefeller Foundation and chairman of the War Camp Community Service for Negro Soldiers. During this period he met major black leaders such as Emmett Scott, Robert Moton, and John Hope, who were involved in war work. Throughout the 1920s, he stayed in close contact with Leonard Outhwaite and Beardsley Ruml, both of the Laura Spelman Rockefeller Memorial, consulting with them about their race-relations and eugenics activities.[23]

In 1917, during Embree's first year as Rockefeller Foundation secretary, Julius Rosenwald was appointed a trustee to the Rockefeller General Education Board. Since childhood Embree had had an interest in different racial groups and hence was attracted to Rosenwald.[24] He admired Rosenwald's individualism, his refusal to subordinate himself, and his support of black education and other controversial causes. Rosenwald's personality and philosophy made a strong impression on Embree, as did his grandfather and Abraham Lincoln. Embree's admiration for these three men was clear—in 1928 he suggested to a close friend that they collaborate on a biography about the three men:

The thing that these three men represent is contributions to American development essentially by revolt against existing one hundred per cent ideals, the revolt by each man being of a very different sort, and expressed in very different ways from any of the others.[25]

At the time that Embree became increasingly restive over the stagnation of the Rockefeller foundations, which prevented him from launching innovative projects, Rosenwald was also becoming impatient with the Rockefeller foundations. He decided to reorganize his own foundation and appointed Embree as president, giving him much autonomy. Embree described to a friend his reasons for leaving the Rockefeller Foundation:

I had been getting increasingly dissatisfied with what seemed to me formalistic attitudes, professionalized viewpoints and bureaucratic tendencies in the Foundation. I kept wanting to do new things, to try out fresh ways of helping, instead of going on doing over and over, however well, types of work, the benefits of which had already been thoroughly established. It seemed to me that the only justification for foundations lay in making social experiments, in launching courageously upon imaginative enterprises, in a word in doing the kind of thing which other governmental or private agencies or individuals were not likely to do and which, therefore, were the unique opportunity for these new, large, untrammeled funds.

The Rockefeller donations did just that in the early days. Mr. Rockefeller and his advisers conceived the idea of a great private university in the Middle West and they created with imagination, courage and with magnificent resources, the University of Chicago, which has influenced the universities of the entire country, particularly that large group of state universities which grew up about the same time throughout the West. These western state universities might have been mediocre to a degree scarcely conceived of today, had it not been for the influence of the abnormally high standards of the University of Chicago.

Other striking ideas put into effect in those early days with magnificent disregard for tradition were the creation of an institute for research in the medical sciences on a scale never before concevied, and the transformation of medical education by ample endowment of a few universitiy centers, first in this country and then on a world basis, in which the emphasis was to be upon getting the best men to give their whole time to teaching and research, working with a select group of students under the best physical conditions.

That is a remarkable record of fine imaginative projects carried out on a grand scale. It is a good enough record to justify any such group as that of the Rockefeller Boards. The thing that troubled me was that I thought the group here was beginning to justify its existence on this past record.

The very brilliance of the initial successes seemed to me to be blinding as to new opportunities. The tendency crept in to do the same things over and over in the same ways. We were afraid—or so it seemed to me—to depart from what had been demonstrated to be sound and successful procedure. The group of officers was growing large, it was developing professional self-consciousness, it was becoming respectable and timid.

Well, just as I was most dissatisfied, Mr. Julius Rosenwald came along and offered me a fairly free hand in directing his giving. He has a foundation and in addition wants to give away a number of millions directly. He wants to give wisely but he is untrammeled by tradition, willing and anxious to do just the kind of creative things that Mr. Rockefeller, Senior, started two or three or four decades ago. Mr. Rosenwald also was ready to give me a good deal more money. So, after going over the whole matter with him carefully both in New York and in Chicago, I decided to leave the Rockefeller Foundation and to cast my lot with Mr. Rosenwald and his new projects.[26]

Rosenwald, who demanded unfailing personal commitment from his employees, liked the much younger Embree because he was loyal. He needed a president who was daring but willing to work within the boundaries he set. Even after Rosenwald died, Embree remained loyal to his family, who enjoyed much informal influence in Julius Rosenwald Fund affairs. In return, the Rosenwald family assured Embree's lengthy tenure as a highly independent president, and continued to support him after the fund dissolved in 1948. Embree's strong pro-Jewish sentiments even inspired one of Rosenwald's sons to refer to Embree as one of the tribe.[27]

EMBREE'S EVOLVING RACIAL WORLD VIEW

Lest Embree's liberal racial world view be exaggerated, his more conventional racial beliefs should be examined. His relationship with writer Clarence Day brings into view his traditional beliefs about the Negro problem, which he held at least through the early 1930s. Clarence Day was born in 1874 into a prominent New England family. He wrote now-classic works such as *This Simian World* and *Life with Father*. Graduating from Yale in 1896, Day served with Embree in the Association of Class Secretaries in the early 1900s.[28]

Embree's attachment to Day can be traced to the writer's prominent Yankee background, exceptional intellect, satiric view of human nature, and most important, his determination not to succumb to a crippling form of rheumatism. (Embree always admired underdogs who beat the odds.) Day sought Embree's opinion on his writings and on world events. Embree also belonged to Day's inner circle of intellectual friends who congregated at the writer's bedside to engage in vibrant conversation. When Embree became president of the Julius Rosenwald Fund in the late 1920s, he often requested his friend's help to get his articles accepted by popular magazines. Through his extensive contacts, Day helped Embree gain access to the New York City literary establishment, which continued to favor Embree through the years between the wars. Embree also had Day review his early foundation reports, which were attempts at literary style, and consulted him on possible candidates to write Julius Rosenwald's biography.[29]

Day had only a vague conception of the Negro problem, once even writing to Embree that he was indifferent to it. But his disdain for the mingling of the races was quite clear.[30] Embree, although he disagreed with his friend's fears of the implications of interracial mingling, did hold some assumptions typical to conventional thinking of his day. For instance, like Leonard Outhwaite, he believed in helping blacks not for reasons of charity or racial equality but because blacks needed such attention lest they negatively affect whites.

In 1929, when Harlem doctors accused the Julius Rosenwald Fund of promoting segregated hospitals, Day asked Embree for his views on racial segregation. Embree's response stressed that segregation was a necessary evil which minimized racial turmoil—a conventional belief held by liberals and conservatives alike.

Your wanting people to stay in their own homes may be sound enough. The Negroes' answer is that he was perfectly willing to stay in that home and that he came here altogether against his own will because he was put in chains and dragged over by American white men and that he was—or she was—encouraged and compelled to multiply rapidly to satisfy the demands of the white masters. Here are ten million descendants of people whom the white man brought to this country. If there ever was a white man's burden, this is it, and a few pious people at one time tried to meet the problem by persuading Negroes to go back to Africa, particularly to Liberia. I am a trustee of one of the funds established by these people to promote such migration and to see that the emigrants were suitably cared for by resident schools and churches. Of course this got no-where. Unless we are prepared to enchain again the whole race and deport them by violence, they are not likely to emigrate from the United States in any great numbers.

Now, since they *are* here and likely to stay here, a sensible procedure would seem to be to educate them and keep them in robust health and give them an opportunity for expression. This will make them assets rather than liabilities economically and socially in the common society and it may make possible distinct additions to the color of our life (other than skin pigmentation). In music and drama and certain of the graphic arts they are making contributions. Read James Weldon Johnson's "God's Trombones" and Countee Cullen's poems, and weep that you have ever suggested annihilating this race![31]

Embree's traditionalism about the Negro problem began to change gradually as he became engrossed in presiding over the Rosenwald Fund's activities in Chicago and the South. An early sign of his shifting world view was his decision to write a definitive book on the sociological plight of black Americans.

. . . so many people whom I talked to seemed to know so little about the Negro and have thought about him even less. I find that when I can spend a couple of hours with a person talking about recent advances and the relation of Negro well being to the prog-ress of the nation as a whole, I can always stir up a lot of interest, but I can't go around spending two hours at a time with a great number of people. Therefore it occurred to me that I might tell the story in a book. A great many people, both white and colored . . . have urged me to do so. When at the trustees' meeting last November so much emphasis was put upon the desirability of giving general publicity to the things in which we are interested, it seemed to me that the attempt to get out such a book was a duty. I am trying to present the Negro as a new race—one with an African background but with a distinctive if limited place in American life.[32]

Before settling on the name *Brown Americans*, Embree toyed with the idea of entitling the book *Nigger: The New Race*. His doubts about this title reveal much about his newly formed attitude on the Negro problem in the 1930s.[33]

By 1950 Embree was a racial integrationist. The expansion of his intellectual network, his fear of fascism, and World War II stimulated the changes in his racial world view. In the early 1930s, Embree began to develop close working relationships with white southern liberals such as Clark Foreman and Will Alexander, and black moderates, most prominently Charles S. Johnson. Through these men, he became involved in southern organizations and universities which were hotbeds of struggle for racial justice if not for racial integration. In Chi-cago, his involvement in Providence Hospital and the American Council on Race Relations began to soften the conventional aspects of his thinking. The Rosen-wald Fund sponsorship of scores of talented black persons made him an ag-gressive believer in black potential. His book *Thirteen Against the Odds*, a cel-ebration of thirteen eminent blacks, emphasized these beliefs.[34]

But the excitement of being a center of controversy contributed most to his change of outlook. His widening circle of moderate and eventually radical black friends and his colorful reputation drew him away from conventional views. Indignant public reaction encouraged Embree to become even more daring and dramatic as the years wore on.

Yet, Embree's gradual shift from traditional belief in racial segregation to racial integration would not have been so dramatic or so quick if it had not been for his fear of fascism and racial turmoil following World War II. Ironically, before the threat posed by Hitler became obvious, Embree smugly embraced an ''anti-democratic'' view of government:

On the whole I am not a believer in democratic government. By definition it is rule by the stupid who make up the majority of the population, and in practice it is the exploitation of those dull, almost illiterate masses by cunning and corrupt individuals and gangs. No business or scientific institution, or church would think of running itself on the basis of the uninformed and uninterested majorities. Why should we trust the increasingly important business of government to the masses? It seems to me that democracy the world over has proved its inadequacy and futility. This fetish seems sufficiently discredited to be removed from the place of superstitious worship so that we can begin to plan for some better method of administering our government.[35]

But, as Hitler's reign in Germany became increasingly dangerous, Embree began to emphasize the necessity of preserving peaceful democracy in America. On the eve of America's entry into World War II, he expressed a growing interest in finding solutions to race problems.

I am going to keep plugging away at this business of human relationships. I am convinced it is the most important problem facing us for the future, and its importance is likely to become acute as Nazism and depotism make their last ferocious stand. I am eager for our group to do something before we step off the map by way of beginning efforts in this difficult but all-important area.[36]

This concern led to the fund's establishment of the American Race Relations Council in Chicago during the 1940s. Embree feared that unless influential liberals acted quickly, a black proletarian movement would emerge and destroy the ''good will'' that had been developing between the races. In the first summer of World War II, Embree, Alexander, and Johnson held a conference to discuss the fund's race-relations program. They drew up a three- to four-year plan which reflected their interest in more aggressive racial reform. Johnson prepared a memorandum suggesting the rationale for shifting from a policy of racial accommodation to one encouraging racial integration:

The characteristic movements among Negroes are now for the first time becoming proletarian, as contrasted to the upper class in intellectual influence that was typical of previous movements. The present proletarian direction grows out of the increasing power of Negroes in labor and increasing general feelings of protest against discrimination, especially in the armed forces and in war activities generally. . . .

There is likelihood (and danger) that the movement may be seized upon by some much more picturesque figure who may be less responsible and less interested in actual improvement in conditions.[37]

"Thus," concludes one of Johnson's biographers, "Alexander, Embree, and Johnson based at least part of their appeal for funding a new and extensive program for race relations upon the fear of a mass movement led by more radical and charismatic leaders like Adam Clayton Powell."[38] This tactic persuaded the more conservative members of the Rosenwald Board of Trustees to support "active race relations programs."

In 1942, Embree obtained approval to establish a race-relations department at Fisk University, headed by Johnson. The race-relations department played a significant role as a data bank for the civil rights movements in the 1950s. The fund's last project was a study of racial segregation in Washington, D.C., which became a model for civil rights activists and policy makers determined to push the issue the Rosenwald Fund had evaded for so many years—integration.

For Embree, liberal race reform efforts—monitoring tense racial areas, lobbying for limited racial integration, and creating courses on intercultural relations for public schools—were far better than chancing a revolution from the bottom. In a letter to Rosenwald Fund trustee Eleanor Roosevelt, he criticized militant integrationists who opposed a plan for the state of Alabama to help subsidize segregated Tuskegee Institute. He believed that revolutionary change would trigger a fascist regime.

It seems to me that the "militant" northern Negroes have made a mistake in attacking this project. Of course the proposed gift is within the framework of segregation, but so are all of the private funds given to Tuskegee in earlier days and for that matter, so are the suits brought by the NAACP to compel equal salaries and equal facilities for Negro schools in the southern states.

The more I think of it, the more I am convinced that those who are willing to accept nothing from the South this side of pure democracy are saying that they will accept nothing this side of a revolution. I do not favor a revolution if for no other reason than because I believe a revolution at present in America would result in a fascist rather than a liberal victory. This side of revolution, the best strategy seems to me to be demanding and welcoming every step forward, meanwhile building directly on one advance toward the next step. This is not revolution, nor utopia, but is democracy.[39]

Embree's concern over the survival of democracy during World War II recalled that of liberals involved in race-relations work during World War I. After the war, the YMCA and other organizations were unable to head off racial violence spurred by the return of black soldiers. Race riots, lynchings, the rise of the Ku Klux Klan, and the resurgence of biologically deterministic theories of racial differences marred the late 1910s and the 1920s. Liberals certainly did not want the same problems to be generated by World War II. During the war years Embree, along with Will Alexander in the federal government and Charles

S. Johnson at Fisk University, did all he could to promote racial peace. He
even began to lobby for complete racial integration toward the end of the decade.

Embree became a flamboyant racial integrationist, but he continued to believe in white domination over nonwhites. In 1927 he described to Clarence
Day his inner struggle between admiration for the ruling ability of Europeans
and for non-European underdogs. But he never questioned the fact of European
domination.

I am much interested in the relations of white and colored people in America. The subject that really intrigues me is that of PEOPLES—both in America and throughout the
world . . . the rise and fall of races; the clash, not so much of nations as of races; the
struggles of the ancient Jews against their neighbors and the conquering Egyptians, Ba-
bylonians, and Romans; the rise of the Greek cities and their decline; the recent surge
of the Nordics and their domination (under difficulties that I hope will prove uncon-
querable) of the Polynesians, the Arabs, the Africans, the Asiatics—all this to me is
exciting. I find myself torn between an emotional devotion to the underdogs in these
struggles and an intellectual admiration for the dominant group.[40]

Throughout his life, Embree expressed this perspective. A Julius Rosenwald
Fund trustee once asked him to clarify what was meant by just employment for
blacks:

It seems to me important that at no time should anyone be able to point to the fact that
through any series of circumstances Negroes are getting preferences they are not entitled
to. With their being underprivileged as they are in almost every instance, it seems to me
we should see that they get only equal opportunities in better situations, because if they
are favored it certainly weakens our case for the underprivileged balance.[41]

Embree responded justice for blacks in employment did not mean that blacks
should surpass whites or in some other way get "more than their share." Blacks
were to be given to labor markets which did not jeopardize "good feelings,"
or "white supremacy".

Finding that there were so few Negro graduate students, the [National Youth] Administration decided to make an extra effort to make possible graduate study by Negroes.
This they did by setting an especially high stipend for Negro graduate work outside the
normal schedule. Since this was an effort to meet a special situation, we should not refer
to it even jokingly as discrimination. I thank you for calling my attention so sharply to
this issue. It is easy for any of us in the midst of a crusade to begin to gloat over obtaining for our side just the kind of unfair advantages which our whole crusade is devoted to eliminating.[42]

But concerning integration of racial minorities into white institutions, Embree was much more radical than many other liberals, who became reactionary
when attacks on Jim Crow increased during the 1940s.[43]

The goals of the Julius Rosenwald Fund activated Embree's southern liberal leanings. He converted the foundation into an organization supporting regional issues and race relations. He believed that southerners were in the best position to handle their problems, and outside financial assistance should be under their guidance. Additionally, he felt that white southerners knew how best to handle "their" Negroes. He said as much to a trustee who wanted names of candidates for a position on the governing board of a prominent black college:

The general suggestion is that whenever possible, it is better to get southerners rather than northerners on such a board. The South is increasingly taking responsibility for whole-hearted cooperation in Negro education, southerners are nearer to the problem, apt to give more attention to it and these days many of them are quite sympathetic and probably on the whole more intelligent about Negro problems than Yankees.[44]

When Embree's trustees were appointed, they were given a copy of his *Brown Americans*, the Rosenwald Fund's manifesto on the Negro question. In it, Embree described the accomplishments of a new race of people developing in the United States—a race brown in color but with its roots in America rather than in some other land. *Brown Americans* was an apology for the doctrines of racial uplift and racial accommodation, though its premises were certainly unconventional for a southern white liberal. Embree claimed that the development of black universities enabled blacks to "learn the civilization"—in other words, black universities were vehicles for the internalization of dominant group norms. Embree's emphasis on black accomplishments in music and art was typical of racial uplift rhetoric, exaggerating the progress of a minority group by emphasizing the success of individuals in economically marginal occupations. Another work by Embree, *Thirteen Against the Odds*, converged with popular beliefs about "proper" black leadership.

THE ROSENWALD FUND AND SOUTHERN LIBERALISM

Embree was granted great freedom in his selection of trustees. The Rosenwald Fund's Board of Trustees between 1928 and 1948 included women, blacks, and Jews at a time when other boards were composed almost exclusively of white Protestant males.[45] Embree's appointments resulted in the fund's domination by southern white liberals and their sympathizers. With the exception of Charles S. Johnson, who was black, the southern board members represented an expanding white middle class, which had no stake in the survival of the plantation South or in the traditional pattern of race relations established by white planters. In fact, they belonged to urban-industrial elites who benefited from the collapse of the plantation system, which led to the migration of black workers to Southern cities. (One of the trustees, Howard Odum, even claimed that the "true" South was not the traditional plantation order, but the middle class.)

In 1937 Embree reorganized the Board of Trustees and strengthened the southern presence by nominating Howard Odum and Edgar Stern to the board, assuming that "two more Southerners on our board would greatly increase our prestige and authority in the South." He told Will Alexander, chairman of the fund's Nomination Committee,

It seems to be inevitable that in the near future we should again be an almost wholly constructive group. There are so many important problems in education and in Southern development. . . . My idea, not yet realized, is that in addition to voting specific sums and programs our group may in itself become sort of a board of strategy for Southern growth.[46]

Embree also expressed concern for southern underdevelopment in his annual reports:

Another weakness in the national structure is the unequal distribution of opportunity among the various regions. The South is a special and complex problem. Most Negroes still live in the South. And by history and traditions this race is under peculiar handicaps and in turn creates peculiar problems. Prejudice against Negroes obscures all social questions, often cloaks abuses which degrade much larger numbers of the poorer whites, prevents a unified front in labor, farm reorganization, decent wages, proper schools, or any other social advances. The South has a quarter of the nation's population, a third of its area. It has a heritage that includes some fine aspects of culture. But it is poor. Because of the collapse of the old plantation system, the South has been impoverished for three generations. This poverty has kept it from taking its proper place in the national economy, has stunted service to its citizens in such fundamentals as education and health.[47]

The trustees' commitment to developing an enlightened southern elite resulted in the establishment of the Rosenwald Fellowship Program for White Southerners.

White Southerners were included in the fellowship program because they, too, had less opportunity for broadening experiences than other groups of the population and needed aid if they were to prepare for social pioneering in the region. Many of these fellows have made notable careers in a variety of fields. . . . One-third are teaching in southern colleges and universities most of whom thus enriched by experience outside their own section. Writers among the white southern fellows include such figures as Lillian Smith, Thomas Sancton, Herschel Brikell, and Harnett Kane. Among the outstanding journalists and editors are . . . men whose ideas are doing much to influence public attitudes through the southern press.[48]

The regional development project ultimately led the trustees to influence the design of New Deal concerning the South and race relations.

Embree's focus on regional and race-relations problems was influenced by Beardsley Ruml. Their association dated back to the early 1920s when both were officers in the Rockefeller foundations. Their mutual fascination with provocative ideas linked them. As dean of the University of Chicago's School of Social Science Ruml gave Embree access to university scholars who became members of his "kitchen cabinet."

Ruml set in motion the foundation's interest in black economic development, particularly in the South. In 1929 he sent Embree a letter he had drafted to President Hoover.

I had a brain storm this morning and drafted the enclosed letter, which I thought might be sent to Mr. Hoover. . . . I should like to know what you and your group think of it. . . . Personally I do not think it is necessary for Mr. Rosenwald to sign the letter in order to get it to Mr. Hoover's attention, but if he would like to do so I think that perhaps it would be a bit more effective.[49]

Embree later described Rosenwald's delight over Ruml's idea:

Mr. Rosenwald is delighted at your idea of calling President Hoover's attention to the possibility of improving the economic conditions of the Negro. We are making a few changes in the letter, with the view to making it a little more personal, and sending it on.[50]

Members of the Hoover administration responded favorably to the idea of studying black economic development problems, but lack of time prevented significant action. However, the idea became central to the planning of Rosenwald Fund funding priorities and eventually was put into effect by the New Deal administration.

Embree was able to implement his funding goals by aligning himself with two southerners who shared his assumptions—Will W. Alexander and Charles S. Johnson. He also took an interest in Howard W. Odum's scientism of regional development. Embree, Alexander, and Johnson set the foundation's policies and supervised its evolution over the years. With the help of these men Embree sought to reform the South through social science.

WILL ALEXANDER

Years before Alexander became a Julius Rosenwald Fund trustee and the permanent vice president of the foundation in 1930, Julius Rosenwald named him the most valuable man in race relations in America.[51] Alexander had a sociologically oriented racial world view. In 1923 he approached Howard Odum about the possibility of starting a southern organization of social science teachers.

Two or three years study convinces me that the thing that hinders the colleges in the South in making a larger contribution to the improving of race relations is their general backwardness in the Departments of Social Science. A great many strong colleges have no Social Science Departments whatever. . . . If there is not already a southern organization of the teachers of Sociology, would it help to bring these people together to discuss their peculiar problems and devise possible means by which the teaching of Social Science could be extended to other schools?[52]

The organization was created early the next year and its members recommended inquiry into the present status and future outlook of undergraduate college work in race relations. This association was a forerunner of the Southern Sociological Society.

The Commission on Interracial Cooperation, founded in 1919 in Atlanta, Georgia, played a key role in incorporating sociology into the curriculum of southern academic institutions. Some of its founders, such as Thomas J. Jones and Willis D. Weatherford, had already established themselves as experts on blacks. Alexander was chosen first as secretary and shortly thereafter became director. The commission was organized to confront increasing hostility toward blacks in the South in the years immediately following World War I. Its administrators confronted the problem of race tension for some twenty-five years, establishing biracial watchdog committees in local communities throughout the South. These committees were comprised of prominent white and black local leaders who participated in conferences and fought to end lynchings and blatant racist statements in newspapers.[53]

The commission was integral to the efforts of southern middle-class elites to develop a new image of the South. New southerners like Alexander strived toward a South where interracial harmony prevailed. The commission was also an indication of the gradual urbanization of the South. Its key administrators, although of rural or small town backgrounds, were urban in outlook. Alexander and other commission administrators assumed that the race problem could be dealt with scientifically. Alexander had been impressed with sociology as a potential medium for social change ever since he had discovered it as a graduate student in theology at Vanderbilt University.

One professor formed the whole department at Vanderbilt in those days, and it was a step-child subject, looked down upon by formal classicists, with indifference at best, suspicion at worst. The first few lectures, on the approach to social problems, were eloquent. Alexander was stirred by new ideas, new tools for understanding people. He resolved to take every course, graduate as well as undergraduate, offered by the department of sociology. . . . I spent a couple of years trying to get a start in sociology. I did some outside research in the area where my boys on the north side of Nashville lived, but my experience with the classroom course was like that of a hungry child forced to satisfy his appetite with the fragrance coming from the kitchen the day before Christmas. Academically, Alexander's interest in deeper knowledge of the society around him was unfulfilled; practically, it would provide the stimulus to drive him into new paths of exploration and experience.[54]

Alexander established a research department which became known as a data bank on southern race problems, especially lynching, in the 1930s. Due to his interest in research there was much interchange between the commission and the University of North Carolina. For instance, in the early 1920s, Thomas J. Woofter, Jr., was appointed as research secretary of the commission. A few years later he joined the sociology faculty of the University of North Carolina. Arthur Raper became research secretary of the commission in the early 1930s while finishing up his dissertation at the University of North Carolina. He had met Alexander before attending the university, and he was reintroduced to him by Odum.

The commission, more than any other organization, should have the credit for establishing courses on race relations in southern academic institutions. As the commission's first research secretary, Woofter wrote the first textbook on race relations expressly for course offerings in academic institutions, *Racial Adjustment*. Many years after the book was published, he described why he had written it:

College faculties and students were increasingly open-minded on race questions but had little ammunition in the way of systematically compiled facts. . . . There was no comprehensive textbook which could be used by those study groups so I was assigned the job of writing one. In rereading it I am impressed by the fact that it was not a very good job and would, in comparison to present day texts, be considered wholly inadequate. I can only plead immaturity and lack of systematically developed facts as reasons for its shortcomings. Nevertheless, it was soon adopted as the basis for courses in race relations in some sixty Southern colleges.

Up to that time analytical literature on race was not too voluminous. Some community surveys gave firsthand descriptions of local situations. A few works have appeared on the plantation system and on educational conditions and a considerable number of essays on the philosophy of race were in print. What I did was try to put these together.

It was not until the late 1920's that extensive, systematic, factual books became common. Since then hundreds of thousands of pages of factual reports, surveys, monographs, and propaganda about the Negro have been published. It is almost beyond the power of human eyesight to read it all. The production of more objectively determined facts soon made it possible to produce more comprehensive and systematic texts for study groups.[55]

Scientific sociology was deemed an objective way to understand the nature of the "race problem," and also a way to make southerners repent their old ways. In this sense, sociology served a civil religious function. It was used as a tool for social change—change of racial attitudes—quite different from its development in the Midwest and East, where it became a tool for the control of problems in the cities.[56]

Like Embree, Alexander publicly supported racial integration by the 1940s. However, he did not share the privilege of distance from the fierce opposition of the southern status quo as Jim Crow began to crumble. By the early 1950s, although he did not withdraw from his friends or his racial stances, he dropped out of the vanguard pushing for racial integration.[57]

NOTES

1. Biographical Materials, Edwin R. Embree Papers, Yale University.

2. Morris R. Werner, *Julius Rosenwald* (New York: Harper and Brothers, 1939), p. 136.

3. Ibid., p. 114.

4. Ibid., p. 12.

5. Ibid., pp. 133–134. Rosenwald also gave generous donations for the construction of black YMCAs.

6. Julius Rosenwald to Abraham Flexner, November 17, 1920, General Education Board Archives.

7. Edwin R. Embree and Julia Waxman, *Investment in People: The Story of the Julius Rosenwald Fund* (New York: Harper, 1949), p. 29.

8. Ibid., p. 31.

9. Ibid., p. 32.

10. Ibid., p. 33; John H. Stanfield, "Dollars for the Silent South," in *Perspectives on the American South*, vol. 2, ed. Merle Black and John Shelton Reed (New York: Editors Gordon and Breach, 1984).

11. *Current Biography*, 1948, p. 190. Academically, Embree was trained in journalism and public relations. His sociological imagination is more than apparent in his numerous articles and books on the social sciences, society, and race relations. He defined racial discrimination sociologically, stressing institutional contexts and patterns of intergroup relations. His philosophy of social science and how (like a secular theology) it was supposed to work toward resolving societal ills was best stated in Edwin R. Embree, *Prospecting for Heaven: Some Conversations About Science and the Good Life* (New York: Viking Press, 1932).

12. John G. Fee's *Autobiography* in the Berea College Archives is the source on which the following paragraphs about his life are based.

13. Philip English, "John G. Fee: A Kentucky Spokesman for Abolition and Educational Reform" (Ph.D. dissertation, Indiana University, 1973). While Fee was a masterful preacher, his grandson Edwin used his public relations talents to develop the Julius Rosenwald Fund into a foundation geared to influencing public opinion. See Embree and Waxman, *Investment in People*.

14. The segregationist policy implemented by Berea College administrations from the early 1900s through the early 1950s greatly disappointed Edwin Embree—so much so that in 1946 he refused to deliver a speech there. Edwin R. Embree to Francis S. Hutchins, July 19, 1946, Edwin R. Embree Papers, Berea College.

15. William Embree became a corporate lawyer who had a deep interest in social issues. While serving as a lawyer for John D. Rockefeller, Sr., he introduced his brother Edwin to the multimillionaire who was looking for a secretary for one of his philanthropies, the Rockefeller Foundation.

16. Edwin R. Embree, "A Kentucky Crusader," *American Mercury* (September 1931).

17. Edwin R. Embree to Edgar Stern, 1945, Julius Rosenwald Fund (hereafter JRF) Archives.

18. Edgar Stern to Embree and E. R. Embree to Edgar Stern, October 5, 1946, JRF Archives.

19. Edwin R. Embree to Julius Rosenwald, May 7, 1931, JRF Archives.

20. Edwin R. Embree to A. R. Levy, 1930, JRF Archives.

21. He was also marginal because although he was periodically dependent upon big foundations for assistance, he was quite critical of their apparent stagnation.

22. See Edwin R. Embree correspondence in Roosevelt University folders, JRF Archives.

23. See Edwin R. Embree–Beardsley Ruml correspondence in Laura Spelman Rockefeller Memorial (hereafter LSRM) Archives and interviews with Beardsley Ruml and

Leonard Outhwaite recorded in Edwin R. Embree's diary, Rockefeller Foundation Archives.

24. Biographical materials, Edwin R. Embree Papers, Yale University.

25. Edwin R. Embree to Clarence Day, August 4, 1928, Edwin R. Embree Papers, Yale University.

26. Embree to Day, December 1, 1927, Edwin R. Embree Papers, Yale University.

27. William Rosenwald to Edwin R. Embree, JRF Archives. Julius Rosenwald's insistence on the unflinching personal loyalty of his nieces, nephews, and children is revaled in surviving personal correspondence in the Julius Rosenwald Papers.

28. Clarence Day, *This Simian World* (New York: Alfred A. Knopf, 1921); Clarence Day, *Life with Father* (New York: Alfred A. Knopf, 1935). The analysis of the Embree-Day relationship is based upon correspondence to and from Day found in the Edwin R. Embree Papers, Yale University. Until his death in 1935, Clarence Day was Edwin R. Embree's best friend.

29. Embree-Day correspondence, Edwin R. Embree Papers, Yale University.

30. Day to Embree, February 23, 1929; March 26, 1929; December 13, 1930; [1929 or 1930?]; and March 1931, Edwin R. Embree Papers, Yale University.

31. Embree to Day, March 26, 1929, Edwin R. Embree Papers, Yale University.

32. Embree to J. Rosenwald, May 6, 1931, JRF Archives.

33. See Embree to Day, March or April 1931, Edwin R. Embree Papers, Yale University.

34. Edwin R. Embree, *Thirteen Against the Odds* (New York: Viking, 1944).

35. Edwin R. Embree to Murray Seasongood, May 22, 1933, JRF Archives.

36. Edwin R. Embree to Frank Sulzburger, June 3, 1940, JRF Archives.

37. John H. Stanfield, "Dollars for the Silent South," pp. 132–136.

38. Patrick J. Gilpin, *Charles S. Johnson: An Intellectual Biography* (Ph.D. dissertation, Vanderbilt University, 1973), p. 488.

39. Edwin R. Embree to Eleanor Roosevelt, May 11, 1943, JRF Archives.

40. Embree to Day, February 19, 1929, Edwin R. Embree Papers, Yale University. Also, Embree occasionally did consultant work for colonial regimes in the 1930s and 1940s. See, for instance, his published works on Dutch Indonesia such as Edwin R. Embree, Margaret Simon Sargent and W. Bryant Mumford, *Island India Goes to School* (Chicago: University of Chicago Press, 1934).

41. Sulzburger to Embree, February 8, 1936, JRF Archives.

42. Embree to Sulzburger, February 10, 1936, JRF Archives.

43. Morton Sosna, *In Search of the Silent South* (New York: Columbia University Press, 1977).

44. Embree to Edgar Stern, some time in the 1930s, JRF Archives.

45. Only highly assimilated Jews such as Abraham Flexner, Simon Flexner, and Julius Rosenwald served on pre–World War II major foundation boards. Besides the daughters of Julius Rosenwald and Eleanor Roosevelt, Embree was reluctant to appoint women to his board. Once, when one of Rosenwald's daughters suggested he do so, he responded:

Frankly, I am not at all keen about women, as women on boards and I do not at the moment think of any woman, who, aside from her womanness, would be within hailing distance of the qualifications for our board, of the men we have been recently considering (Charles S. Johnson and Robert M. Hutchins). After a long and turbulent life and after extensive perusal of the classics, my conclusion is that women are valuable (a) for social purposes including the perpetration of the species, and; (b) exploitation—women can be had for accurate, devoted, and sometimes brilliant service at much less cost than men. As a hard headed executive I am in favor of using various groups for the greatest returns, in general men for counsel and women for work. [Edwin R. Embree to Edith Stern, November 2, 1934, JRF Archives]

The following persons served terms as Julius Rosenwald Fund trustees between 1928 and 1948: Will W. Alexander, Marion R. Ascoli, Harry W. Chase, Will W. Clayton, Donald Comer, John J. Coss, Edwin R. Embree, Mark Ethridge, Marshall Field III, A. Richard Frank, O. Max Gardner, Charles H. Houston, Robert M. Hutchins, Charles S. Johnson, Charles H. Judd, Adele R. Levy, Franklin C. McLean, Howard W. Odum, Leonard M. Rieser, Anna Eleanor Roosevelt, Julius Rosenwald, Lessing J. Rosenwald, William Rosenwald, Beardsley Ruml, Murray Seasongood, Bishop Bernard J. Sheil, Alfred K. Stern, Edgar B. Stern, Edith R. Stern, Frank L. Sulzberger, Harold H. Swift, Robert E. Wood.

46. Edwin R. Embree to Will Alexander, August 20, 1937; September 29, 1937, JRF Archives.

47. Edwin R. Embree, *Julius Rosenwald Fund: Review for the Two Year Period, 1938–1940*, pp. 7–8.

48. Embree and Waxman, *Investment in People*, p. 151.

49. Ruml to Embree, November 25, 1929, JRF Archives.

50. Embree to Ruml, December 12, 1929, JRF Archives.

51. Leonard Outhwaite to Beardsley Ruml, April 6, 1926, LSRM Archives.

52. Will Alexander to Howard W. Odum, June 1923, Howard W. Odum Papers.

53. The best published accounts about the Commission on Interracial Cooperation are: Wilma Dykeman and James Stokely, *Seeds of Southern Change: The Life of Will Alexander* (Chicago: University of Chicago Press, 1962) and Morton Sosna, *In Search of the New South* (New York, 1977).

54. Dykeman and Stokely, *Seeds of Southern Change*, pp. 13–14.

55. Thomas J. Woofter, Jr., *Southern Race Progress* (Washington, D.C.: Public Affairs Press, 1957), pp. 167–168.

56. James T. Carey, *Sociology and Public Affairs: The Chicago School* (Beverly Hills, Calif.: Sage Publications, 1975).

57. At least through the 1954 *Brown* decision, Alexander participated in Southern Regional Council meetings from whence early school desegregation strategies were drawn. Patrick Gilpin, *Charles S. Johnson: An Intellectual Biography*, p. 608.

6

Charles Spurgeon Johnson

In the history of American social science, no man did more for the advancement of modern "black social science" than Fisk sociologist Charles S. Johnson. But historians continue to be uncertain about his activities as race statesman, foundation consultant, and sociologist. All they know for sure is that Johnson possessed extraordinary stability, self-confidence, and reserve, allowing him to design a most unusual career, which was largely behind the scenes.

Johnson's place of birth and family explain much about the origins of his unusual strength. Johnson was born in 1893. His father was a Baptist clergyman, and the family was solidly middle class. Although racial problems have always been present in the Appalachian region where Johnson grew up, they have usually been hidden under a surface of tolerant race relations. This environment certainly contributed to Johnson's later ability to get along with whites, even those who insulted him or black people in general.[1] He had a reputation for charm and tact, and he was also skilled at getting what he wanted from whites for his institutions, family, friends, and students without selling out to whites, or to blacks for that matter. He never allowed success to go to his head.

Johnson's Appalachian background, his middle-class upbringing, and his religious background developed in him an inner strength which freed him from many of the identity conflicts that afflicted other black social scientists of his era. Unlike Horace Cayton, for example, he did not fret over whether he really wanted to be black or white. Unlike E. Franklin Frazier, he did not spend years trying to climb into another social class.[2] Instead, he dedicated his life to liberating blacks from racial discrimination by conducting scientific research, advising white policy makers, and developing black talent. He married an assertive middle-class woman who strengthened his personal and social stability, and he joined the "proper" black middle-class organizations. In his studies of poor blacks, he did not claim to be one of them, nor did he interpret their plight as pathological—he wrote as a sympathetic but detached and empirically grounded observer.[3] His stability allowed him to be a highly prolific scholar while serving numerous foundations, government agencies, and other organizations.

Johnson's home environment contributed to his ability to communicate with people from all walks of life. His father, one of the most prominent black leaders in Bristol, Virginia, opened his house to strangers passing through the town. Thus, Charles Johnson learned that middle-class status should be used for stewardship, not for conspicuous consumption or prestige. He went to college intending to pursue a career which would allow him to help people. This eventually led him to sociology. The Johnson home, being the way station and sociological laboratory it was, also inspired at least two of his siblings to enter the social sciences.[4] After finishing his undergraduate work at Virginia Union University, Johnson enrolled in the sociology department at the University of Chicago in 1917.

The story of how Robert E. Park "discovered" Johnson in one of his classes characterizes Johnson's unusual self-confidence, brightness, and unassuming presentation of self. Park called on students in one of his classes one day to read papers. He was especially impressed by the report of the black youth in the back of the room who detailed his paper's conceptual premises and methodology with extraordinary insight.[5] From that point on, Johnson's career soared. Because of his administrative skills and exceptional talent for data collection and analysis, Park appointed Johnson the first director of research (1917–1919) of the Chicago Urban League.[6] The timing could not have been better. Soon after Johnson became director, the Chicago race riot of 1919 broke out.

The race riots in the late 1910s made it more than apparent that sociological race-relations theories and policies were inadequate. Their explanation and recommendations, steeped in the theories of biological determinism, could not make sense out of the rapid, conflict-ridden changes in white-black relations occurring in Chicago and other urban areas. In Chicago, a commission on race relations was organized to sponsor a study of race-relations conditions in the city. The commission, which was heavily financed by Julius Rosenwald,[7] hired Robert E. Park and Charles S. Johnson. (This sort of policy-oriented race-relations research was to become Johnson's forte.)

Their published study, *The Negro in Chicago*, became a classic for two reasons. It was the first study published in the University of Chicago Press Sociology Series, and it was the first comprehensive social scientific analysis of post–World War I white-black relations. *The Negro in Chicago* continues to enjoy a peculiar immortality. Although Park has been called the senior author, Johnson wrote over half of the study, as indicated in a copy of the work he gave to his father with this dedication and confession:

Here is contained the work of 2 years. In transmitting the volume to you, I waive the anonymity customary in publications of this nature and command to your special attention, Chapters III, IV, V, VI, IX, X, XI which are my contributions exclusively.[8]

From the Chicago Urban League, Johnson went to National Urban League headquarters in New York City. It was there, as editor of *Opportunity* (a black literary and social commentary journal) that Johnson developed an interest in sponsoring young black talent. He published the work of Harlem Renaissance artists and sponsored benefits on their behalf. Sometime during his tenure with the Urban League he became acquainted with Leonard Outhwaite. Their meeting undoubtedly had to do with the large sums of money the memorial contributed to the New York City Urban League in the 1920s.[9] Leonard Outhwaite and Edwin Embree were able to observe Johnson's skill as a race-relations analyst during the New Haven Negro Problems Conference, which was composed of foundation officers and black leaders concerned with long-range race-relations planning in the foundation sector.[10] Outhwaite and Embree were quickly impressed with Johnson's analytic powers.

After the conference Outhwaite and other memorial officers began working toward the establishment of a social science research center at Fisk University. For some years, the Rockefeller foundations had been interested in developing Fisk into an important liberal arts center for blacks. The appointment of Thomas E. Jones as its president in 1926 increased their regard for the institution. The Negro Problems Conference and the National Interracial Conference convinced Outhwaite and his colleagues that Fisk should become a center for social scientific data collection on blacks. In his attempt to make Fisk attractive to the memorial, its recently appointed president defined race-relations research as one of the necessary functions of a black college.

Each time the memorial assisted in the establishment of a social science research center, its officers formally or informally influenced the selection of the center's director. Fisk was no exception. In fact, memorial influence over the organization of the Fisk social science research center was most explicit and deliberate. Although the correspondence does not reveal their attitudes explicitly, Outhwaite and the other memorial officers were well aware of the danger of placing the wrong black in charge of this well-financed social research center, lest he study the wrong things, violate caste etiquette, or, worst of all, rebel against foundation dominance. A black who was theoretically or philosophically oriented would not be useful, since the center was to be a clearing house for data on the Negro problem, not a place where scholars might develop theories applicable to other populations. Negro problem social science was ultimately for social and political control—it was not meant as a contribution to mainstream academic literature about human nature.

Charles S. Johnson was selected as the director of the center. In early 1928 Outhwaite, Edwin Embree, Alfred Stern, and Julius Rosenwald held conferences with Johnson about his new position.[11] Johnson wrote a lengthy letter to Thomas E. Jones which mentioned his dissatisfaction with his Urban League post, his relationship with Embree and the newly reorganized Julius Rosenwald Fund, his plans for Fisk, and an offer by Julius Rosenwald.[12]

The reasons why Johnson became dissatisfied with the Urban League remain unclear. Since he liked to be in complete control, he may have become restless in his subordinate position. There is also some indication that *Opportunity* was suffering from financial difficulties.[13] Johnson may also have disliked spending so much time on the road, away from his young family.[14]

In formulating the race-relations plans of the future Rosenwald Fund, Embree consulted with memorial officers Ruml and Outhwaite and with Raymond Fosdick of the Rockefeller Foundation. When the idea of Johnson's directorship of the Fisk Social Science Department was first considered, Embree wanted him to do a comprehensive survey of the race-relations field to assist the Julius Rosenwald Fund's program development. A few weeks later, Embree changed his mind, deciding that Johnson was more valuable as a consultant who would do studies on behalf of his foundation. Johnson agreed that Fisk social science programs should emphasize data collection and training of students.[15]

Edwin Embree and the memorial officers were aided in their attempt to lure Johnson to Fisk by Julius Rosenwald, who offered to give Johnson the financial backing necessary to make Fisk a superior race research center. Julius Rosenwald was willing to do this because he had been so deeply impressed by Johnson during his tenure on the Chicago race-relations commission. Throughout the 1920s, Johnson had continued to correspond with Rosenwald, often asking for support for Urban League activities.[16]

JOHNSON AND EMBREE

Charles S. Johnson was more than a consultant, trustee, and officer during and after his years with the Julius Rosenwald Fund. After Clarence Day's death in 1935, Charles S. Johnson became Edwin R. Embree's closest friend until Embree died in 1950. His close friendship with Embree greatly influenced the gradual evolution of the foundation from a supporter of racial caste to a promoter of racial integration. Both were candid about their feelings toward various events. This was particularly true of Embree. Johnson, in his more reserved fashion, occasionally wrote to "Mr. Embree" about what at least appeared to be cases of racial discrimination.[17]

Embree was greatly influenced by Charles S. Johnson's ideas about the plantation society. Johnson, along with his graduate students, designed the study entitled *Collapse of the Cotton Tenancy* (authored by Johnson, Alexander, and Embree). Johnson's statistical analyses of the South were consumed in large quantities by Embree. As originally planned, Julius Rosenwald Fund officers frequently called on Johnson to supply them with the statistical data needed for their speeches, reports, and books. Johnson also served as a major sounding board for Embree's books, especially *Brown Americans*.[18] Embree also relied on Johnson's judgment of candidates for Julius Rosenwald Fund fellowships, especially in the social sciences. He shared with Johnson news about the careers of other black academics and sometimes asked him to intervene informally. He held Johnson's recommendations about black institutions and persons in high esteem.[19] Embree appointed Johnson to every board within his domain which was involved in racial issues.

Embree also had a subtle influence on Charles S. Johnson, beside the obvious and important financial role of patron. Johnson never willingly risked his source of institutional stability; thus, he hesitated to strike out boldly against racism, even when the proper occasion presented itself. Although he was always a racial integrationist, he avoided leftist solutions and tried to maintain a moderate perspective. This moderation meant that for years he put up with racial segregationists claiming to be friends of the black. Johnson was able to become more openly integrationist as the president of his major source of support, the Julius Rosenwald Fund, leaned in that direction. But had Embree moved to the right in response to the racial changes wrought by the depression years and World War II, Johnson probably would not have risked criticizing racial segregation, criticizing white liberals as racial gradualists, or joining the pro-integration American Race Relations Council (ARRC). He may not have risked publishing the Fisk Race Relations Institute's *Monthly Review of Trends*, which was financed by the Julius Rosenwald Fund and distributed by the ARRC.[20]

After the death of Julius Rosenwald in 1948 and of Edwin Embree in 1950, Johnson, who had become president of Fisk in 1947, endeavored to make the university the information center for the emerging civil rights movement. He attracted funds from the newly established Ford Foundation to establish the Southern Educational Reporting Service.[21]

Johnson's friendship with Embree and his connections with Jackson Davis and Albert Mann of the General Education Board allowed him to build a tremendous center for the training of graduate students and for race-relations research. Due to an informal pact he had with Embree, which was also respected by the General Education Board, Fisk received most of the choice fellowship and scholarship recipients in its social science graduate program. Johnson supervised and analyzed most of the data collected by his students.

He not only found money for his students but also looked after them—his students received the best jobs the segregated economy had to offer. Every time an opening was announced by Embree, another foundation, or a government agency, Johnson recommended at least one of his students. Contrary to some claims, Johnson did not habitually exploit his students and then "dump" them.[22]

JOHNSON'S CONCEPTUAL CONTRIBUTIONS TO THE ROSENWALD FUND

Charles S. Johnson gave Embree and Alexander both methodological expertise and conceptual tools for presenting regional and racial problems. He offered empirical documentation for their belief that the South was an underdeveloped region, afflicted with a disintegrating plantation base, in need of reform led by indigenous elites. Borrowing from Robert Redfield's and especially Robert E. Park's studies of the disintegration of folk culture, Johnson portrayed rural blacks captive in the shadow of the plantation and thereby isolated from civilization.[23] But Embree's foundation commissioned Johnson to do studies of regionalism and black folk culture which often caused contradictions in Johnson's interpretations of race in the plantation South. Two works authored by Johnson and Fisk graduate students—*Shadow of the Plantation* and *Collapse of the Cotton Tenancy*—serve as examples.[24]

VENEREAL DISEASE AND *SHADOW OF THE PLANTATION*

In 1949 Edwin Embree recalled the circumstances surrounding the initiation of his foundation's involvement in a health project some twenty years before:

In 1929 the United States Public Health Service sought the Fund's cooperation in demonstrating the possibility of mass control of syphilis among southern Negroes. Dr. O. C. Wenger of the United States Public Health Service had just completed an investigation in Mississippi which revealed that syphilis was a much more serious public-health problem in the South than malaria, hookworm, or pellagra. On the basis of this investigation, the U.S. Public Health Service, through Dr. Thomas Parran, then assistant surgeon general, approached Dr. Michael M. Davis, the general director of the Fund's medical program, with the suggestion that a joint demonstration project be undertaken in several areas of the rural South. A Plan covering investigation and experiment in six communities selected as typical of different sections of the South was worked out and carried through with the cooperation of the Fund, the U.S. Public Health Service and the state and county authorities.[25]

This was the inception of the Julius Rosenwald Fund's four-year study on syphilis among rural southern blacks in collaboration with the United States Public Health Service and other agencies.

In 1931 Michael Davis of the Julius Rosenwald Fund wrote to Charles S. Johnson inviting him to participate in the ongoing venereal disease project as a social scientist.[26] "I am especially eager about these demonstrations," wrote Johnson in reply, "principally because I want to get into some of these rural areas. I believe the plan can be worked out for a large measure of personal participation in the sociological and economic aspects of the study."[27] Davis wrote back to Johnson to inform him of his exact duties in the project and the reasons why he, as a social scientist, was being asked to become involved in the project.[28]

It was understood when these demonstrations were planned that the fund would wish to have a study made of the work after they had been in operation for sometime. The primary purpose of the study is to furnish suggestions as to how the plans and methods adopted might, perhaps with certain modifications, be applied in other areas and be supported financially. It was also intended that the studies would include some technical evaluation of the methods used in diagnosis and treatment of syphilis so as to judge the value of the medical results achieved and to suggest improvements in the method applicable to rural conditions in other areas.

Consideration of the details of these studies led to the tentative conclusion that it would be advisable to have at least one of these areas studied carefully from at least two points of view (1) that of a physician expert in syphilis and (2) that of a sociologist who would form judgments as to the social and economic conditions and the paying ability of the area and who would also investigate the manner in which the demonstration had been conducted with reference to its effectiveness in reaching the people whom it was to serve and the psychological reactions to the demonstration of both Negro and White groups in the locality. The economic relationships of the local medical practice to the treatment of syphilis are also a matter of interest and might be approached jointly by the syphilologist and the sociologist.[29]

About the aim of the Macon County demonstration O. C. Wenger said: "The aim of the work undertaken was to determine the number of positive Wassermanns in a group of unselected rural negroes of all age groups in a given area of Macon County and to arrange treatment for all cases uncovered."[30]

Macon County, Alabama, was one of the most useful settings for examining the prevalence of syphilis. It had the largest number of reported venereal disease cases in the South. Alabama claimed to have one of the best organized state health programs in the country, including the facilities of the Tuskegee Institute and Hospital. The county health administrators, social workers, and others concerned with this problem were "more favorable to this type of social experiment than one usually found in southern counties." Most important, the black population in the area made docile, cooperative subjects.

The cooperation of the Negro people is easily secured and a reasonable degree of regularity in clinic visits can be expected . . . the large Negro attendance is due in part to the fact that in the minds of these people, there is nothing to suggest that syphilis is not entirely acceptable.[31]

Through public relations work in black schools and churches and through the legendary name "Rosenwald" ("even though its ways are not always understood"),[32] the project administrators managed to secure a large turnout in their drive to collect blood samples.

We have seen that the administrators assumed that widespread incidence of syphilis among their black subjects was due to their lack of social or moral inhibitions about the disease. In fact, they came to believe that the pervasiveness of this disease caused other diseases. This assumption distracted physicians from realizing that black people were also suffering from diseases which were *not* the result of being infected with syphilis. In fact, of course, the increased incidence of syphilis and other diseases was due to the lack of economic resources among blacks and their systematic exclusion from white health care institutions. Davis agreed with Wenger that:

it is useless to attempt to cure syphilis in the rural Negro population in Macon County, Alabama until and unless some way is found to treat the large number of cases of tuberculosis, malnutrition and pellagra, and also to give some fundamental training in living habits, with the necessary attention provided to enable one to earn a living.[33]

Unfortunately, the Rosenwald Fund health administrators did little to resolve this health problem, for if they had attempted to do so, they would have violated the ''gentlemen's agreement'' between northern philanthropists and southern state governments that the foundations were not to promote changes in the traditional structural positions of the races.[34] Rosenwald officers and administrators from other agencies apparently felt that it was more appropriate to assume that poor health conditions among rural blacks were caused by moral and cultural deviation, rather than by the exclusion of blacks from white-dominated institutions. Based upon the assumption that the culture and morals of blacks caused pervasive syphilis, the monograph they put together described the sociological and cultural characteristics assumed to be the major conductors of this repugnant state of affairs. Thus enters *Shadow of the Plantation*.

PUTTING THE SHADOW ON THE PLANTATION

Shadow of the Plantation is Johnson's descriptive sociological analysis of black community life in Macon County, Alabama. In a letter to Davis, Johnson offers an overview of the rationales for the study:

I realized, as its preparation proceeded, that it would be utterly useless to present simply a statistical analysis of this situation. It could be misleading and could not convey to you the vital elements of community life which should be known in order that a proper health program might be devised. Moreover, rural communities have been studied less frequently than more advanced urban communities, and there is, as a consequence, less standardization of technique and criteria for measurements. Most of the elements in this situation fall so far below minimum standards that it would have been useless to attempt to relate them to these standards. The study thus takes a descriptive slant and presents the social patterns against the questions originally set by you to be answered, and offers more or less through the materials themselves the answers to these questions.

I have not attempted in this report to offer specific recommendations of programs because it occurred to me that this is what your office would want to do, in the light of your own plans with reference to the section and your field of health work. I can, however, send suggestions and even a closer summary of the observations of this study if you desire these.[35]

Johnson's study began in June 1931. Three field workers interviewed 612 families. Since the area they surveyed was in the southwestern portion of the county, which was heavily canvassed by project administrators, in most of the families interviewed, at least one member had been given the Wassermann test. Some controversy arose among the administrators as to whether Johnson should link the venereal disease demonstrations (or ''medical materials'' as they called them) and the conditions among blacks he described. But referring to the letter which outlined his duties in the project, Johnson pointed out:

I have never proposed to handle the medical materials. That was not my job, but I did include on our social and economic questionnaire items regarding the families in which some or all members had shown positive Wassermann results and families with negative results. The notation was made with a view to providing a basis for comparing the racial backgrounds of these two groups. In addition, we included several complete communities as a means of gauging the representations of the families in contact with the clinics.[36]

Therefore, Johnson barely mentioned the venereal disease control demonstration in the monograph, using it only to point out poor health conditions among the blacks.[37] But while Johnson did not tie syphilis explicitly to his descriptions, it obviously influenced his emphasis on certain characteristics of the black population. The lack of a direct link between social conditions and "medical materials" allowed Johnson to generalize about how the poverty in the community led to social conditions which were incongruent with surrounding civilized society, such as illiteracy, variations in family structure, and ineffective social control institutions. This last point deserves further elaboration.

The "shadow" on the plantation was the obsolete economic system used by white planters to get the most out of black tenants. This system led to the development of cultural lag and social isolation, two social circumstances which were the central issues in the book:

the early social organization of this group . . . has taken form, naturally, outside the dominant current of the American culture. At the same time, and unfortunately, the very fact of this cultural difference presents the danger of social disorganization in any sudden attempt to introduce new modes of living and conceptions of values. The situation is one clearly of isolation and cultural lag. Changes are occurring slowly, however, and it is possible to observe and to measure them.[38]

In his analysis of rural black social life, Johnson emphasized the social, cultural, and economic consequences of exploitation and ineffective social control institutions.

This approach to the study of racial inequality created a contradiction in the published study. On one hand, Johnson insisted that social phenomena such as "quasi-family" types and loose sexual mores were normative aspects of the culture of these "folk Negroes" even though they deviated from the norms of mainstream society. Intolerance for such social forms and behavior developed only when some members of folk society attained a higher cultural level via education and travel. On the other hand, in his presentation of case studies, Johnson portrayed a disorganized community, plagued with a variety of social and economic pathologies. This led to a discrepancy between his presentation of the data and its analysis. Johnson emphasized that "invading" social forces had a disorganizing effect on folk society. In this claim he contradicted himself, because these so-called outside forces could not disorganize a community which was already disorganized.

Johnson effectively illustrated the precarious conditions of "folk Negroes" through presenting statistical and case study data on the failure of black institutions. Schools did not even teach the essentials of reading and writing because white landlords benefited from the illiteracy of their laborers. Churches served as social centers but did not fulfill more central functions such as moral regulation and spiritual development: "there is a widespread gap between doctrine and behavior and the behavior which leaves the traditional doctrine empty and unconvincing in relation to the normal currents of life."[39]

Johnson conceptualized black rural life in this manner because it was his responsibility, as a researcher on behalf of the Rosenwald Fund, to describe the social and cultural conditions which generated the prevalence of syphilis in the area. Health officers of the Julius Rosenwald Fund already assumed that the "pathological" quality of rural black life caused such severe health problems. Johnson was expected to supply data to substantiate, or at least complement, the picture of black rural life they already saw. Johnson's conceptualization of the shadow on the plantation gave the work a critical edge. He demonstrated how an obsolete agrarian economy produced an "isolated and culturally backward people" who suffered under various demeaning conditions, including a chronic syphilis problem. This view, which the fund endorsed, was, in part, a variation of Parkian sociology and congruent with what would be called the "ideology of the disintegrating plantation system"—the conception, shared by Embree, Johnson, and Alexander, of the South as an underdeveloped region.

THE COLLAPSE OF THE COTTON TENANCY AND THE COMMITTEE OF THREE

The noticeable gaps in *Shadow of the Plantation*, brought about through the priorities of Johnson's patrons, can be analyzed by comparing the publication with another one supported by the Julius Rosenwald Fund: *The Collapse of the Cotton Tenancy*. In 1934 a Julius Rosenwald Fund task committee composed of Edwin Embree, Will Alexander, and Charles S. Johnson met to decide how best to spend $50,000 secretly given to them by the Rockefeller Foundation. The funds were to be used for the development of a project to provide a more adequate basis for economic and social planning within the New Deal administration in respect to the black population. They named the project "The Negro and Economic Reconstruction Project."[40] The activities of the committee, as Embree, Alexander, and Johnson called their group, represented their foundation's response to the lack of black social and economic stability and inadequate New Deal assistance programs. The committee dealt with several problems, but their funding priorities and political strategies were geared primarily toward bringing about agrarian reform in the plantation South. The committee agreed on six general provisions:

- The work was to be concluded within the current year.
- The emphasis would be placed upon information leading directly and promptly to action.
- The basic studies would lead to clear-cut proposals of social and economic plans.
- The committee would restrict its interest to a small number of projects selected for effective and prompt demonstration.
- Both agricultural and industrial inquiries and programming would be included.
- The work of the committee would be set up under three divisions—observation and current reporting, agricultural studies, and industrial studies.

The last provision depicts the division of labor among members of the committee. The observation and reporting by Will Alexander described to government agencies and to the press the impact of various New Deal programs on the black population.

Before the southern agricultural studies began, Alexander organized three conferences to insure "essential interest and cooperation in the agricultural field." The first conference included selected black leaders who were to make suggestions about possible future developments. John Hope, W.E.B. DuBois, and Robert R. Moton were recommended participants. The second conference was to include farm agents, and the third selected large planters, bankers, and specialists who could "provide a means of testing the probability of practical difficulties in recommended action and to provide information and suggestions regarding lands, credit and marketing and excess labor problems." The makeup of these conferences emphasizes the fact that the committee was planning an elitist reform movement. Those who were to be the subjects of reform—the sharecroppers, renters, and small landowners—were not invited. The participants of these conferences were part of a developing southern elite set on creating new economic organization in the South. The masses—the tenants—were not consulted about these plans. At most, their precarious living conditions served as the data which this developing elite would use in order to present their demands in national policy—making circles.

The committee's central concern was the agricultural demonstration studies, directed by Charles S. Johnson and carried out by graduate student field-workers. The studies stimulated political action in Congress, the Department of Agriculture, and the White House. Data was collected on conditions of the tenant and other problems associated with the retirement of submarginal lands. Three studies, now considered sociological classics, came out of this phase of the committee's project: *Human Geography of the South*, by Rupert Vance of the University of North Carolina, *The Collapse of the Cotton Tenancy*, by Charles S. Johnson, Edwin R. Embree, and Will W. Alexander, and *Preface to Peasantry*,[41] by Arthur F. Raper, research secretary of the Commission on Interracial Cooperation. *The Collapse of the Cotton Tenancy* was the only one of these works to focus on the economic conditions of the tenant farmer, thus it was considered the work most likely to instigate immediate political action.

The industrial studies addressed the problems surrounding the integration of black workers into the iron and steel and meat-packing industries. The study investigated the Negro problem in industry primarily in northern cities. Birmingham, Alabama, was the only southern city included in the survey. George Mitchell and Horace Cayton supervised these investigations, which were published in 1939 as *Black Workers and the New Unions*.[42] The committee did not use this work to push for political reform. They did not organize a campaign for national support, nor did they fervently push for the book's publication. (These were major concerns for *The Collapse of The Cotton Tenancy*.) The lack of interest in industrial reform is again symbolic of the committee's emphasis on the problems of the rural South.

THE COLLAPSE OF THE COTTON TENANCY AND *SHADOW OF THE PLANTATION*

From the preface of *The Collapse of the Cotton Tenancy* to its appendices, Johnson, Embree, and Alexander expounded on the necessity to convert southern cotton tenants into small landowners—that is, peasants. The work became the manifesto of southern agrarian reformers. The adherents of this ideology believed that peasantry was the only feasible way to improve the tenant's living standards.

Compounded of bad economics and degrading social conditions, cotton culture faces sweeping changes. What is to become of the half-million to million families—the two million to five million individuals—who no longer are needed as cotton tenants? The alternatives seem to be (1) starvation, (2) permanent support on the relief rolls, (3) the finding of new work in the cities, (4) reorganization of farming in the old cotton states. The fourth is the only acceptable and feasible choice. . . . Some reorganization of farming in the cotton states must be devised whereby these former tenants can make their own livelihood and develop a self-respecting as well as self-supporting way of life.[43]

In order to educate their intended audience—the president, the secretary of agriculture, congressmen, and influential southern opinion leaders—about the problem, they presented analyses of tenants' income, living conditions, and resources; the credit system; and the failure of federal recovery programs such as the Agricultural Adjustment Act. The study portrayed cotton tenancy as an oppressive, archaic system. Tenants were fatalistic about their precarious economic situation while landlords and their creditors were forced to participate in a perpetually vicious cycle of exploitation and economic counterproduction. This portrayal convinced the public that the existence of the cotton tenancy was a barrier to what the authors called "the best American tradition"—individualism. Through this fusion of political ideology and national folklore the authors attempted to gain the support of influential people of all political and regional affiliations.

The authors' conception of the cotton tenancy as a faulty system which somehow mysteriously operated beyond human control avoided critical examination of the activities of power holders who created and profited from this pattern of labor exploitation. Ironically, the very people who profited from the creation and perpetuation of cotton tenancy played a central role in implementing the changes these reformers pushed for.

In developing and presenting the ideological framework of their problem, the committee became somewhat obsessed with emphasizing not only that the cotton tenancy was an oppressive economic mechanism which had outlived the "Old South," but also that by the 1930s the majority of the tenants were white. (This certainly was true, at least in the Old Black Belt region, because the great out-migration of rural blacks was followed by an increase in the rural white population.) This emphasis, made explicit in both text and tables, was necessary to gain the attention and support of key national policy makers. The fact that whites were being exploited by a ruthless system traditionally confined to blacks shocked these policy makers, who were, of course, also white. Conversely, when the victimization of blacks was emphasized, political mobilization for reform did not occur—it could not, without the risk of alienating southern political supporters.

Shadow of the Plantation and *The Collapse of the Cotton Tenancy* differ radically in their conceptualizations of southern rural social life. In the former work, the conditions of white tenants are not discussed, even though, as Table 2 indicates, the number of white tenants in Macon County was increasing while the number of blacks was decreasing. *Shadow of the Plantation* fails to analyze the structural relationships between black and white tenants and their mutual oppression by the landlords.

Johnson contended in *Shadow of the Plantation* that the nature of the plantation, rather than slavery (an incidental by-product of the plantation system), caused the development of black folk culture and its concurrent problems. Logically, it follows that the nature of the plantation would affect the cultural development of any group over which it cast its shadow. But Johnson's study emphasized ideological, not logical, consistency. *Shadow of the Plantation* was intended to describe the social and cultural conditions which generated a high rate of syphilis in the rural black population. Many of Johnson's assumptions about folk culture pertained only to black rural life. A similar analysis of rural whites in the area would have led to politically dangerous questions because cultural backwardness among the rural whites would have had to be explained in terms other than slavery. In *Shadow of the Plantation*, Johnson asserted that social change was cultural and internal while in *The Collapse of the Cotton Tenancy*, he and his collaborators claimed it was structural and external. In *Shadow of the Plantation*, social change is brought about through norms and values internalized when individuals are exposed to "mainstream" society through

Table 2

Number of Farm Tenants by Race and Percentage Change from Decade to Decade in Macon County, Georgia, 1900–1935

Year	Number of Tenants in Macon County	
	White	Negro
1900	280	624
1919	238	1123
1920	304	1082
1930	352	1022
1935	393	832

Year	Percentage Change	
	White	Negro
1900–1910	−15.0	79.9
1910–1920	27.7	− 3.7
1920–1930	16.0	− 6.4
1930–1935	11.6	−18.6

Source: Figures taken from Arthur F. Raper, Preface to Peasantry (Chapel Hill, N.C.: University of North Carolina Press, 1936), table 38, p. 144.

schooling, travel, or in other ways. Johnson was very concerned about children and their schooling:

Children of parents who are zealous to have the mystery of letters mastered have a new sentimental value for their parents. They have the key to power, and the great pride of these parents is to hear them read, not so much because they are interested in what is read as in the demonstrated ability to understand a printed page. ''Come here, Markus,'' a parent shouted, ''and let the man hear how you can read.'' . . . The children become, thus, a link with the new culture. New notions of sanitation and hygiene percolate into the new homes: the value of screening, the dangers of infection from careless and ignorant habits, the hazard of open wells and careless waste disposal. The slow rate of transition, generally, through this medium appears to be due quite as much to the inadequacy of the present local elementary schools as to the inability or unwillingness of the older members of the group to abandon their traditional ways.[44]

On the other hand, in *The Collapse of the Cotton Tenancy*, social change is discussed in terms of the intervention of certain external forces which must inevitably lead to the radical reorganization of the plantation South. One of these outside forces was the mechanical cotton picker. As these machines were increasingly used, fewer human laborers were needed. Thus it became necessary to restructure the traditional rural economic system in order to sustain those who were threatened with eviction and unemployment in the face of such rural automation. The committee and its supporters felt that a solution lay in reorganizing the inefficient plantations into smaller landholdings. In *Shadow of the Plantation*, Johnson emphasized that he did not think machinery was an effective means for social change in the rural South:

Strangely enough, the changes appear to have come in this setting least rapidly through the introduction of machinery. Farming implements are practically the same as they were three or four generations ago. On the other hand, however, there has been definite cultural penetration through the medium of the school, the church, the influence of persons educated outside the community; the exposure to demonstrations in health and agriculture, and through returned migrants. Throughout, the weight of tradition, as would be expected, has resisted these changes.[45]

In order to make sense out of these contradictory conceptions of southern rural society, it is necessary to take into account changes in the interests and ideological stances of those who supported the studies. Changes in the vested interests of Johnson's patrons resulted in different points of focus in his studies of social life in the rural South.

CONCLUSION

In the short run, the committee and other "southern agrarian reformers" were successful in gaining a national hearing. However, they failed to bring about substantial long-term reform in the South. They also failed to incorporate the "need" for the South to industrialize into their ideology. Some (Alexander, for instance) disapproved of industrialists, while others (such as Johnson) were ambivalent.[46] Their failure to see the need for industry made their orientation obsolete in the 1940s when changes in the world's cotton market critically reduced the need for southern cotton.[47]

The Julius Rosenwald Fund not only gave Johnson an opportunity to expand the ideas of Robert E. Park, but it also gave him a power base from which to develop and explore his own ideas. Unfortunately, many of these ideas were too liberal or radical for his patrons and his commercial publishing contacts. *Bitter Canaan*, a manuscript that he finished in his earliest years at Fisk, is perhaps the most significant example. The work was a historical sociological analysis of the exploitative roles and political economic dilemmas of the Afro-American–descended elite in Liberia who ruled over an unstable caste-ridden society. Johnson wrote *Bitter Canaan* shortly after returning from Liberia as a member of a League of Nations commission investigating slavery there.

For at least fifteen years, Johnson tried to get the manuscript published, but it was too politically sensitive. His theory of race relations, which went beyond Park's, was too power oriented, too pessimistic. His analysis of the role of the Firestone Rubber Company and Liberia's European colonial neighbors in the country's internal affairs suggested the perspective that scholars today call the "development of underdevelopment." In that respect, Johnson was far ahead of his time. But as indicated earlier, Johnson's patrons only allowed him to popularize a liberal image of the Negro problem, which portrayed a race slipping into mainstream society as formal segregation crumbled.

The most serious damage done by the Rosenwald Fund was its institutionalization of a racial division of labor which confined black talent to black institutions. This was evident even in the fund's treatment of Charles S. Johnson. The fund made Johnson quite secure at Fisk, but he still had no significant mobility within white power structures. He never became an executive officer of the Rosenwald Fund or of any of the other foundations with which he was associated. When it came time to decide whom to send to Washington to head the Farm Settlement Program after Rexford Tugwell stepped down, Johnson candidly noted:

Tugwell asked one of our trio (to) take over a post in his office to see that the program was carried out. Embree could not leave the Fund and I was a Negro; that left Dr. Alexander, he went as Tugwell's assistant. When Tugwell was turned out of office, Alexander was left to head the Resettlement Program (formally called the Rural Rehabilitation Administration) and later the Farm Settlement Administration.[48]

NOTES

1. Charles S. Johnson, "Charles S. Johnson," in *American Spiritual Autobiographies: Fifteen Self-Portraits*, ed. Louis Finkelstein (New York: Harper and Brothers, 1948), pp. 192–195.

2. For a comprehensive analysis of Frazier's preoccupation with social status, see Grace E. Harris, *The Life and Work of E. Franklin Frazier* (Ph.D. dissertation, University of Virginia, 1975), pp. 175–217.

3. Charles S. Johnson's *Shadow of the Plantation* (Chicago: University of Chicago Press, 1934); and *Growing Up in the Black Belt: Negro Youth in the Rural South* (New York, Washington, D.C.: American Council on Education, 1941), are major examples of how the Fisk sociologist developed "social conditioning" rather than pathological interpretations of the black non-affluent.

4. Interview with Lillie Ida Johnson Epps and Julia Mae Johnson (Charles S. Johnson's sisters), June 1983.

5. Interview with G. Franklin Edwards, September 1982.

6. Arvarh E. Strickland, *History of the Chicago Urban League*, (Urbana: University of Illinois Press, 1966), pp. 41–42; also see Ralph L. Pearson, *Charles S. Johnson: The Urban League Years: A Study of Racial Leadership* (Ph.D. dissertation, Johns Hopkins University, 1970).

7. Chicago Commission on Race Relations correspondence folders, Julius Rosenwald Papers.

8. Autographed copy of *The Negro in Chicago: A Study of Race Relations and a Race Riot: Report of the Chicago Commission on Race Relations* (Chicago, 1922), in the possession of Lillie Ida Johnson and Julia Mae Johnson. This dedication gives first-hand evidence to what informed persons and Johnson's students had been claiming for years. See Patrick J. Gilpin, *Charles S. Johnson: An Intellectual Biography* (Ph.D. dissertation, Vanderbilt University, 1973), pp. 20–21.

9. New York Urban League folders, Laura Spelman Rockefeller Memorial (hereafter LSRM) Archives.

10. Negro Problem Conference proceedings, LSRM Archives.

11. Charles S. Johnson-Edwin Embree correspondence, Julius Rosenwald Fund (hereafter JRF) Archives.

12. Ibid.

13. Nancy J. Weiss, *The National Urban League, 1910–1914* (New York: Oxford University Press, 1974), p. 221.

14. Charles S. Johnson-Marie Johnson correspondence in the 1920s, in the possession of Patricia Clifford.

15. Charles S. Johnson-Edwin Embree correspondence, JRF Archives.

16. Charles S. Johnson folder, Julius Rosenwald Papers.

17. Johnson-Embree correspondence, in JRF Archives and Charles S. Johnson Special Collection.

18. Charles S. Johnson, Edwin R. Embree, and Will Alexander, *The Collapse of the Cotton Tenancy: Summary of Field Surveys and Statistical Surveys, 1933–35* (Chapel Hill: University of North Carolina Press, 1935); and Edwin R. Embree, *Brown Americans* (New York: Viking, 1943).

19. Johnson-Embree correspondence in JRF Archives and Charles S. Johnson Special Collection.

20. See American Race Relations Council correspondence files, Julius Rosenwald Fund Archives.

21. Patrick Gilpin in his *Charles S. Johnson*, pp. 600–623, offers the most comprehensive account of the Southern Educational Reporting Service (SERS). This Ford Foundation–financed agency was organized in 1954 in Nashville as a race-relations information dissemination center to assist peaceful transitions in the midst of the *Brown* decision controversy and afterwards. Johnson developed the idea of the SERS, using the Department of Race Relations and the Institute on Race Relations newsletter *Monthly Trends* as models. He never received full public credit for doing so. Moreover, although SERS was supposed to have an integrated staff, it did not have any black members well into the 1960s after Fisk sociologist Bonita Valien was terminated under controversial circumstances soon after the organization began operations. The governing board, which included Johnson and one other black through the 1950s, remained a predominantly white body which included segregationists as well as integrationists. (This was because the organization was supposed to collect and disseminate information no matter what its ideological flavor was, but clearly segregationists and traditional liberals were in control.)

Johnson's failure to get the SERS board to live up to its internal integration policy and to hire back Bonita Valien through his discreet lobbying style is indicative of his decline in power as the white opposition to desegregation stiffened and as a new generation of foundations and foundation administrators began to emerge who were willing to ignore his wishes. The SERS affair and the rising resistance to racial integration, which included not a few "friends of the Negro," contributed to the less than optimistic stance on race relations Johnson took shortly before his death in 1956. See Charles S. Johnson, "A Southern Negro's View of the South," *New York Times Magazine*, September 23, 1956, pp. 15, 64.

22. In "Black Sociologists in White America," *Social Forces* 56 (1977):259–270, August Meier suggested that Charles S. Johnson often did not give student research assistants deserved credit for their contributions to research projects he supervised. This claim can be debated, since correspondence in the Charles S. Johnson Special Collection and in the Julius Rosenwald Fund Archives illustrate Johnson's conscious efforts to give students due credit for their contributions in book projects such as *The Collapse of the Cotton Tenancy* and *Shadow of the Plantation*. Furthermore, the Johnson Special Collection is replete with correspondence which exemplified Johnson's sincere efforts to assist students and colleagues in their careers (such as Horace Cayton, Thelma Ackiss, Mozell Hill, Lewis Jones, Earl Moses, Herman Long, and Bonita Valien).

The sponsorship of "junior Black scholars" by those in more influential positions has always been a precarious business. No matter whether we focus on the Age of Jim Crow or the Civil Rights Era and its aftermath, there has been a grave scarcity of positions with authority powers for Blacks and other racial minorities. This scarcity, which is produced through white monopolization of institutional authority rights, is compounded by a cultural and sociopolitical phenomenon I prefer to call the rule of one. White elites who are in control of major institutions and task organizations tend to promote images of racial fairness while blockading significant racial minority mobility into institutional circles of power and authority, through creating and legitimating one "Super Negro." Since white elites consider one to be more than enough Blacks to interact with on a more, usually less intimate basis, the rule of one limits the opportunity structure for mobility into influential positions. This produces tension and obsessive envy between Black mentors, their students, and among peers.

A major example of this point was the Charles S. Johnson-E. Franklin Frazier relationship. Throughout the 1920s, Johnson was Frazier's major sponsor into professional sociology. As editor of the National Urban League's *Opportunity*, Johnson encouraged Frazier to write critical social commentaries, sometimes under a pseudonym. He helped to pave the way for Frazier's admission into the doctoral program at Chicago through his friendship with Robert E. Park and was instrumental in assisting Frazier in receiving a Laura Spelman Rockefeller Memorial doctoral fellowship. Throughout his graduate school career, Johnson ran interference for him when he had problems with Robert E. Park, William Ogburn and other Chicago faculty. Johnson, who was supportive of Frazier's predoctoral and doctoral Black family perspective, gave Frazier advice about how to approach the Social Science Research Council to continue his line of research after earning the Ph.D. (William Ogburn was chair of the Social Science Research Council Policy Committee which considered Frazier's grant.)

Soon after Johnson became Director of the Fisk Social Science Department in 1928, he gave Frazier his first job as a professional sociologist. Throughout this time period, it was obvious that Frazier was Johnson's student. Besides giving Frazier advice and helping gain access to valuable resources, Johnson on a number of occasions attempted successfully to exploit Frazier's research issues, calling on him to assist in major research projects, even when he was still in graduate school. But while Frazier was a student of Johnson's, he was also a competitor, often for the same few positions open to black social scientists in a segregated economy and academia. Frazier had applied for the position with the National Urban League which was eventually given to Johnson. And was, of course, greatly disappointed that he did not get it. He was even more bewildered when his radicalness prevented him from being lured by Fisk President Thomas E. Jones as Director of the newly organized Department of Social Science in the late 1930s. The job went to Johnson.

Frazier only stayed two years at Fisk not only because of his ideological differences with Johnson but also because he was in competition with him over the only available position for a black interested in doing and administering social science research. The next best place was Howard, which in 1933 made Frazier Chairman of the Sociology Department. But, given the continuous power struggles with Howard President Mordecai Johnson, Frazier was never able to build a research center comparable to that at Fisk. Also, the white powers already had their "super Negro"—Johnson—and that was enough. The most Frazier could do was climb the narrow staircase of professional sociology with a few prestigious plums thrown his way. The paradoxical competition between Johnson and Frazier, which was a product of chronic scarce resources in a Jim Crow social science as well as ideological differences, made the men outwardly cordial toward each other, but inwardly resentful and suspicious of each other. See Charles S. Johnson and William E. B. DuBois folders in the E. Franklin Frazier Papers, Howard University.

23. Robert Redfield, *Tepoztlan, A Mexican Village: A Study of Folk Life* (Chicago: University of Chicago Press, 1930); see comments on Park's views on culture and civilization in Chapter 3.

24. Johnson, *Shadow of the Plantation*; and Johnson, Embree, and Alexander, *The Collapse of the Cotton Tenancy*.

25. Edwin R. Embree and Julia Waxman, *Investment in People: The Story of the Julius Rosenwald Fund* (New York: Harper, 1949), p. 113.

26. Michael M. Davis to Charles S. Johnson, February 1930.

27. Johnson to Davis, February 19, 1930, JRF Archives.

28. Davis to Johnson, March 3, 1931, JRF Archives.

29. Ibid.

30. "The Macon County Alabama Demonstration for the Control of Syphilis Among the Rural Negro Population," April 16–May 24, 1930, by O. C. Wenger, Surgeon Director, U.S. Public Health Clinic, Hot Springs, Arkansas, p. 1, JRF Archives.

31. Memo to M.M.D. from H.L.H., October 1, 1930, JRF Archives.

32. Charles S. Johnson, "Report on Visit to the Macon County Demonstration for Control of Syphilis," March 28, 1931, JRF Archives.

33. Memo to M.M.D. from H.L.H., October 1, 1930, JRF Archives.

34. Louis R. Harlan, *Separate and Unequal: Public School Campaigns and Racism in the Southern Seaboard States, 1901–1915* (Chapel Hill, N.C.: University of North Carolina Press, 1958).

35. Johnson to Davis, October 3, 1931, JRF Archives.

36. Charles S. Johnson to Clyde Frost, August 25, 1931, JRF Archives.

37. Johnson, *Shadow of the Plantation*, acknowledgments section, pp. 187–189, 202–204, and 206.

38. Ibid., p. 209.

39. Ibid., pp. 150–151.

40. What follows is based upon background correspondence about the Negro and Economic Reconstruction Project found in Box 309, especially Folder 13, JRF Archives. See, in particular, "Memorandum of Conference of Johnson, Embree and Alexander, on Negro Social and Economic Planning and Current Observation Project," January 28, 1934 (folder 13).

41. Arthur Raper, *Preface to Peasantry* (Chapel Hill, N.C.: University of North Carolina Press, 1936); Rupert Vance, *Human Geography of the South* (Chapel Hill, N.C.: University of North Carolina Press, 1935).

42. Horace R. Cayton and George R. Mitchell, *Black Workers and the New Unions* (Chapel Hill, N.C.: University of North Carolina Press, 1939).

43. Johnson, Embree, and Alexander, *Collapse of the Cotton Tenancy*, p. 64.

44. Johnson, *Shadow of the Plantation*, pp. 148–149.

45. Ibid., p. 209.

46. W. W. Alexander to C. D. Barr, vice president of the American Cast Iron Pipe Company, August 17, 1934, JRF Archives. Charles S. Johnson's ambivalent views about the advantages of industrialization was a major way he differed from Chicago school urbanologists.

47. See "Industrialization of the South," March 1, 1945, Bureau of Agricultural Economics Archives, National Archives, Washington, D.C.

48. Charles S. Johnson interview for unknown person(s), October 17, 1944, JRF Archives.

7

Myrdal, Carnegie, and the Natives—In a Hurry

I have gone through these chapters in a great hurry, but I fully agree with you that they need major repairs. I shall do my best within the next two or three days to get them off to you—Louis Wirth to Frederick Keppel.[1]

The Carnegie Corporation Negro Problem Study was published by Swedish economist Gunnar Myrdal in 1944 under the title *An American Dilemma*.[2] An example of "big science," the study cost the Carnegie Corporation half a million dollars and employed over fifty researchers. After World War II, *An American Dilemma* became the seminal thesis on the Negro problem for liberal social scientists and anathema to Marxist ones. For decades, any sociology textbook containing discussions of race relations and any scholarly book on race relations which failed to give at least lip service to Myrdal's study was considered inexcusably incomplete. The work's most popular passage, frequently quoted, proclaims:

The American Negro problem is a problem in the heart of the American. It is there that the interracial tension has its focus. It is there that the decisive struggle goes on. This is the central viewpoint of this treatise. Though our study includes economic, social, and political race relations, at bottom our problem is the moral dilemma of the American—the conflict between his moral valuations on various levels of consciousness and generality. The "American Dilemma," referred to in the title of this book, is the ever-raging conflict between, on the one hand, the valuations preserved on the general plane which we shall call the "American Creed," where the American thinks, talks, and acts under the influence of high national and Christian precepts, and, on the other hand, the valuations on specific planes of individual and group living, where personal and local interests; economic, social, and sexual jealousies; considerations of community prestige and conformity; group prejudice against particular persons or types of people; and all sorts of miscellaneous wants, impulses, and habits dominate his outlook.[3]

Carnegie's sponsorship of Gunnar Myrdal's Negro problem study was, to say the least, ironic. The Carnegie Corporation seemed the least likely foundation to address the Negro problem in America so boldly. Carnegie officers were reluctant to become directly involved in domestic race-related issues, more so than the Rockefeller foundations and definitely more than the Julius Rosenwald Fund. In the first half of the century, Carnegie administrators carefully integrated projects focused on blacks into general programs. This bureaucratic procedure, which only appeared liberal, was frequently touted in the corporation's public reports.[4]

The reluctance of the Carnegie Corporation to openly support race-related causes was mainly due to the influence of its president, Frederick Keppel. Keppel, born in New York City in 1875, was the first long-term president of the Carnegie Corporation after Andrew Carnegie. Although Keppel had a board of directors, like Edwin Embree of the Julius Rosenwald Fund, he *was* the Carnegie Corporation. He brought style to the foundation sector with his scholarly essays and books on philanthropy and his informal behavior. But during Keppel's reign the Carnegie Corporation tended to stay aloof from pressing social issues.[5]

The Carnegie officers' timidity in the face of the domestic Negro problem contrasted with their fascination with the native problem in South Africa. This contrast clearly revealed their conservative race-relations philosophy. They believed that white South Africans should learn from American southern whites how to handle their Negro problem—that is, they believed that Jim Crow was a successful form of apartheid. Keppel and his colleagues worked hard to transplant American ideals of interracial cooperation to South Africa and other parts of colonial Africa. Both the Carnegie Corporation and the Phelps-Stokes Fund sponsored Jeanes teachers programs and endorsed YMCA race-relations programs in various parts of Africa. At one time, Anson Stokes strongly suggested to Keppel that Carnegie officials should urge South Africans visiting the United States to visit the American South—to observe successful management of the Negro problem:

visitors from South Africa coming over with the help of the Corporation should first as far as possible be encouraged to visit some of the Negro institutions in the South and to get some insight into the interracial work. I realize that your visitors come for many purposes: art, education, library, agriculture, science, etc., but in one way or another they will all face the racial problem when they return and our experience is that it helps them to see what has become of the Negro in this country and what he has done for himself. Perhaps the thing that impresses these visitors most of all is the potentiality of the Negro—a thing which is most important for South Africa to realize.[6]

Considering Frederick Keppel's racial conservatism, why did he and his foundation decide to sponsor a Negro problem study which would impartially— and dangerously—probe the depths of the issue? The official response is that the Carnegie Corporation's southern-bred trustee, Newton Baker, persuaded his colleagues of the pressing need for a study on the Negro problem. Specifically, Keppel recalled:

In 1931, the late Newton D. Baker joined the Corporation Board. He was the son of a Confederate officer, attended the Episcopal Academy in Virginia and the Law School of Washington and Lee University, and spent the greater part of his early years in the Border states of West Virginia and Maryland. His services first as City Solicitor and later as Mayor of Cleveland gave him direct experience with the growing Negro populations in Northern cities, and as Secretary of War he had faced the special problems which the presence of the Negro element in our population inevitably creates in time of national crisis. Mr. Baker knew so much more than the rest of us on the Board about these questions, and his mind had been so deeply concerned with them that we readily agreed when he told us that more knowledge and better organized and interrelated knowledge were essential before the Corporation could intelligently distribute its own funds. We agreed with him further in believing that the gathering and digestion of the material might well have a usefulness far beyond our own needs.[7]

It would be more appropriate to ask why Keppel and his Carnegie associates decided to organize a Negro problem study with a European director and such a massive American staff.[8] Even this question has an official answer, found in Keppel's forward to *An American Dilemma*:

There was no lack of competent scholars in the United States who were deeply interested in the problem and had already devoted themselves to its study, but the whole question had been for nearly a hundred years so charged with emotion that it appeared wise to seek as the responsible head of the undertaking someone who could approach his task with a fresh mind, uninfluenced by traditional attitudes or by earlier conclusions, and it was therefore decided to "import" a general director—somewhat as the late Charles P. Howland was called across the Atlantic to supervise the repatriation of the Greeks in Asia Minor after the close of the first World War. And since the emotional factor affects the Negroes no less than the whites, the search was limited to countries of high intellectual and scholarly standards but with no background or traditions of imperialism which might lessen the confidence of the Negroes in the United States as to the complete impartiality of the study and the validity of its findings. Under these limitations, the obvious places to look were Switzerland and the Scandinavian countries, and the search ended in the selection of Dr. Gunnar Myrdal, a scholar who despite his youth had already achieved an international reputation as a social economist, a professor in the University of Stockholm, economic advisor to the Swedish Government and a member of the Swedish senate.[9]

This official reasoning fails to put the Carnegie Negro problem study into proper historical and political context. Actually, there was nothing new about the foundation's attempt to undertake a comprehensive study of the Negro problem. During the late 1920s and 1930s other foundations financed comprehensive studies on the Negro problem, though at a more modest scale.[10] Carnegie's effort differed from the other studies because Keppel's conservatism led the corporation to find a European who would not be overly protective of blacks or unduly influenced by interracial cooperation strategies.

Keppel, acutely aware of the floundering interracial effort of Stokes's Negro Encyclopedia project (see Chapter 8), realized the futility of allowing blacks to share decision-making power in research endeavors.[11] The Carnegie Corporation was the most racially exclusive of the major foundations and was very supportive of white supremacy in apartheid societies.[12] It dared not allow blacks any decision-making power in areas such as race-relations research and the development of black libraries. According to Carnegie Corporation protocol, black destiny was to be decided by whites only.

Thus, a black or non-European director was out of the question. One can only speculate why the corporation did not choose a native white American director. The official answer to this question is rather superficial. As we shall see, as impartial as he supposedly was, Myrdal was very dependent upon "biased" native researchers to coordinate and develop "his" study. The Carnegie Corporation may have chosen a European because he would be easier to control—knowing nothing about American race relations, he would have to rely on others to construct a proper interpretation. The corporation also wanted a European scholar who was devoted to the interests of foundations and who would not raise embarrassing issues.

By July 15, 1937, several candidates for the Negro problem study directorship were under consideration (See Table 3). Candidates from colonial powers had proved to be inadequate, although they were given first consideration (especially Hendrik Mouw and Roy F. Harrod). In addition, Donald Young of the Social Science Research Council warned Keppel of the folly of assuming that all European scholars would be unbiased toward the Negro problem:

If the choice of directing personnel has to be between a reasonably objective specialist in race relations and one of special ability in a related social field but with the advantage of absolute freedom from factional entanglements, in my judgement the former would probably produce the more significant results. After all, lack of familiarity with the United States and the American Negro does not assure freedom from prejudices, but only a somewhat novel set of practices or naivete with reference to existing prejudices.[13]

Table 3
Negro Study Directorship and Personnel Suggestions October 1936 through July 1937

Professor Melville Herskovitz, Northwestern University	Suggested by ELT. Endorsed by Kidder. Crane said H. was very able but not always tactful.

Table 3—*Continued*

Malinowski	Macadem and Frederick P. Keppel have doubts about him.
Gerald Campbell	Suggested by Macadem.
Rev. J. H. Longenecker, Tennessee	Suggested by ELT; Endorsed by Rev. Emory Ross. Suggested by J.
Schrieka-Rosenwald Study	TH. Moll; Frederick P. Keppel said he didn't want to start from educational end.
Mr. Hendrik Mouw, Holland; 50 years old; retired from Netherlands Indies Government Serv.	Suggested by Moll. HUD favorably impressed by this recommendation. Huizinga said Mouw had done excellent reports but doubted his capacity for independent research; somewhat narrow mind, political bias; doubted ability to get along with people, and of having fresh point of view. Malcom Davis could find out nothing about Mouw.

Table 3—*Continued*

Lord Hailey	Oldham thought we might get him when he finished the African job.
Professor Metraux, Swiss Anthropologist	Suggested by Melville Herskovits; Malcolm Davis thought the idea of a Swiss was good and later got a favorable comment on Metraux from the director of the Institut Universitaire de Hautes Etudes Internationales at Geneva and also from Prof. Rivet of Museum d'Histoire Naturelle.
Lindbacha, Royal Swedish Museum	Suggested by Melville Herskovits.
Wm. Rappart, ex-head of University of Geneva	Suggested by Melville Herskovits; Macadem said he was ruled out.
Abram E. Harris, black former Guggenheim fellow	Suggested as member of committee by Herskovits.
Dr. Nicholas John Spykman, Yale University	Raymond Fosdick thought he might have valuable suggestions.

144

Table 3—*Continued*

Kekkanbach, Belgium	Suggested by Macadem; did first-rate work in Upper Silesia and as legal advisor to Plebicite Committee. Had Canadian-born wife.
Arthur Salter	Suggested by Vincent Massey. Lothnian doubted if Salter was up to the job.
Roy Forbes Harrod, Christchurch New Zealand	Suggested by Sadler. 39 years old; bachelor; well-trained, observant. WGS commented on Harrod, thought a man of much wider experience was needed. Appiget memo-bright young man combining realistic, hard-boiled viewpoint with considerable personal courage. Unsentimental. Only doubts about Harrod related to his ability to go beyond logical factors and correctly

Table 3—*Continued*

	evaluate intangible emotional ones. Lindsay told Frederick P. Keppel at Oxford that Harrod might be a very good man to consider. Donald Young commented--worried about Harrod's lack of evidence of ability to run a team and perhaps lack of appreciation of social and cultural factors as contrasted with economic.
E. A. Radicz, Oxford University	Suggested by Sadler--a former Commonwealth student in 1938 (probably too young).
McCartney, at Chatham House	Suggested by Malcolm Davis.
Sir Donald Cameron	Suggested by Coupland--much experience in Africa.
A. Victor Murray, Professor of Education, University of Colorado; at Hull from 1933.	Suggested by F. Clark--knew Africa well but had never held position of authority there. See Who's Who.

Table 3—*Continued*

Dr. W. W. Vaughan	Suggested by F. Clarke--former headmaster of Rugby. Chairman of Central Council for School Broadcasting; member of Colonial Office Commission on Education. Clarke prefers Vaughan to Murray.
Miss Matthis	Frederick P. Keppel suggestion.
Douglas Brown	Suggested by Beardsley Ruml--a Canadian.
Billy Blatz	Suggested by Beardsley Ruml-a Canadian.
Heinze, of National Bureau	Suggested by Beardsley Ruml--a Canadian. Frederick P. Keppel disapproved.
Karl Gunnar Myrdal, Stockholm, Sweden	Suggested by Ruml; Frederick P. Keppel asked Larry Frank about him. Frank said he was able, energetic, and competent in the social field, well-oriented psychologically;

Table 3—*Continued*

had worked in crime and
disorders. Thought he
would be good, if we
could get him. Had
responsible position
on Social Board for
Sweden.

Source: Table in Carnegie Corporation Archives. Table did not
include complete names in most cases.

GUNNAR MYRDAL

Gunnar Myrdal received a 1930–1931 Rockefeller Foundation Fellowship to study methodological issues in American social science (his wife Alva received a Laura Spelman Rockefeller Memorial Fellowship probably in the late 1920s). Although his fellowship records have been destroyed as are all Rockefeller fellowship records after a ten-year lapse of time, apparently he received a travel fellowship that enabled him to visit major American centers of social research. Apparently Myrdal spent his time in the United States completing his *The Political Element in the Development of Economic Theory*, based upon a series of 1928 lectures delivered at the University of Stockholm and published in 1932. *The Political Element in the Development of Economic Theory* was Myrdal's first comprehensive attempt to explain how valuations or, "political speculations," played a role in the development of the social sciences and the general problem of valuations in human ideologies and behavior. Myrdal wrote this sociology of knowledge analysis as a youthful critique of the laissiez-faire epistemology of the older economists who dominated in academic and policy circles in Sweden. In the process, he also questioned the conservative valuation qualities of conventional economists in other European countries and in the United States.

Through his one- or two-year stay in the United States, he became a good acquaintance of Beardsley Ruml. When Ruml and one of his former memorial colleagues, Lawrence Frank, recommended Myrdal for the directorship, he was no stranger to Keppel.

Gunnar Myrdal certainly would not have received serious consideration from

Keppel and the Carnegie Corporation trustees if he had not had Beardsley Ruml's recommendation. Ruml, a former Carnegie officer and part of the selective Carnegie fraternity, served as a Carnegie contact for Keppel, often sending him inside information about Rockefeller foundation activities.[14]

In 1937 Keppel wrote to Myrdal offering him the Negro problem study directorship. Donald Young had outlined the study's parameters and offered the informal assistance of his organization to Myrdal. Keppel wrote:

I am discussing with some of the members of my Board of Trustees the desirability of financing a comprehensive study of the Negro in the United States to be undertaken in a wholly objective and dispassionate way as a social phenomenon. We have, as you know, many people in the United States, members of both races, who are giving all that they have to the improvement of the conditions under which the Negro is living, but, so far as I know, there is not one of them whose thinking is not influenced by emotional factors of one type or another, and many are also under the influence of earlier environmental conditions, family or community traditions of the abolition movement on the one hand or of the old regime of the South on the other. For this reason, it has seemed to me that it might be desirable to turn to someone who would approach the situation with an entirely fresh mind.

If the Corporation goes into this enterprise, it would be ready to meet the expenses of a director and provide a suitable honorarium, as well as to pay whatever would be necessary to provide adequate assistants and also for the preparation and publication of the report.

Our idea, so far as we have developed it, would be to invite a man to be responsible for the Study as a whole, but to place at his disposal the services of a group of associates, Americans, who would be competent to deal as experts with the anthropological . . . and social aspects of the question, including public health and public administration . . . the Social Science Research Council would be willing to sit as an informal adviser in the selection of a team of colleagues of this kind . . . which I think would be much better than for us to try to find them ourselves or to place the responsibility upon the director. Donald Young, whom I consulted about this whole matter, agrees with me that whoever takes up this responsibility would probably have to spend two years, less vacations, in this country, but it would be wise to precede this residence by a visit to the United States about a year earlier for a few weeks during which the team could be expanded and the selection of certain essential material set in motion.[15]

In their selection of Myrdal the foundation officers put more faith in a member of their fraternity (Ruml) and minimized risk by carefully selecting a scholar to do sponsored research in this highly controversial area. Myrdal was devoted to Keppel and had great admiration for America. In the preface to the twentieth anniversary edition of *An American Dilemma*, Gunnar Myrdal acknowledged Keppel and his role in the Negro problem study in glowing terms:

At this time, I want to refer somewhat more fully to the role of the late Dr. Frederick P. Keppel, at that time the president of the Carnegie Corporation, in the preparation of this study. He was a truly great American, an open, warmhearted, generous, truthloving human being of highest culture and unflinching courage. I reckon it as one of the great fortunes in my life that, for some years, I was closely associated with him. He always referred to Newton D. Baker, who had been one of the trustees of the Corporation, as the man who conceived the idea of this study; but from circumstantial evidence, it is clear to me that Keppel was the major force in planning and pushing this undertaking even before I was engaged to carry it out. He then followed the study with intense interest. I know that it meant much to him, and not only because—as he told me once in a letter after the work was finished—he had risked so much of his own reputation upon it.[16]

Initially, Myrdal turned down Keppel's offer, citing his heavy academic and public responsibilities.[17] Keppel kept the position open for several weeks hoping Myrdal would change his mind. In October, Myrdal reconsidered the offer through the persuasion of Beardsley Ruml. He wrote Keppel a lengthy letter outlining his expectations of the study.[18] Before even crossing the ocean, Myrdal decided that rather than emphasizing practical solutions to the Negro problem, the study should be a comprehensive analysis of "the facts," which would later benefit policy makers.[19]

Myrdal requested that Swedish economist Richard Sterner be allowed to accompany him as his chief assistant.[20] He also wanted to bring his wife, Alva, and their three children.[21] Myrdal wanted complete control over the administration of the study and over the writings of collaborating researchers,[22] and he wanted to begin the study in the summer of 1938, after delivering lectures at Harvard University in May of that year. He planned to use the summer and autumn months to review literature about the black experience and to travel and reflect before meeting with American race-relations specialists. The actual study would begin early in 1939 and would be finished in 1941.[23]

Finally, Myrdal told Keppel that the study would be worth his time only if it promised to be highly significant and mentioned the great sacrifices he was making by leaving his academic and Senate Posts. The Swedish economist was obviously more concerned about the potential academic prestige afforded by the study than he was interested in its subject. This became apparent especially in Myrdal's attempt to distance himself from race-relations research after completion of the study.[24]

Keppel agreed with Myrdal's observations and promised to fulfill his requests. Thus, Myrdal, who knew virtually nothing about blacks and the vast literature on race relations, became the director of the most comprehensive study on the Negro problem ever attempted. He later qualified his ambitions, which had originally been to complete the study in two years, but the Carnegie Negro Problem Study was still done in a flurry. His lengthy return to Sweden when his country became involved in the war and his hurried backtracking to the United States to complete the study aggravated the intellectual travail.

THE STRANGER AND THE NATIVES

In American anthropology and sociology the stranger is an observer and interpreter. Since the stranger is not a member of the society he is observing, he is not contaminated with the styles of cognition, values, and norms which prevent the natives from understanding the routines of their own society.[25] Thus, the stranger has the capacity to be impartial or objective in the collection and interpretation of data from the host society. Carnegie officers and Gunnar Myrdal were true believers in the virtues of stranger objectivity.[26]

The premises of stranger objectivity are questionable. In order to maneuver and survive in an alien society and to interpret events and phenomena accurately, the stranger must select reliable natives to serve as informants. Thus what a stranger learns about the inner workings of the host society is gathered from personal impressions developed through observation and reading and from the informants' interpretations. The more alien the society, the more the informants influence the stranger's personal impressions and interpretations. A society can be so strange that the alien researcher does not dare trust personal impressions but views them as secondary to the words and deeds of "trustworthy" natives.

Myrdal's acknowledgments and prefaces in *An American Dilemma* lack a discussion of the methodological and cultural flaws of his role. Not surprisingly, an analysis of the politics underlying the Carnegie Negro study is also missing. Understandably, Myrdal displayed a lack of critical awareness of how the Carnegie Corporation foundation influenced what was said and not said in *An American Dilemma*.

This point cannot be overemphasized, since Myrdal, as impeccable as his credentials as a Swedish economist were, knew little about blacks, race relations, or race-relations literature in the United States. He did travel extensively in America, especially in the South, and certainly formed strong personal impressions which helped shape *An American Dilemma*. But his great ignorance about American racial issues made him chronically dependent upon native researchers and consultants, who ended up, in effect, writing his book for him. Perhaps the most obvious indication of Myrdal's lack of knowledge was his decision to emphasize American social science as a central theme of *An American Dilemma*, which distracted attention from a sorely needed radical analysis of the moral basis of racism. *An American Dilemma* is known for its value paradigm of sociological inquiry but certainly not as a coherent, comprehensive book on the Negro problem.[27]

From the very beginning Keppel and his advisors realized that the "stranger" would need native assistance in selecting his staff and in becoming acquainted with the race problem and race-relations literature. Donald Young wrote to Keppel in the early stages of the study that his organization would be willing to recommend researchers and other staff members.[28]

In Keppel's first letter to Myrdal about the directorship, he stressed that his foundation would give the economist extensive assistance. Myrdal in turn emphasized his need for collaborators to compile and synthesize materials.[29] Myrdal's request exemplified a contradiction inherent in "stranger objectivity" only hinted at thus far—since Myrdal's staff, researchers, and consultants were American, they were burdened with the very prejudices the study was supposedly trying to avoid. The monographs produced by Myrdal's contributing researchers, several of which became chapters in *An American Dilemma*, show that there was a continuity between the work these men and women did in the past and the work they did for Myrdal. They gave Myrdal summaries of their long-held perspectives and prejudices, rather than breaking new, "value-free" ground.[30]

This ideologically diverse and contradictory body of native knowledge shaped Myrdal's work on the Negro problem. Even though Myrdal claimed that the novelty of *An American Dilemma* lay in its reinterpretation of data, it actually only reproduced the collective biases of native researchers because the study failed to question the meaning of its data.

Upon arriving in America in the autumn of 1938, Myrdal was given a tour of the South by General Education Board officer Jackson Davis. Myrdal recalled in the preface to an *An American Dilemma*:

On Mr. Keppel's advice, we started out in the beginning of October on a two months' exploratory journey through the Southern states. Jackson Davis of the General Education Board, who has behind him the experiences of a whole life devoted to improving race relations in the South and is himself a Southerner, kindly agreed to be our guide, and has since then remained a friend and an advisor.[31]

JACKSON DAVIS

Jackson Davis was born in Virginia in 1882. After graduating from William and Mary College in 1902, Davis became a public school administrator in Virginia. In this capacity, he developed an innovation in black education which assured him a place in the history of southern liberal education: the concept of the roving Jeanes teacher, which was an integral part of rural black schooling for decades. The Jeanes teacher went from place to place carrying important advice and information.[32]

The idea of the roving teacher attracted the attention of Hollis Frissell, president of Hampton Institute, and James Dillard of the Jeanes Fund. James Dillard made Davis's idea the funding centerpiece of the Jeanes Fund. Both James Dillard and Hollis Frissell recommended Jackson Davis as the first state agent for Negro education in 1910 when the General Education Board officers decided to launch a program to promote black public education in the South. Davis's mentors played a major role in his appointment to the General Education Board staff in 1915.[33] From then on, Davis was his foundation's major authority on race relations, black education, and the South. By the time of the Carnegie Negro Problem Study, Davis was the most widely respected southern-born administrator in the foundation sector. He had spotless credentials in the southern liberal establishment.[34]

Davis dedicated his life to promoting interracial cooperation, especially separate but equal education in a biracial society. As the 1920s progressed into the 1930s and the 1930s into the 1940s, Davis increasingly sympathized with those who denounced racial segregation. Yet, like other liberals of his generation, his criticism of racial segregation did not lead to consideration of its immediate eradication. That was too risky; it would alienate the good white people and encourage destructive tendencies among militant blacks.[35]

Davis did not panic or become a reactionary in the face of a growing black militancy generated by the racial contradictions inherent in America's involvement in World War II. Instead, he sought ways to give dissident voices legitimate channels of expression. In the early 1940s, William T. Couch, an editor at the University of North Carolina, Chapel Hill, Press, solicited from Howard historian Rayford Logan an anthology of essays by black leaders and scholars which represented a wide range of black thought. In 1944, when the anthology was about to be published, a disturbed Couch expressed to Davis his concerns about the antisegregation tone of some of the essays. Davis recorded in his diary:

He discussed the book which he is editing "What the Negro Wants" (possible title—"The Negro Speaks for Himself"). WTC [Couch] said 11 of the 14 had at once launched an attack on segregation. He still thinks the book ought to be published, but he is worried about the reaction which he knows he will get. He says there is no objection from the Press or the University to publishing the book, but he knows there is a great deal of dynamite in it. . . . He is not decided whether he ought to have a very brief introduction simply saying that we believe in free discussion and we want to know what the Negro really thinks and wants. He would add that the volume is brought out to present this fact and not present the view of the University or any of the people connected with it. WTC feels that there is need of a presentation of what is possible in the South and feels that the sociologists have not always had a broad enough viewpoint. . . . Anticipating the bitterness of discussion, he has taken a great deal of pains in pointing out certain statements by the different writers so that the publication will represent their considered views. I told him I would be glad to see his introduction.[36]

Davis, after reviewing his friend's introductory remarks, advised him that such essays, published by a major press, represented an effective safety valve.

I recall that you were very doubtful whether you ought to write an introduction to this book in which you would attempt to inject a different viewpoint. After thinking the matter over, I share these doubts with you. The University of North Carolina Press is doing a wonderfully fine thing in bringing out this book. I don't think you have to worry about the dynamite that it may contain. It will be in the nature of a safety valve and will let the whole colored world know that they can say what they really think and that the educated people of the South want to know their opinions. Therefore, it seems to me the effect of this book would be enhanced by a very brief introduction merely stating that the University believes in discussing current issues; that while the book does not represent the views of the University, it is the policy of the University to foster complete freedom of discussion.[37]

Keppel had a deep respect for Jackson Davis. He used Davis as an informal consultant for the Carnegie Jeanes Teachers Program in colonial Africa and sponsored Davis's first trip to Africa.[38] In June 1938 Keppel asked General Education Board president Raymond Fosdick about the possibility of Jackson Davis taking Gunnar Myrdal on a tour of the South soon after his arrival in the United States:

Myrdal wants to see the general situation in the South more or less incognito before public announcement is made of his appointment, and there is no one who could show him what he ought to see half so well as Jack Davis. Perhaps I oughtn't to remind you that we stole him once before for a trip to Africa and that was a great success.[39]

Davis was glad for this opportunity, feeling it was a good way to get the Carnegie Corporation more interested in blacks. Ultrasensitive about how outsiders viewed the South, southern liberals exercised their influence over others' interpretations.

Gunnar Myrdal and Richard Sterner toured the South for a little over a month. Jackson Davis developed their itinerary contacts with numerous liberal friends and acquaintances, most of whom were General Education Board state agents for Negro education. These people arranged local appointments and sightseeing for Myrdal and Sterner (see Table 4).

Table 4
Jackson Davis's Trip with Gunnar Myrdal and Richard Sterner, October 3–20, 1938

Date(s)	Place(s)	Conferences
Oct. 3, 4	Richmond, VA	L. R. Reynolds, Commission on Interracial Cooperation; Virginius Dabney, Times Dispatch editor; W. T. Sanger, president of Medical College of Virginia and staff members; Douglas S. Freeman, News Leader editor; Met Tennant Bryan, Richmond Inter-racial Committee chairman; American Tobacco Company; I.N. Tobacco

Table 4—*Continued*

Date(s)	Place(s)	Conferences
		Stemming Plant; secretary, State Planning Board; F. M. Alexander, A. G. Richardson, and T. C. Walker, State Department of Education
Oct. 5, 6	Hampton, VA	Miss Curtis, Hampton Institute Library and Library Chool; President Howe, Hampton Institute; Trade School; People's Building and Loan Associations Purves; groups of Hampton Institute faculty and students; Principal Ross, Phoenix Training School
Oct. 6, 7	Norfolk, VA	Dean W. T. Hodges, Norfolk Division, College of William and Mary; H. Aspergren, Swedish Consul; Proctor and Gamble plant; chief of police; toured Norfolk black community with two policemen; P. B. Young, Journal and Guide editor; visited Norfolk Division, Virginia Union University
Oct. 7	Petersburg, VA	Visited Virginia State College for Negroes
Oct. 8, 9 10, 11	Raleigh, NC	N. C. Newbold, state agent for Negro education; Miss H. L. Triff; State Superintendent Erwin and staff; state Governor Clyde Hoey; Frank Graham, president, University of North Carolina, and Howard Odum, University of North Carolina
Oct. 11, 12	Chapel Hill, NC	Howard Odum, Rupert Vance, Guy B. Johnson, and Dean Bradshaw, University of North Carolina
Oct. 12	Hartsville, SC	Dr. Coker, cotton plantation owner; tour of Coker plantation by George Wilds, in charge of plant breeding

Table 4—*Continued*

Date(s)	Place(s)	Conferences
Oct. 13	Columbia, SC	President Starks, Benedict College (J.D.), Booker T. Washington High School (M. and S.); Superintendent Hope and dept. heads, State Department of Education; Dr. Josiah Morse, University of South Carolina professor of Sociology
Oct. 13	Orange, SC **(sic)**	With W. A. Schiffley, assistant agent of Negro rural schools, talked with Jeanes agents, President Shelton Phelps, Winthrop College (J.D.), visited the State Colored Normal, Industrial, Agricultural, and Mechanical College
Oct. 14	Augustus, GA **(sic)**	President E. C. Peters, Paine College (J.D.); visited class on the family; F. L. Steeley; L. B. Furtick, G. I. O. organizer, black former secretary of Bricklayer's Union; toured countryside; stopped at black church; visited a white sharecropper's home; visited two black homes and a cotton gin
Oct. 14, 15	Atlanta, GA	President Florence Read, Spelman College, W. E. B. DuBois and Ira de A. Reid, Atlanta University; J. R. McCain; President W. A. Fountain, Morris Brown College; Trevor Arnett, Chairman of Board of Trustees, Spelman College; and Bacotes, Atlanta University; visited textile mills at La Grange, West Point and Lanett
Oct. 15, 16, 17	Tuskegee, AL	President Frederick Patterson, Tuskegee Institute; Monroe N. Work; T. M. Campbell, W. T. B. Williams, Mr. Fry, and Allen

Table 4—*Continued*

Date(s)	Place(s)	Conferences
		(Tuskegee Institute); Dr. M. O. Bousfield, Julius Rosenwald Fund; Mr. and Mrs. Colin Maher, Nairobi, Kenya; visited black church; visited tenant home on Huddleston plantation ("mean" white man); visited Mr. and Mrs. Martingale, Martingale plantation ("good" white man); Mr. T. N. Roberts, Prairie Rural Settlement Project; Myrdal's Tuskegee talk on Sweden; Dr. Perry, a black physician; visited a rural schoolhouse
Oct. 17	Jackson, MS	Alfred Stone, state tax commissioner; Pitt Easom, state agent; Mr. Travis
Oct. 18	Greenwood, MS	Will Garrett, manager of the Delta Staple Cotton Cooperative Association
Oct. 18, 19	Clarksdale, MS	Visited the homes of three black sharecroppers; visited a white farm family with black sharecroppers; P. F. Williams, former superintendent of Coahoma County; visited the Williams plantation and observed some of its tenants; visited Coahoma Agricultural High School
Oct. 19	Rochdale, MS	Mr. McDonald, a bookkeeper and the farm manager of Delta Cooperative Farms; Mr. Toler, assistant manager of the Delta and Pine Land Company Plantation; went back to Jackson
Oct. 20	Baton Rouge, LA	A. C. Lewis, state agent, who was to take M. and S. to Teche County sugar planations after J. D. departed for New York; Barrows would drive them to Houston, Prairie View, and

Table 4—*Continued*

Date(s)	Place(s)	Conferences
		Little Rock; McCuiston agreed by phone to meet them in Litte Rock on Oct. 25 and accompany them as far as Birmingham, putting them in touch with James Saxon Childers there. J. D.
Oct. 20	Baton Rouge, LA	gave M. Letters of introduction for T.V.A. in Knoxville and Birmingham trips.
Oct. 20	Scotlandville, LA	State Superintendent Harris, President Clark and staff members of Southern University; J. D. catches train to New York City from New Orleans.

Although Myrdal later recalled that he and Sterner had visited a host of different persons, actually the majority of their time was spent with liberal-minded educators. Seldom did they converse with politicians or industrialists. They also encountered planters and their tenants. Most of the blacks they met with were involved in foundation-sponsored education and advocates of interracial cooperation. Myrdal did not have the opportunity to converse with white reactionaries or with militant blacks. He spent ten days in the more liberal Southeast, especially in Virginia, and only three days in the more caste-ridden deep South. Although he spent much time conversing with tenants, both black and white, there is little indication how much time he spent visiting with urban dwellers.[40] The tour greatly influenced the impressions and opinions Myrdal developed— such as an unwarranted optimism for inevitable racial improvement—which appeared later in *An American Dilemma.*

Jackson Davis, Fred McQuiston, and their liberal friends were impressed with Myrdal's intelligence but disturbed about his slowness in arriving at what they considered appropriate interpretations. But they spent much time helping him get his bearings—again within the context of their world views.[41]

Jackson Davis was instrumental in getting *An American Dilemma* accepted by southern liberals. He wrote a book review of the study for circulation among General Education Board trustees and his friends. The review, which pointed out strengths and weaknesses of *An American Dilemma*, gave southerners a needed ideological filter, and assured them of the non-threatening value of the book. Davis also assisted Keppel in distributing *An American Dilemma* among state agents and other liberal friends.[42]

THE JANUARY 28, 1939, MEMORANDUM

Between his tour of the South and consultations with race-relations experts, Myrdal, with Sterner's assistance, attempted to formulate the premises for the project, which were drawn from his observations, his limited reading in race-relations literature, and his knowledge of his homeland and Europe. In a lengthy confidential report to Keppel written shortly after he returned from his tour, Myrdal outlined the premises of what was to become *An American Dilemma*.[43] The major premises, or biases as they might be called, demonstrate that even strangers have opinions about the alien society they are in and such impressions greatly determine how they use selected natives to help them construct plausible interpretations. In this sense, the biases a stranger develops through combining personal knowledge with initial observations in an alien society are in dialectical relationship with the native knowledge on which he depended so much. Many of the ideas in *An American Dilemma*, well substantiated with empirical documentation, were derived from interpretations Myrdal developed before consulting race-relations experts or reading the race-relations literature. He may have arrived in America with no preconceptions of the Negro problem, which is questionable, but by the time he had organized his staff, he had already formulated ideas about what the study was going to do and say.[44]

Myrdal's intellectual biases, which played major roles in the development of ideas found in *An American Dilemma*, were a critical attitude toward the weakness of American race-relations literature; a strong environmental bias about black capacities and abilities, a moralistic and anti-popular view of the origins and dynamics of race prejudices and pathological assumptions about black culture, a bias toward southern views of black problems in America, historicism, and a practical focus.

In his report, Myrdal conveyed a deep disappointment with the poor quality of literature about the Negro problem.[45] He wanted to reorganize and reinterpret the literature through a new paradigm.[46] This strategy worked toward the development of the value argument that *An American Dilemma* became known for, but worked against exploration of the larger political realities of racial caste which stifled the development of a relevant literature on the Negro problem. Even this study could not contend with certain issues, such as the role of southern liberals, without raising controversy. The inability of American social scientists to understand the virtues of state intervention as a solution to the Negro problem was a reflection of a conservative racial order rooted in laissez-faire principles.

Myrdal's tendency to reinterpret data in a new framework rather than exploring the reasons why such data were so poor enabled him to avoid critical dilemmas in the development of interracial civil rights organizations. He failed to understand that mainstream civil rights organizations such as the National Association for the Advancement of Colored People (NAACP) and the Urban

League not only included "some white members" but were controlled by them. He failed to realize, understandably, that the inconsequentiality of black "protest movements" was linked to their dependency on whites who convinced their black colleagues of the virtues of working from within the system and the dangers of working outside it.[47] His reified views about black civil rights organizations materialized in *An American Dilemma* chapters on black improvement and protest organizations.[48]

Myrdal de-emphasized the importance of the nature versus nurture debate about black capacities and abilities. Thus unlike other major social studies of blacks both before and after the Carnegie study, *The American Dilemma* does not contain countless pages regurgitating the nature versus nurture debate.[49] Myrdal agreed with the popular liberal view that racial prejudice was "the result of a social tendency and distorted reality interpretations and felt that associating opinions with knowledge would have to be a high priority in the study."[50] This definition of racial prejudice randomized and individualized racism in a society Myrdal strongly believed was a democracy. It also inhibited a power and privilege understanding of racism through evading the elite origins and preservation of racial inequality. Conveniently, it emphasized the need to research the racially biased ideologies and practices of lower classes rather than affluent classes, workers rather than corporation managers and owners. In his criticism of *An American Dilemma*, historian Herbert Aptheker claimed that Myrdal chose not to use opinion-poll data, which would have pointed out the racial prejudice of white affluent classes.[51]

The argument that racism originated in the consciousness, ideologies, and policies of the affluent classes was too power-oriented a perspective for Myrdal and his liberal friends, both southern and northern, to accept. Myrdal not only rejected the conservative ideas of Park (although he relied upon his students) but also criticized Marxist perspectives. The moral argument of Myrdal's work gave middle-class liberals clean hands and pure hearts and a justified indignation against less fortunate whites and others who dared to violate the American Creed.[52]

Although at one point in the memorandum Myrdal appeared to have an open mind about the African culture survival issue in relation to blacks in America,[53] he spent most of his time and space expressing views similar to cultureless scholars. Cultureless scholars, such as Chicago and Chapel Hill trained social scientists and major folklorists, argued that black personality traits, black community formations, the black church, and black customs were deviations from lower class white culture or from obsolete European cultural forms.[54] Myrdal agreed with cultureless scholars on these and other black culture matters, which gave his initial impressions about black culture a pathological character.[55]

Myrdal's assumptions about the pathological nature of black culture helped him to develop a deep affinity for social scientists trained at Chicago and Chapel Hill, who dominated in the contributions of advice and materials to the study.[56] He gravitated away from cultural pluralists such as Melville Herskovits, who because of a dispute with Myrdal, published his monograph, *The Myth of the Negro Past*,[57] separately. The pathological perspective on black culture permeated *An American Dilemma* but was especially explicit in his chapters entitled "The Negro Community," "The Negro Church," and "The Negro School."

Myrdal told Keppel in the memorandum that except for his frequent tourist excursions into Harlem, he had not seen much of northern black life.[58] He presumed that the Negro problem as a racial caste phenomenon was confined to the South, and this view was nourished through Carnegie officers, Jackson Davis, and contributing researchers.[59] This regionally biased presumption agreed with conventional wisdoms which suggested that only the South, and not the West, Midwest, and East, had white elites and lower classes which discriminated against Negroes as "to create and preserve a stable racial caste order premised on white supremacy."[60]

Myrdal's *An American Dilemma* has a chronological rather than an analytical framework, since he was more concerned about exploring blacks as a policy problem than as an academic issue. This was in keeping with the study's goals, which Donald Young and Frederick Keppel had agreed upon.[61] A chronology was needed to give background information about various aspects of the Negro problem.

The emphasis in *An American Dilemma* on "contemporaneous conditions" and its lack of appreciation for analytical history (as opposed to chronological history) was, ironically, also characteristic of the stagnant race-relations studies that Myrdal had criticized. Lack of understanding of the historical foundations of race relations led Myrdal to make unrealistically positive predictions about the future. *An American Dilemma* was unable to grapple with the changes in race relations stimulated by World War II. Comparing Myrdal's work with Quincy Wright's study of war, Howard Odum noted:

each study was begun at a time when there was expectation of both objectivity and uninterrupted study and of optimistic trends and both ended in the unpredicted chaos and turmoil which made some of their assumptions and conclusions appear out of date before they could be published. Thus Professor Wright says of his study that it was "begun in the hopeful atmosphere of Locarno and completed in the midst of general war." Similarly, in his introductory note to *An American Dilemma*, the late Frederick P. Keppel wrote, "When the Trustees of the Carnegie Corporation asked for the preparation of this report in 1937, no one (except possibly Adolf Hitler) could have foreseen that it would be made public at a day when the place of the Negro in American life would be subject of greatly heightened interest in the United States . . . when the eyes of men of all races the world over turned upon us to see how the people of the most powerful of the United Nations are dealing *at home* with a major problem of race relations." So, too, Dr. Myrdal's italicized conclusion on page 1003 that "The gradual destruction of the popular theory behind race prejudice is the most important of all social trends in the field of interracial relations" strikes hard against the rising tide of race prejudice and conflict the world over, but particularly in America.[62]

Most of the book discusses the problems of black migration, economic inequality, persistent slavery traditions, the southern plantation economy, business and professional occupations, housing, politics, intraracial and interracial stratification, and the legal system. The practical emphasis of *An American Dilemma* followed the social science convention through ignoring the more normative features of black experiences. This tendency was buttressed by Myrdal's overreliance on quantitative data, which were thought "scientific." Most data on blacks were official statistics developed by governmental agencies, especially the U.S. Census Bureau. Few qualitative, ethnographic studies of Afro-American experience or white attitudes towards blacks existed. Myrdal also assumed, as did most social scientists of his generation, that quantification was an effective way to cross national and cultural boundaries. It was easy for Richard Sterner to study black income and consumption statistically because he had done the same kind of analyses in Sweden. It stands to reason, especially considering the time constraints of the study and Myrdal's limited knowledge about America and blacks, that he felt more comfortable with quantitative data and with phenomena that could be quantified.

Myrdal planned to do the comprehensive Negro problem report in two years— a tremendously fast pace for any researcher, no matter how intelligent, who had to become familiar with an alien society, a strange people, and the American mode of social research organization. The time pressure meant that he only had an opportunity to read cursorily and was forced to depend on native researchers for details. Myrdal was aware of the inevitable contradictions that resulted.

In the memorandum to Keppel, Myrdal pointed out that there were unanticipated initial difficulties in familiarizing himself with the research area. Although he still believed strongly in the virtues of stranger research, he was becoming increasingly aware of his nearly complete lack of knowledge about the Negro problem which resulted in handicaps he initially underestimated. The major handicap was his lack of awareness of the complexity of the American race problem and the magnitude of work needed in doing background reading and organizing the collection of materials.[63] Since Myrdal was so unfamiliar with the Negro problem research area, he requested assistance in organizing a small executive staff to coordinate the work of commissioned race relations authorities and to help him write the main report. He stipulated that the executive staff, to be headquartered in New York City, ought to have at least an efficient secretary, a competent sociologist and a research assistant.

Myrdal wanted twenty experts to write monographs on aspects of the Negro problem and cultural annotated bibliographies on the literature of that subspecialty.[64] Due to the time constraints, researchers would be asked to review or synthesize existing literature rather than embark on original studies (as we shall see, Myrdal's attempt to recruit Horace Cayton was a distinct exception).[65] Thus, Myrdal's *An American Dilemma* was at best an attempt to reorganize existing race relations knowledge through the fresh though highly dependent perspective of an outside researcher.

As a new elaboration of old data, *An American Dilemma* was and is only useful as an example of stranger research and as an indictment of American social science. It did not offer new empirical insights about blacks or race relations (innovative theories such as cumulative causation were poorly tested or confirmed). It merely reiterated what liberal race-relations scholars had been saying for years, especially in its treatment of the moral premises of racism and its contradiction with theoretical democracy.[66] Although Myrdal was aware of the problems caused by rigid time constraints and by his lack of knowledge, this awareness did not save the project from being poorly coordinated, rushed, and full of discrepancies, repetitions, and ideological contradictions.

The major organizational components of the Carnegie study, and Myrdal's main sources of information, consisted of executive staff members, contributing researchers, informal consultants, and an advisory committee. With the exception of contributing researchers, the whole organization was exclusively white or at least rigidly controlled by whites. Blacks participated in the study only as collectors or sources of data.[67] Although the study was plagued with disorganization, deep ideological conflicts, and Myrdal's dissatisfaction with the work of his executive staff and contributing researchers, this did not disturb the project's exclusive white control or its use of prominent black social scientists as field hands. With few exceptions, black social scientists not only failed to criticize the project but continued to contribute passively to it. Some, such as E. Franklin Frazier and Charles S. Johnson, became friends with the congenial Gunnar and Alva Myrdal.[68]

Myrdal's closest executive staff members were Richard Sterner and Arnold Rose. Sterner, although he had been formally invited to assist Myrdal with the Negro problem study, was apparently not always free to do so. Like Myrdal, Sterner's activities in the United States were greatly influenced by Jackson Davis. Davis served as mediator between Myrdal and Sterner when the former requested the reluctant Sterner to take a three-month leave of absence from his position at a population studies center (which he had secured with Davis's assistance) in order to put more time into the Negro problem study. Sterner revealed to Davis his disinterest and discontent with the Carnegie project.

The problem of my work on this manuscript has really bothered me for some time. Up until now I have not been able to do much about it since I have had to devote most of my "work nights" to the editing of Mrs. Myrdal's book on Swedish population policies. . . . . The consequence however, is that I will have to speed up the work on my own MS as much as possible. Since it is not a question of revision but also of supplementing, particularly in regard to 1940 Census material, I do not think that I will be able to do it by working only after office hours.[69]

Chicago sociologist Louis Wirth, who was Myrdal's most instrumental informal consultant, had two of the most brilliant graduate students in the 1930s and 1940s: Horace R. Cayton and Arnold Rose. It is interesting to reflect on why Rose rather than Cayton was selected as Myrdal's major American assistant.

HORACE CAYTON

By some accounts, Cayton was the most brilliant sociologist of African descent in the so-called Johnson-Frazier generation. Others claimed that he was a confused man, entangled in a life-long identity crisis which ended in a broken spirit and alcoholism. The two perspectives are not contradictory, but complementary. Cayton's upbringing in a predominantly white environment, sheltered from major race problems, gave him both a high degree of self-confidence and an acute sense of marginality.[70] As he began to move into the black world in Chicago, his keen self-confidence began to convert him into an articulate "race man" while his marginality, his identification with whites, prodded him to become an astute, detached sociologist of Afro-American society. These mixed priorities resulted in his tragic career in Chicago and his obscure status in the annals of race social science.

Although Cayton originally went into the University of Chicago Sociology Department hoping to get a Ph.D., those plans gradually changed as he became torn between the two poles of his inner conflict. Cayton idolized Louis Wirth, his mentor, and Wirth adored Cayton. Early in his graduate career, Cayton wrote to his mentor and friend:

We will not complete this study until the first of January, 1935. At that time, if you can use me, I would be very glad to work for you again. I will have some money saved, and so the amount of wages that I will receive from you is not important. I am very anxious to continue in your study and work on a thesis in that field. I will be in Chicago from October on and can assist you in putting any one to work on the material which I have started.[71]

In return, Wirth wrote Cayton sparkling letters of recommendation. He even loaned Cayton money at times, and his wife, social worker Louise Wirth, employed Cayton's first wife.[72]

Cayton began to gravitate away from graduate school and toward the Chicago black community in the mid–1930s. Continuing his interest in research, he became director of the Parkway Community House in 1940. He became an influential community leader, speaking against local patterns of racial discrimination in housing and writing a widely read column for the *Pittsburgh Courier*. He went on to become the director of the largest Works Progress Administration (WPA) program in Chicago's black community. This represented to him an ideal way of synthesizing his dual roles as a black community leader and social researcher. During his directorship at the WPA he attempted to launch a definitive study of the black community: *Black Metropolis*.[73] This power base, besides giving Cayton an opportunity to do community-based research, gave his sense of racial identity a significant boost.

Wirth profited from Cayton's movement into the black community, since both men were deeply involved in Chicago housing issues, and Cayton became Wirth's contact in the black community. This contact was important, since during the 1930s and 1940s black community leaders vehemently opposed the University of Chicago's encouragement of restricted housing on the South Side and its exclusion of blacks from medical school and hospitals.[74]

Cayton and Wirth sometimes debated on opposite sides, although still retaining respect for each other. On one occasion, Cayton, in appearing before the Metropolitan Housing Council of which Wirth was a member, accused his mentor of vacillation on the issue of restricted housing covenants. He commented to the president of the council:

Dr. Wirth's question as to whether we would want the Metropolitan Housing Council to come out flatly against restrictive covenants, though it might wreck the organization, was not exactly a fair one. In the first place, it resembled to an extent the question which is often raised in connection with giving a Negro any occupational advancement, a vote, or some other change in the conventional racial pattern—"Do you want your daughter to marry a Negro?" The council could make any of a number of statements. Any statement which it did make might not injure the organization, according to its stand on the issue. No one knows how far in this particular crisis an organization could go in liberalizing its policies.[75]

Wirth gave the typical liberal line about being more concerned about civilities, reason, and patience than direct action, which could destroy the goals of the commission. He gravitated away from this view after World War II.

I think I need not tell you that I am unequivocally, both on principle and for practical reasons, opposed to restrictive covenants. I think I need not tell you either of my concern about the inadequacy of housing of Negroes and the serious repercussions I think their inadequate housing will have upon American community life not only in Chicago but elsewhere. I am anxious about, and I shall do all I can to improve this situation through every method I find to be useful to that end. . . . It is my opinion that if the organization were to put itself on record unequivocally as opposing restrictive covenants it would become a less effective organization than it now is in the advancement of Negro housing and it might even cease to exist as an organization. . . . I need not tell you that I think restrictive covenants are one reason why we have not been able to get adequate housing for Negroes, so that it is not altogether a matter of one versus the other, but, considering how the Metropolitan Housing Council gets its support and the basis on which it enjoys whatever power it may have to advance the cause of Negro housing, it is a question of one versus the other at the present time.[76]

But Cayton always resolved the differences with his mentor (claiming to have continued faith in him):

It's funny but now issues aren't half as clear as I thought they were a few years ago. Probably I've seen more of the ramifications and possibly things are just so mixed up that it's hard to find any decent stand to take on anything, including being a Negro, believer in democracy, or anything else. One faith that I've always had, however has been in you and your integrity and I don't think that will ever be shaken either by the amount of insight I might get or any extent to which I might differ with you or any possible action of your own.[77]

Another factor that contributed to Cayton's conflict was his effort to compile and analyze the data which eventually found its way into *Black Metropolis*. Ever since the mid–1930s, Cayton had contemplated doing a comprehensive study of the Chicago black community.[78] He needed assistance in gathering, organizing, and storing raw data. When he met Lloyd Warner, the Harvard anthropologist who arrived at the University of Chicago in 1935, Warner was impressed with his ideas and supported his plan to establish an Institute on the Negro, which would be a repository for bibliographies, unpublished and published documents, and other materials on Afro-Americans. Their major concern was financing. At one point in their planning, Cayton wrote to Wirth about possible foundation support:

It seems to me that if the persons who are interested in having this study made are sufficiently interested in the Negro they should be willing to make an initial contribution to the organization of an Institute. This would give us an opportunity to attempt to match funds with one of the foundations. What we would like is a budget of, say, $6,000 a year over a ten-year period which we might match from the Rockefeller and/or the Rosenwald Foundations. Under the circumstances I think this would be a very praiseworthy and thoroughly justifiable expenditure for it would be a demonstration of an interest, and a continued interest, which this group feels in the Negro population.[79]

Cayton was assured by Dean Robert Redfield that if the institute received funding, he would house it at the University of Chicago.

If such a grant is made Doctor Redfield has promised to house the institute at the University. With the aid of the staff which would be possible from the budget which we hope to obtain, and the assistance of a staff of at least 126 W.P.A. workers we can, within a very short period of time, have an excellent and exhaustive report. The Institute, I am sure, will receive the hearty support of members of the Negro community and we envisage an interracial committee who are interested in research as well as race relations.[80]

This was not truly the case, since Chicago's black community leaders were avidly opposed to research on blacks generated by the University of Chicago.[81] But the only way Cayton could become a high-powered social scientist was to have the nod of the University of Chicago social scientists, especially that of his mentor, Louis Wirth.[82]

The institute never materialized. Cayton and Warner parted over an issue that revealed Cayton's continued academic marginality and racial subordination.

Apparently, Cayton had planned to co-author Warner's *Color and Human Nature* for the American Youth Commission's Negro Youth Committee (financed through the General Education Board chaired by Will W. Alexander). For unknown reasons, Warner later decided to co-author the study with Buford Junker but not before Cayton had spent much time and money on the project. He wrote Warner a bitter letter:

My recent trip to Washington was, as you know, primarily to feel out the possibilities for obtaining publication of the study. I had decided before I left that I was not going to accept a federal study, but was going to use the opportunity to present to the group the results of the large research, and to ask them to help in the publication. You will perhaps remember that on March 23, I wrote you asking the possibilities for getting transportation for me to the A.Y.C. meeting in New Haven. I suggested that we could continue from there to Washington to meet with the group. You stated at that time, that it was necessary for you to take Junker with you, and as there was going to be considerable discussion about social organization, I concurred in your feeling that it was just as well for me to not attend. However, I found that the week following my trip to Washington another of the A.Y.C. was scheduled to which you took both Mr. Junker and Dr. Adams.

It seems to me that in view of the facts, first, that I was supposed to write the A.Y.C. report jointly with you, and second, that by postponing the engagement for one week, both of us could have appeared before the committee in Washington regarding the large research, your failure to include me was an injustice. It was understood at the beginning that I was to direct all research in the field of the Negro, but I was included in none of the meetings in New York and have not even been able to read any of the manuscripts. Incidentally, in going to Washington, it was necessary for me to spend over seventy-five dollars of my own money. It was also necessary that I drive straight through for a thousand miles each way under extremely uncomfortable and tiring circumstances. It is obvious that if my Washington trip had been put off for one week the expenditure of money and the tediousness of the automobile trip could have been avoided and you could have assisted me in the presentation in Washington. This was especially true in view of the fact that, as you state, the controversial issues were settled in the first meeting.

In view of this and a number of other misunderstandings in the past, I feel quite definitely that I would like to work independently in the future. I will outline, what seems to me, a possible program for the fulfillment of my obligations, both to you and the Works Progress Administration.[83]

Cayton's hostility toward Warner, and his academic marginality, prevented him from gaining due credit for his significant contributions to *Black Metropolis*.

Myrdal wanted access to Cayton's data. In his memorandum to Keppel, he outlined his interest in doing a community-based study as part of his comprehensive report (following perhaps an earlier suggestion by Donald Young).[84] Cayton accompanied Wirth to New York City early in 1939 to confer with Myrdal. In exchange for data about blacks in Chicago which Cayton had been collecting for several years, Myrdal promised Cayton much autonomy, credit for the data analyses, an appropriate professional fee, and time to write a book.[85]

A year later, Myrdal changed his mind. Cayton was to take a leave and pay cut from his Parkway Community House directorship for two months, come to New York City, and give Myrdal liberal access to his data. This, needless to say, infuriated Cayton, who wrote to Wirth:

I am enclosing the correspondence which I have had with Dr. Myrdal to let you know how things stand. Myrdal has reversed his entire position and I am now of the opinion that either he is pretty erratic and temperamental, or that he was dishonest in his conversation with me in New York.[86]

Myrdal and Cayton never came to an agreement. Myrdal argued that there was no longer ample time for Cayton to do a comprehensive study and that the Carnegie Corporation could not possibly afford to pay him a stipend.

I read your letter very carefully and discussed the matter both with the few colleagues who are here and with Mr. Dollard of the Carnegie Corporation. . . . As I told you, for certain reasons I am not at present in a position to propose that the Carnegie Corporation make an additional grant and even if I can squeeze $1,000 out of the budget I cannot very well allocate it for a purpose which is not directly of great importance for our own work. We cannot give you a stipend out of our budget to write a book. Within our time schedules, the collaborators cannot make use of any raw material which is not submitted to them within the next few weeks. Such memoranda as we planned that you should prepare and which eventually could also be of use for you too in writing a book must be in our hands within the next few months (in any case before June 1) in order to come within our time schedules. Under these circumstances, the only thing I can suggest is that you come here for two months, bringing with you your material and your secretary, and that before you come you arrange to have sent to the various collaborators such manuscripts, tables and other material as we discussed during your stay in New York.[87]

Cayton said no. He did not want to involve himself in a study which denied him of deserved academic credit and compensation.[88]

There is no indication that Wirth defended Cayton in his clashes with prominent white social scientists, or if he did, that his defense had any effect. In fact, Wirth was ineffectual in his attempts to secure Cayton a job outside his own research activities. Wirth was also unsuccessful in getting Cayton focused academically. Although he commended Cayton for his organizational skills, his astute research abilities, and his personality, Cayton drifted away from graduate school. After leaving his community work in the mid–1940s, Cayton began to realize the costly long-range effects of his lack of a doctorate. In 1948, he wrote to Wirth:

Dear Louis: As you may have heard I have a one year leave of absence. We are at present living in New York. I am feeling very well now having taken a month's rest in the country.

At present I am beginning to make some plans for the future. In regard to this I want to ask your advice and assistance. I can, of course, return to my job at the Center, but confidentially, I don't want to. What I would most like would be a teaching post in some college near New York, like Bennington. Do you know of any openings? In addition to what sociological training that I have, I have completed a number of courses at the Institute for Psycho-analysis. As you know I am rather conversant with the field and the literature of race relations. What I would really like would be to give courses in elementary sociology, something in the field of community organization and perhaps a course in social pathology or criminology and then conduct a seminar on race and culture, employing an eclectic approach—sociology, literature, psychoanalysis, etc. That's what I would like, but of course, what I would take would be a job. I have taught political science, economics and labor.

I have also thought of returning to school and getting my doctor's degree. But having been out of school so long, this prospect rather frightens me. In any case I would like to talk to you about it.

In case there are no teaching jobs I would be interested in the general field of research. Also I would like to know what opportunities there are in the field of race relations, but am not particularly keen on such things as mayor's committees.[89]

Wirth responded several weeks later:

Dear Horace: I have been away from the office for some time and have just got a chance to answer your letter of some weeks ago in which you tell me of your whereabouts about which I have been wondering and something of your plans. It seems to me that unless you went through the ritual of taking academic degrees about which you have some understandable trepidations, it would only be an unusual academic institution that would take you on its staff and offer you expanding opportunities, but there might be such an institution and if I should come across any clues, I will certainly do what I can to open this door. Aside from the academic field, there is, of course, little in the race relations area that would pay you enough to make it worthwhile outside of Government. With your contacts, I would think that some of the strategic positions in the federal service might want to consider your candidacy in connection with the President's program on non-discrimination; if it is actually carried out, there will no doubt open such positions.[90]

Cayton's non-academic standing led to his inability to defend his academic accomplishments and personal ambitions in his later years. His autobiography, *Long Old Road*, published shortly before his death, was a pitiful attempt to do so.[91]

Since Louis Wirth recognized and appreciated Cayton's incredible capacity for work, his profound knowledge about Afro-American experiences, his brilliant writing ability, and his superb organizational abilities, Wirth's recommendation of Arnold Rose to Myrdal was surprising. Wirth often attested to Rose's brilliance.[92] But as intelligent as he was, Rose knew virtually nothing about blacks, and he experienced problems writing on the subject. At one point, Keppel complained to Wirth about the poor quality of the chapters Rose wrote for *An American Dilemma* and even asked Wirth to rewrite sections of them.[93] Rose's dissertation on non-attached persons in urban areas was part of Wirth's urban growth project for the National Resource Planning Board.[94] It was at best only vaguely related to Afro-American conditions.

Why was Rose chosen rather than Cayton? More than likely, Carnegie officers would not have approved of a black like Cayton being intimately involved in their study's decision-making circles.[95] Myrdal's private opinions about this are unknown, but he conformed to the wishes of his foundation superiors. Cayton's tendency to be outspoken and independent also made him an undesirable candidate. To assure that things were done properly especially during Myrdal's absence, it was necessary that his American assistant do nothing without the approval of the directors of the project. Correspondence between Keppel and Wirth describes Rose's willingness to jump at every Wirth order.[96] It is doubtful that Cayton would have conformed to such authoritarian rule. This independence, and his deep knowledge about the Negro problem, made Cayton's expertise too threatening.

Arnold Rose's participation in the Carnegie Negro problem project paved the way for his successful career as a race-relations expert. Quite a different fate awaited Wirth's other brilliant, but black, student.

Myrdal's dependency on various American men and women to produce information at a rapid pace for his consumption and synthesis resulted in an avalanche of memos from the Negro study headquarters—reminders about deadlines and queries about delayed reports.[97] When Myrdal did not get what he wanted, Carnegie officers intervened, reminding researchers of Myrdal's special needs as a foreign scholar. Shortly after Myrdal returned from Sweden to begin reading through a rough draft of the study, which his staff had prepared in his absence, Charles Dollard conveyed to the contributing researchers Myrdal's disappointment over the lack of "promised" comprehensive bibliographies. The condescending and demanding tone of his letter illuminates the authoritarian relationship Carnegie officers and Myrdal developed with contributing researchers, due to their chronic dependency on the native experts.[98]

Myrdal did not publish ideas that conflicted with his own presumptions or with those of foundation officers and informal consultants. For example, he did not incorporate Herskovits' cultural pluralism perspectives into the study because they conflicted with his own opinions about the "cultureless" roots of contemporaneous Afro-American experiences.[99] Furthermore, Myrdal gave Jackson Davis free reign over Doxey Wilkerson's monograph on black education. Wilkerson, a leftist black education specialist at Howard University, relied on Davis for data and contacts, and the foundation officer reviewed his report.[100] Davis made sure Wilkerson did not do or write anything that might upset his fellow white liberals. For example, when Davis and his friend, North Carolina state agent for Negro education N. C. Newbold, checked the questionnaire Wilkerson was planning to mail to school officers, they both agreed that questions about interracial marriage, among others, should be deleted:

In regard to the questionnaire which would deal, as you say, somewhat with the intangible elements of the program in education, I agreed to help him get information on ninety-three of the points, suggesting that he eliminate the other three which had to do with eliminating inter-marriage and certain biological facts. These, it seems to me, would not weaken the material he wanted and would certainly make the paper more *palatable* to our southern people in general.[101]

When Wilkerson did not conform totally with liberal strategies, he was considered too leftist to be taken seriously. Jackson Davis's clearest intrusion was his critical review of the rough draft of Wilkerson's monograph, which, interestingly enough, even criticized the author for overstating the role of foundations in black education. After telling Samuel Stouffer, Myrdal's temporary substitute, that "the [manuscript] reflects a super-sensitive, highly critical mind, with a rather hopeless attitude towards the part education can play in basic changes which will set the world alright," Davis said:

Chapter X (pp. 59–60) questions the evolutionary method of social change of which education is the main hope, and implies much more. One does not question his right to his opinion, but since in many parts of the world new forms of tyranny have been accepted under the guise of reform, one does question the soundness of his "bias. . . ."
  I don't suppose the MS is for publication. It is too voluminous for that. It is padded with excerpts and summaries, and the reader gets lost and confused in the mass of details. . . . The treatment of Educational Foundations is not satisfactory. They deserve well, but he gives them credit for too much.[102]

The southern focus of *An American Dilemma* was in part due to the abundance of data on southern black conditions, an indication of the gap between the knowledge base of race studies and demographic changes in black America. More importantly, the southern composure of the study was due to the biases of the native researchers and consultants Gunnar Myrdal depended on for data collection and interpretation. Reliance on southern liberals such as Jackson Davis assured that the study would give no attention to racial miscegenation as a possible solution to the Negro problem.
  Myrdal respected Davis, Keppel, and Charles Dollard because he admired the institutions they represented. His great appreciation for foundations and the evaluation of his work by foundation officers and others in agreement with foundation interests assured a distorted interpretation of foundation contributions to racial issues.[103] Other than these three, Myrdal's most important informal consultant was Chicago sociologist Louis Wirth. In fact, most of the major ideas expressed in Myrdal's book originated from Louis Wirth's contributions.[104]
  Wirth was a student of Park whose first published book, *The Ghetto*, discussed Jewish communities in Europe and the United States. Wirth was also a sociologist of knowledge with a keen interest in the role of values in social

research.[105] Unlike his Chicago colleagues Robert E. Park, William Ogburn, and Charles Merriam, Wirth worked mostly behind the scenes and thus has never received full credit for many of his accomplishments. In the late 1930s, he obtained large W.P.A. grants for Chicago. Some of the money went to the black community, under the supervision of his student Horace Cayton. Wirth also organized and directed a massive study on the city for the National Resource Planning Board at the same time as he was assisting Myrdal on the Carnegie Negro Problem Study.[106] (Other reasons for Wirth's obscurity were his Jewish background and his increasing activism in the 1940s at a time when it was considered proper for liberals to retreat or turn reactionary in the course of rapid race relations changes.)[107]

Myrdal and Wirth met just before the end of the initial planning stages of the project. More than likely due to their common interest in the sociology of knowledge, Myrdal accepted Wirth's recommendations for his executive staff and advisory committee. Thus, Arnold Rose became Myrdal's chief American researcher and Wirth's Chicago colleagues—Samuel Stouffer and William Ogburn—were appointed to the three-man Advisory Committee (Donald Young of the Social Science Research Council was the third person).[108] Two other Wirth students—Edward Shils and Herbert Goldhammer—wrote monographs for the study. Meanwhile, all three did the research for their dissertations as assistants in Wirth's city project for the National Planning Board.[109]

Wirth's more intensive participation in Myrdal's work began in the spring of 1942. Myrdal had returned from Sweden to look over the prepared rough draft. Since Myrdal planned to return to Sweden in August, he needed fast reviews and revisions on the book's chapters. He chose Wirth to write a comprehensive review of the book in June and July.[110]

Wirth rapidly wrote lengthy reviews of most of the chapters. He criticized the poor academic quality of several of the chapters. He also criticized the pessimism of the portrayals of black conditions and suggested including more optimistic data displaying areas of black progress.[111] Optimistic views of black progress were a trademark of the Chicago school of race relations.[112] Wirth was concerned about the overall quality of the manuscript and suggested that Myrdal employ someone to do a comprehensive editing job.[113]

Myrdal followed Wirth's advice on virtually every editorial point he made, but he did not hire someone to smooth out the repetition and disjunctures in the book chapters. Myrdal gave no time for adequate synthesis of data analyses by his native collaborators, and of course, given his lack of experience in race relations, he could not do it himself. He even justified the repetition and the multitude of uncoordinated perspectives which convoluted the book's paradigm.[114]

Myrdal's gratitude to Wirth was shown in a most unusual way. In the acknowledgments in *An American Dilemma*, Myrdal singled out the work of Richard Sterner and Arnold Rose while merely listing Wirth as one of many contributors and consultants.[115] That may have been how Wirth wanted it, perhaps in order not to embarrass Myrdal, but it slighted his career while giving Myrdal,

Richard Sterner, and especially Arnold Rose more praise than they deserved.

An American Dilemma was a sideshow in Gunnar Myrdal's career, and it had been done in a hurry. The ideas developed in the text about race relations belonged more to his native collaborators than to him. Even the meanings of the American Creed and the moral basis of racial prejudice were not novel—in fact, they had been well developed in liberal circles for years.

The claim that Myrdal was an "objective" researcher by virtue of his "stranger" status has been questioned. Points made about Myrdal's selection and his January 28, 1939, memorandum to Keppel reveal that he did have preconceptions which influenced the writing of *An American Dilemma*. The issue of preconception, or to borrow one of Myrdal's own terms—*valuations*—is reinforced when we once again turn to his *The Political Factor in the Development of Economic Theory*.

While discussing the "obstacles to the accurate determination of attitudes," Myrdal reflected in passing about an issue which would become a major concern in *An American Dilemma* fifteen years later: " . . . we cannot always believe what people tell us. When asked the account for our political connections, we are liable to use conventional and stereotyped stock phrases which may have little bearing on our actual behavior. Thus American sociologists have found the people's declarations about their views on the Negro problem have very little to do with that conduct in everyday lives." [116]

In the 1954 edition of *The Political Element in the Development of Economic Theory*, Myrdal reveals perhaps the most important preconception that would shape how he explored the Negro problem: the valuation paradigm. At first glance, *An American Dilemma* served as an acid test for critical views on valuations in economic research that Myrdal presented in his *The Political Element in the Development of Economic Theory* and was trying to refine. Explaining why he did not bother to radically revise *The Political Element in the Development of Economic Theory* for English translation, Myrdal said:

Rewriting the book would have forced me to make it conform more closely with the views on the value problem which I have reached after further experience and study. I might here be permitted to refer in particular to "Das Zweck-Mittel-Denken in der Nationalokonomie" (*Zeitschrift fur Nationalokonomie* vol. IV, no. 3, 1933) and to the methodological appendices to *An American Dilemma—The Negro Problem and Modern Democracy* (New York, 1944). [117]

But really, Myrdal "wrote" at least two books in one: a successful critique of American social science which was an extension of long held professional beliefs and a massive convoluted discussion about the Negro problem. The twine met only inconsistently; mostly in the first chapters and in the appendices.

The uneven quality of the contents of *An American Dilemma*, which was intended to be a definitive study on race relations, can be seen in its reviews. The study is cited for its novel methodology, its American Creed concept, and its comprehensive character. No one has applauded it for consistency, because it has none. No one has lauded its theoretical framework, because there is none. Its conservative southern composure and mysticism made the work obsolete before it even came off the press.

An American Dilemma has been viewed as a seminal work because it is too big for most people to read and because at least through the early 1980s no other agency or foundation has successfully attempted such a comprehensive analysis about blacks.[118] More importantly, it has survived because it was done by a great "democratic organization" which selected an alleged objective European who preserved the European-descent interpretation of the Negro problem during a time in which race relations were once again in radical flux. *An American Dilemma* quickly became the convenient bible of post-World War II liberals in policy and social science circles in need of a race relations paradigm that stressed the moral and value dimensions of the Negro problem in a society characterized by state intervention and the delegitimization of Jim Crow. Such a paradigm continued the liberal avoidance of power and pluralistic solutions to the oppression of blacks while midwifing post-World War II liberal advocacy of racial integration.

The words of a French observer of American race relations in the late 1940s conclude this chapter quite sufficiently:

In liberal circles in the United States, however, the book has achieved a reputation that calls for serious reservations. It has been widely hailed as an "exhaustive and objective analysis," a "definitive" study. Abridgements have been published. The book has become a sort of bible for innumerable interracial and cultural clubs, committees and groups. Yet though the book may be without criticism so far as *description* goes, it is feeble in its *interpretation*. It does not answer the question which seems to me to be fundamental: that is, it does not explain *how, by whom* and *why race prejudice was brought into being*. Without calling into question Myrdal's good faith, we must nevertheless make the observation that his method is quite in harmony with the concerns of those who subsidized his work, and serves their interests quite well. For what did the trustees of the Carnegie Corporation actually want? They wanted the evil of race prejudice frankly described, for the same reasons . . . that periodically inspire large-scale public inquiries in the United States. But they didn't want much emphasis given to the remedies for the disease, because they understand thoroughly that no real remedy exists within the framework of the present economic and social system. And they most certainly didn't want the real causes of the evil to be laid bare; for if a cause-and-effect relationship were established between capitalist oppression and race prejudice, the victims of race prejudice would be likely to draw conclusions dangerous to the established order. . . . Myrdal's inquiry could be acceptable to his subsidizers only if it steered clear of these dual reefs and helped conjure away this dual danger.[119]

NOTES

1. Louis Wirth to Frederick Keppel, December 29, 1942, Louis Wirth Papers.
2. The full title is *An American Dilemma: The Negro Problem and Modern Democracy*, but *An American Dilemma* will be used in this chapter.

3. Gunnar Myrdal, *An American Dilemma* (1944; new edition New York: Harper and Row, 1962), p. lxxi.

4. See Carnegie Corporation of New York City Annual Reports.

5. One could argue that the peculiar funding constraints Keppel was under limited his actions, but certainly such restrictions did not prevent him from commenting on contemporary social issues in his annual reports. But as one observer claimed:

The 1930s and 40s when he [Keppel] headed the corporation were marked by severe strain and friction in American life, caused by sweeping changes in mores and values and the accelerated pace of an increasingly urbanized, mobile society. By the early 1930s the tensions were exacerbated by a worldwide depression. Keppel's tenure at Carnegie coincided with the Calvin Coolidge and Herbert Hoover years, the depression, and the early days of the New Deal; when he retired World War II was raging in Europe. Yet, his annual reports contain hardly a hint of the great issues and problems of the times. In the isolated environment of the corporation, training for librarians, adult education conferences, and the distribution of art teaching sets were its preoccupations. [Waldemar A. Nielson, *The Big Foundations* (New York: Columbia University Press, 1972), p. 39]

Other points about Keppel and his Carnegie Corporation leadership style are derived from the same source, pp. 36–40.

6. Anson Phelps Stokes to Frederick Keppel, October 24, 1933, Anson Phelps Stokes Papers.

7. Gunnar Myrdal, *An American Dilemma* (New York: Harper and Brothers, 1962), p. xlviii.

8. William E. B. DuBois had a more critical interpretation of Newton Baker's interest in the race question:

It [the Myrdal study] was made at the suggestion of a prominent American statesman who was a liberal and yet not too liberal. He was a signer of an anti-Jewish pact in Cleveland which kept Jews out of certain residential districts. He hesitated considerably when Secretary of War, as to just how far he should champion the Negro soldier. He came to be a staunch defender of the Negro effort in the war, but when after the war, as member of the Carnegie Board, Newton Baker was asked to vote for certain projects concerning the Negro he said bluntly that he needed more light and he wanted a study of the Negro which would tell what real conditions were. [William E. B. DuBois, Review of *An American Dilemma: The Negro Problem and Modern Democracy*, by Gunnar Myrdal. *Phylon* 5 (June 1944):121]

9. Myrdal, *An American Dilemma* (1962), pp. xlviii-xlix.

10. The following foundations sponsored comprehensive Negro problem study projects in the late 1920s and 1930s: the Laura Spelman Rockefeller Memorial (Charles S. Johnson, *The Negro in American Civilization* [1930]); the Phelps-Stokes Fund (Negro Encyclopedia Project, 1930s and 1940s), and the Julius Rosenwald Fund (B. Schrieke [a Dutchman], *Alien Americans: A Study of Race Relations* [1936]).

11. See Keppel folders in Anson Phelps Stokes Papers. Anson Phelps Stokes wrote extensively to Frederick Keppel about the origins, problems, and prospects of his Negro Encyclopedia project.

12. Unlike the other foundations discussed in this book, the pre–World War II Carnegie Corporation did not appoint blacks to its governing board or "kitchen cabinet."

13. Donald Young to Frederick Keppel, June 14, 1937, Carnegie Corporation (hereafter CC) Archives.

14. Points made in the two preceding paragraphs are based on: Gunnar Myrdal, *The Political Element in the Development of Economic Theory* (Cambridge: Harvard Uni-

versity Press, 1953); Ruml and Frank comments in May 1937 Correspondence Files of the Negro Study, CC Archives. About Myrdal's 1930–1931 fellowship, see Rockefeller Fellowship Directory, Rockefeller Archive Center. Ruml acted as an informant for Keppel while serving as a Julius Rosenwald Fund trustee, as well as when he was a Rockefeller Foundation officer. Once Keppel noted in a memo about a meeting with Ruml, "He is a trustee of the Rosenwald Fund and absolutely confirmed everything Embree said." June 17, 1932, Keppel memo in Beardsley Ruml of the Spelman Fund correspondence, CC Archives.

15. Frederick Keppel to Gunnar Myrdal, August 12 or 13, 1937, CC Archives.

16. Myrdal, *An American Dilemma* (1962), p. xxv.

17. Myrdal to Keppel, August 30, 1937, CC Archives.

18. Myrdal to Keppel, October 7, 1937, CC Archives.

19. Ibid.

20. Ibid.

21. Ibid.

22. Ibid.

23. Ibid.

24. Shortly after *An American Dilemma* was published, Louis Wirth as associate editor of the *American Journal of Sociology* wrote to Gunnar Myrdal in part:

Since you are the arch authority on race relations and particularly the Negro, we would like to ask you to write a little review or as long of a review as you want to do on Horace Cayton's and St. Clair Drake's *Black Metropolis*. If your office or time forbids you, perhaps you can induce Alva to do it. I think the American audience would like to hear what you think about one of the Negro studies which has come out since your magnum opus. [Wirth to Myrdal, October (?), 1945, Louis Wirth Papers]

Myrdal responded in part:

I was happy to receive Cayton's and St. Clair Drake's *Black Metropolis*. Please forward to them my cordial greetings and congratulations. I will not be able, however, to write the review on the book. I am far away from the scene and the problem. *An American Dilemma* was my first and last contribution to the discussion of the Negro problem in America, and of course I am terribly busy in my new office. . . . [Myrdal to Wirth, October 24, 1945, Wirth Papers] Also see, *An American Dilemma* (1962), XIV.

25. For an overview of stranger or "outsider" social research, see Robert K. Merton, "Insiders and Outsiders: A Chapter in the Sociology of Knowledge," *American Journal of Sociology* (July 1972).

26. Myrdal to Keppel, October 7, 1937, CC Archives.

27. At most, *An American Dilemma* is known as a comprehensive work in the sense of being replete with data presentations about numerous aspects of the Negro problem as a policy issue. It is not comprehensive in examining the quality of the inner workings of Afro-American life.

28. Donald Young to Frederick Keppel, January 30, 1937, CC Archives.

29. Gunnar Myrdal to Frederick Keppel, October 7, 1937, CC Archives.

30. Particularly the following monographs were instrumental in shaping *An American Dilemma*: Louis Wirth and Herbert Goldhamer, "The Hybrid and the Problem of Miscengenation"; Guy Johnson, "The Stereotypes of the American Negro"; Ralph Bunche, "Conceptions and Ideologies of the Negro Problem," "The Programs, Ideologies, Tactics, and Achievements of Negro Betterment and Interracial Organizations,"

"A Brief and Tentative Analysis of Negro Leadership," "The Political Status of the Negro"; Allison Davis, "Negro Churches and Associations in the Lower South"; E. Franklin Frazier, "Recreation and Amusement among American Negroes," "Stories of Experiences with Whites"; Edward A. Shils, "The Bases of Social Stratification in Negro Society"; Doxey Wilkerson, "The Negro in American Education" (fragment); T. J. Woofter, Jr., "The Negro and Agricultural Policy"; and Charles S. Johnson, "Patterns of Negro Segregation."

31. Myrdal, *An American Dilemma* (1962), p. XIX.

32. Mildred M. Williams, *The Jeanes Story: A Chapter in the History of American Education, 1908–1968*, (Atlanta: Southern Education Foundation, 1979); Arthur D. Wright, *The Negro Rural School Fund* (Washington, D.C.: The Negro Rural School Fund, Inc., 1933).

33. James Dillard and Hollis Frissell correspondence, General Education Board Archives, Rockefeller Archive Center.

34. This is best seen in the letters of sympathy from southerners written to the General Education Board when Jackson Davis died in 1947. See Jackson Davis folders, General Education Board Archives.

35. See excerpts about race relations in Jackson Davis diary, General Education Board Archives.

36. Interview with William T. Couch, January 29, 1944, Jackson Davis, General Education Board Archives.

37. Jackson Davis to William T. Couch, February 11, 1944, General Education Board Archives.

38. Jackson Davis folders, General Education Board Archives.

39. Frederick Keppel to Raymond C. Fosdick, June 8, 1938, CC Archives.

40. Fred McCuiston to Jackson Davis, November 10, 1938, and Howard Odum to Jackson Davis, October 28, 1938, General Education Board Archives. The major urban dwellers Myrdal and Sterner did see were the businessmen and journalists referred to in the text as well as law enforcement officers.

41. There are two points which cannot be overstressed. First, the disappointment of foundation officers and informants over Myrdal's and Sterner's difficulty in catching on. The following excerpt from Jackson Davis's (JD) diary, which is a record of a meeting with Carnegie officers Charles Dollard and R. M. Lester (RML) soon after the trip reveals this disappointment and the interest of Davis in giving the Myrdal study a southern composure.

We discussed JD's recent trip with Myrdal and Sterner. JD brought out some misgivings on the part of persons of both races which seemed to indicate that Myrdal's quick mind and remarkably successful work in Sweden made him jump to conclusions about southern problems, instead of keeping his mind open with a willingness to hear and appraise discussion by people most concerned with the several aspects of southern life. However, Myrdal's remark to JD that he came back from his trip feeling that he knew nothing about the situation and that he wanted now to read and study and think through his own plans before taking any further steps in the field, indicated that he had sensed this difficulty himself, and it would be best to say nothing further about it. RML said that Myrdal had made the same statement to FPK [Frederick P. Keppel].

JD suggested that Myrdal spend considerable time in the South. The value of his study would inhere chiefly in his own first hand study and observation in the field. The interpretation of his observations from his detached point of view and background of Swedish experience would then give us the findings of a competent foreign observer. It is necessary that he spend . . . considerable time in the South and make wide contacts in order to validate his study in the public mind. Otherwise, it would be discounted as an academic effort of a person unfamiliar with the history, traditions and general framework in which race relations and southern social problems must be worked out. [Jackson Davis interview with Charles Dollard and R. M. Lester, November 17, 1938, Jackson Davis diary, General Education Board Archives]

Second, to make sure that the Swedish social scientists developed a positive or at least not too negative impression of the plantation South, at least on one occasion, tenants were screened for interviews—in Clarksdale, Mississippi. Davis wrote to the planter after visiting his plantation these compliments:

Your tenants were in simple homes, but they were screened, they were well kept, and they all had gardens, live stock, and the farmers had an attitude of interest and hopefulness in contrast to much that we had seen. [Jackson Davis to P. F. Williams, October 26, 1938, General Education Board Archives]

42. Jackson Davis, Review of *An American Dilemma: The Negro Problem an Modern Democracy* by Gunnar Myrdal, March 30, 1944, General Education Board Archives.

43. Gunnar Myrdal, January 28, 1939, Memorandum to Frederick Keppel, CC Archives.

44. Thus I am arguing that although in the spring of 1939 Myrdal met with numerous American social scientists who reviewed the memorandum and helped him modify some of his ideas and plans, Myrdal did not deviate very much from most of his original assumptions and strategies as seen in the organization of the research project and in the contents of *An American Dilemma*.

45. Gunnar Myrdal, January 28, 1939, Memorandum to Frederick Keppel, CC Archives.

46. Ibid.

47. Ibid.

48. Gunnar Myrdal, *An American Dilemma*, Chapters 33–36.

49. Gunnar Myrdal, January 28, 1939, Memorandum to Frederick Keppel, CC Archives.

50. Ibid.

51. Herbert Aptheker, *The Negro People in America: A Critique of Gunnar Myrdal's "An American Dilemma"* (New York: International Publishers, 1946).

52. Aptheker, *The Negro People*; and Daniel Guerin, *Negroes on the March: A Frenchman's Report on the American Negro Struggle* (René Julliard, Paris, 1951). See Myrdal, *An American Dilemma* (1944 ed.), pp. 592–598; 667–688; 787–788; 890–892.

53. Gunnar Myrdal, January 28, 1939, Memorandum to Frederick Keppel, CC Archives.

54. Ibid.

55. Ibid.

56. Especially Samuel Stouffer, William Ogburn, E. Franklin Frazier, Louis Wirth (all trained at Chicago or on the Chicago faculty); Guy B. Jonnson and Arthur Raper (Chapel Hill). Particularly E. Franklin Frazier, Charles S. Johnson, Louis Wirth, and Guy B. Johnson did not believe in a unique Afro-American culture and wrote fervently against the plausability of it.

57. Melville Herskovits, *The Myth of the Negro Past* (New York: Harper and Brothers, 1941; repr. Boston: Beacon Press, 1969).

58. Gunnar Myrdal, January 28, 1939, Memorandum to Frederick Keppel, CC Archives.

59. Ibid.

60. Ibid. There is some evidence that Myrdal was aware of a possible southern bias in his study; his concentrated travels in the South and his dependence on native collaborators lead to the regionally biased focus of *An American Dilemma*. See Carnegie Negro Study folders, E. Franklin Frazier Papers.

61. Donald Young to Frederick Keppel, January 30, 1937, CC Archives.

62. Howard W. Odum, Review of Gunnar Myrdal's *An American Dilemma*, GEB Archives. This was a draft paper later published in Odum's *Social Forces*.

63. Gunnar Myrdal, January 28, 1939, Memorandum to Frederick Keppel, cc Archives.

64. Ibid.

65. Ibid.

66. This is especially apparent when one compares the major themes of *An American Dilemma* with the ideas of Robert E. Park, Charles S. Johnson, Louis Wirth, and Guy B. Johnson. See John H. Stanfield, *Race Rationalization as a Cohort Experience* (Ph.D. dissertation, Northwestern University, 1977) and John H. Stanfield, "Race Relations Research and Black Americans Between the Two World Wars," *Journal of Ethnic Studies* (Fall 1983): 61–93.

67. Black political scientist Ralph Bunche, though an executive staff member, did not have as much formal decision-making power as his white colleagues. When Myrdal or other senior principal investigators were absent or busy elsewhere, white social scientists such as Arnold Rose or Guy B. Johnson were given the reins of the project or a part of it. See correspondence generated from the central Negro Study Office, CC Archives, and Guy B. Johnson to Louis Wirth, correspondence in the spring of 1940 when Myrdal returned to Sweden for almost a year, Louis Wirth Papers.

68. Johnson became an especially good friend of the Myrdals. See Myrdal folder, Charles E. Johnson Special Collection. Louis Wirth was impressed enough with Gunnar Myrdal to recommend him for a honorary degree from the University of Chicago; Louis Wirth to Theodore Schultz, February 1, 1949, Louis Wirth Papers. See note 111 about Frazier's friendship with the Myrdals.

69. Richard Sterner to Jackson Davis, April 30, 1941, General Education Board Archives.

70. Horace R. Cayton, *Long Old Road* (New York: Trident Press, 1965). He was born in 1903 and reared in Seattle, Washington.

71. Horace R. Cayton to Louis Wirth, July 8, 1934, Louis Wirth Papers.

72. Horace R. Cayton–Louis Wirth correspondence, Louis Wirth Papers.

73. There is much evidence that Cayton's work, which would be published in 1945 with St. Clair Drake as *Black Metropolis*, was planned in the mid–1930s. Cayton wrote extensively to Robert E. Park, Charles S. Johnson, and Louis Wirth about the study's research design. Whenever Wirth wrote to correspondents about *Black Metropolis* he referred to it as Cayton *and* Drake's work. As the correspondence reveals, *Black Metropolis* was to be and became the last great Chicago school urban race-relations study rooted in Parkian conceptions. St. Clair Drake and Horace R. Cayton, *Black Metropolis* (New York: Harcourt, Brace and Company, 1945). This point is not meant to take credit from St. Claire Drake, who certainly contributed to the writing of *Black Metropolis*, but to give overdue credit to Cayton as the work's progenitor and senior author.

74. See unsigned and undated memorandum from black community leaders criticizing the University of Chicago, in Horace R. Cayton folder, Louis Wirth Papers.

75. Horace R. Cayton to Fred Kramer, March 3, 1944, Louis Wirth Papers.

76. Wirth to Cayton, March 7, 1944, Louis Wirth Papers.

77. Cayton to Wirth, March 8, 1944, Louis Wirth Papers.

78. Horace R. Cayton, Memorandum Regarding the General Study of the Negro Community in Chicago, no date [1939?]; Cayton to Wirth, April 14, 1936, Louis Wirth Papers; Robert E. Park to Horace R. Cayton, April 22, 1939, Louis Wirth Papers.

79. Cayton to Wirth, May 28, 1937, Louis Wirth Papers.

80. Ibid.

81. See unsigned and undated memorandum from black community leaders criticizing the University of Chicago in Horace R. Cayton folder, Louis Wirth Papers.

82. This dependency relationship between Cayton and the University of Chicago was apparent in the absence of mention about the contributions of the University of Chicago to the maintenance of Southside Chicago racial caste relations in his *Black Metropolis*.

83. Horace R. Cayton to W. Lloyd Warner, no date [1939], Louis Wirth Papers.

84. Considering how much time community fieldwork would take, it is amazing Myrdal toyed with the idea of doing such a study. The only way it could be done would be if someone such as Cayton was already well into data collection and analysis.

85. Horace R. Cayton to Gunnar Myrdal, February 26, 1940, Louis Wirth Papers; and Memorandum on Collaboration Between the Study of the Negro in Chicago and the Negro in America, Louis Wirth Papers.

86. Cayton to Myrdal, February 29, 1940, Louis Wirth Papers; Cayton to Wirth, March 4, 1940, Louis Wirth Papers.

87. Myrdal to Cayton, March 1, 1940, Louis Wirth Papers.

88. Cayton to Myrdal, March 2, 1940, Louis Wirth Papers. While, for reasons which can only be speculated, a large number of prominent race relations scholars allowed the Negro problem study staff to exploit their skills and deprive them of proper academic credit, Cayton and a few others stood up for their academic rights. Cayton's expression of concern to Myrdal about proper academic recognition raises ethical questions about how the Carnegie Negro Problem Study was carried on:

One of the principal difficulties is the matter of my obtaining academic credit for the study. As I have devoted approximately three years to this study as well as considerable finance, I would like to publish a small volume outlining the findings. As you are aware, I had about 18 research assistants who were responsible for individual monographs. Some of which have been mimeographed. I allowed each research assistant to sign his own monograph and I was to synthesize them and sign the general statement. If the monographs are released over the signatures of these individuals and if the "cream" of the material is skimmed by the study of *The Negro in America*, I will not receive the type of credit which I had in mind. [Memo from Cayton to Myrdal entitled Collaboration Between the Study of the Negro in Chicago and the Negro in America, Wirth Papers]

Since Cayton did not wish to be in the position of denying use of material to any study which would find such material useful (same memo), being a believer in cooperative scientific research, he proposed his alternative plan to Myrdal which would have preserved his academic integrity. Since Myrdal was reluctant to accept Cayton's suggestion, Cayton went his own way, transforming "The Study of the Negro in Chicago" into *Black Metropolis*.

89. Cayton to Wirth, December 1, 1948, Louis Wirth Papers.

90. Wirth to Cayton, January 17, 1949, Louis Wirth Papers.

91. Horace R. Cayton *Lond Old Road*.

92. Letters Wirth wrote on behalf of Arnold Rose and Horace R. Cayton are in the Louis Wirth Papers.

93. Frederick Keppel to Louis Wirth, December 23, 1942; Keppel to Wirth, January 25, 1943. In the December 23rd letter Keppel said in part,

I am worried about the Community chapters which Rose has written for the Myrdal book. Chapter 43 (Institutions) seems to lack the direction of a mature mind, although on the surface, it reads smoothly enough. To me little things appear to be over-supported and the big things too often merely asserted. Also there is a patronizing and pitying tone about the Negroes which Myrdal himself has avoided, and which I think is very bad medicine. The succeeding Chapter 44, is better, although it seems to me that Rose has not used his material very intelligently in the section on Negro Culture and Personality, but here again there is throughout a note of immaturity.

94. Arnold Rose Folders, Louis Wirth Papers.

95. The fact that Myrdal chose Ralph Bunche rather than a more eminent and critical black race relations researcher such as E. Franklin Frazier or Charles S. Johnson to be in his inner circle is even more proof of his interest in controlling interpretations of the Afro-American experience. Interview with E. Franklin Edwards, May 1984.

96. For instance, Keppel, who retired while the Negro Problem Study was in progress, wrote this letter of thanks to Louis Wirth:

Though my connection with the Carnegie Corporation's affairs has been pretty tenuous, I do want to thank you for the fine job you have done for us on the community chapters. Mrs. Anderson has told me all about it. The fact that Rose adopted your suggestions, bait, hook and sinker, is not the least of your achievements. [Keppel to Wirth, January 28, 1943, Louis Wirth Papers].

After Myrdal left for Sweden in September, 1942, Rose wrote to Wirth, asking him to look over additional materials, stating, "I don't suppose—with all the other work you are doing—that you are too anxious to get this extra burden, but we wouldn't feel safe without your criticism first" (Rose to Wirth, September 30, 1942, Louis Wirth Papers).

97. At least the following individuals contributed to *An American Dilemma* through writing monographs for Gunnar Myrdal: M. F. Ashley-Montagu; Margaret Brenman; Sterling Brown; Ralph Bunche; Barbara Burks; Allison Davis; Harold F. Dorn; J. G. St. Clair Drake; G. James Fleming; Lyonel C. Florant; E. Franklin Frazier; T. Arnold Hill; E. C. Isbell; Guion G. Johnson; Louise K. Kiser; Dudley Kirk; Ruth Landes; Gunnar Lange; T. C. McCormick; Paul Norgren; E. Nelson Palmer; Arthur Raper; Ira deA. Reid; Edward A. Shils; Bernhard J. Stern; Samuel A. Stouffer; Lyonel C. Florant; Doxey Wilkerson; T. J. Woofter, Jr.; Melville J. Herskovits; Charles S. Johnson; Richard Sterner; Otto Klineberg; Benjamin Malzberg; Louis Wirth; Herbert Goldhamer; Eugene L. Horowitz; Guy Johnson.

98. Prior to leaving for Sweden for what would be almost a year away from the United States in the spring of 1940, Myrdal asked his American collaborators to work towards completing the study and developing comprehensive annotated bibliographies for his use when he returned. After Myrdal returned and looked over the work done in his absence, Charles Dollard wrote a "Memorandum to Collaborators on the Negro Study" (March 31, 1941), which began:

As all of you have doubtless heard, Dr. Myrdal returned to the United States two weeks ago and has now retreated to Jackson, Mississippi to read over the manuscripts which you have prepared for him in his absence. In leafing through the memoranda, he was rather disturbed to note the absence of the critical bibliographies which he had requested from all collaborators in a special memorandum dated October 31, 1939.

Dollard proceeded to remind the researchers that through binding rules they promised Myrdal annotated bibliographies of major sources which were "concise, descriptive, and critical." About monograph preparation, Dollard said,

If a "Major Source" has been commented upon extensively in the body of the report, it should be listed in the bibliography without annotation. However, page citations should be given to those sections of the report in which it is discussed [Dollard quoted this from the October 31, 1939 memorandum]. To an American scholar preparing a report on the Negro, such critical evaluations of the sources of data would be perhaps only of evidential importance, since he would himself be in a position to make judgments concerning the relative weight of authority which should be assigned to each source and the degree of bias to be discounted. In Dr. Myrdal's case, however, it is of central importance that his collaborators gave him the benefit of their own great familiarity with the literature in their respective fields, since he himself has not been able, in the very nature of things, to read even a small portion of the thousands of books and articles from which the data have been gathered. Accordingly he urges that all of the collaborators forward annotated bibliographies to me at their earliest convenience. *If the pressure of other work keeps you from doing the complete job, I hope that you at least send me within the next ten days a list of the major works of first importance in your particular area, so that we can supply him with reviews of these which appeared at the time of their publication.* [Dollard's emphasis] Memorandum found in the Louis Wirth Papers.

99. R. Fred Wacker, "Culture, Prejudice, and An American Dilemma," *Phylon* 42 (1981):255–261.

100. Doxey Wilkerson–Jackson Davis correspondence, General Education Board Archives.

101. N. C. Newbold to Jackson Davis, April 13, 1940, General Education Board Archives.

102. Jackson Davis to Samuel Stouffer, August 12, 1940, General Education Board Archives. See excerpts in Jackson Davis diary which allude negatively to Wilkerson's leftist orientation. General Education Board Archives.

103. Guerin, *Negroes on the March*, pp. 1–26.

104. Myrdal to Wirth, August 5, 1942, Louis Wirth Papers.

105. Louis Wirth, *The Ghetto* (1928; repr. Chicago: The University of Chicago Press, 1956).

106. Albert J. Reiss, Jr., Interview, August 1983.

107. Ibid. Also one should not discount the negative impact of anti-semitism in academia and policy circles on Louis Wirth's career. Albert J. Reiss, Jr., Interview, August 1983.

108. This made the Carnegie Negro problem study a peculiar extension of Chicago sociology, especially since Louis Wirth heavily edited the entire manuscript and his colleagues on the advisory committee supervised the completion and publication of monographs.

109. Albert J. Reiss, Jr., interview, August 1982.

110. Wirth's hectic schedule prevented him from joining the Myrdal staff until the summer of 1942 (Myrdal to Wirth, March 24, 1939, April 13, 1939, Louis Wirth Papers) but apparently his student Arnold Rose served as his representative. In an April 2, 1942, letter, Myrdal first approached Wirth about editing his manuscript so he could complete it as much as possible before returning to Sweden in September 1942:

Under normal circumstances I would, perhaps, have liked to have had a great number of critics read the manuscript before publishing it. Now a major consideration must be that I don't have space in my time schedule to utilize more than a bare minimum. In order, nevertheless, to be able to benefit maximally, it is more important that the critics are selected with utmost care and with a view to their effectiveness, Mr. Keppel and Mr. Dollard are giving me the very best type of critique from the viewpoint of the cultivated layman-citizen. In addition, we will probably want one of the outstanding newspaper editors of the south to read through the manuscript. The most important thing for me is, however, to get an overall reading by an experienced fellow social scientist with broad experience and interests in methodology. It is not to be assumed that such a person, more than the general reader, will agree with me on every point or even on all of the main approaches. In a work which is not a committee work, that should not even be desirable, but, nevertheless, such an overall criticism by a competent social scientist will be most valuable in my final version of the manuscript. In the letter to Mr. Keppel, which I so far have been mainly quoting, I continued, "There is actually only one person who, I think, would be ideal for the purpose; namely, Professor Louis Wirth of the University of Chicago." Mr. Keppel agrees with me and I am now writing you to ask formally if you will do me—and the Carnegie Corporation—this highly valued service.

Wirth said yes, he would do the editing and spent June through August 1942 in New York City completing it. Myrdal's selection of Wirth over more seasoned black scholars such as Charles S. Johnson or E. Franklin Frazier indicated either his own reluctance or that of Carnegie officers to give blacks significant decision-making power in the Negro study. All cited correspondence is in the Louis Wirth Papers.

111. Extensive comments on chapters are in Gunnar Myrdal folders, Louis Wirth Papers. Besides Louis Wirth, Gunnar Myrdal contacted E. Franklin Frazier to do extensive editing work for him. Initially he was asked to work two weeks but ended up helping Myrdal revise his chapters from June through December 1942.

Unlike in the case of Wirth, Frazier was not asked from the start to come to New York City and join the Myrdal fraternity. Only a little later did Dollard extend an invitation to Frazier but, obviously, it was not of the same status as the offer extended to Wirth. Also, Frazier assisted Myrdal in a way which was quite patronizing. He openly disagreed with fellow black scholars, calling them by name and gave Myrdal personal anecdotal information about white/black relations. Not a few of the "personal observations by Negroes" found in *An American Dilemma* are E. Franklin Frazier's experiences. Many were taken from the Memo Frazier did for Myrdal (Carnegie Negro study folders, E. Franklin Frazier Papers, Howard University, interview with G. Franklin Edwards, May 1, 1984).

Although Myrdal relied greatly on Frazier to give him a "Negro" view of things, some times to the point of pressuring him explicitly to do so, he paid little attention to Frazier's more critical editorial comments. Myrdal listened more to the substantive remarks of the more conservative Wirth. This is a crucial point since although Frazier agreed with Myrdal that the Negro problem was basically a moral dilemma in a democratic society, he disagreed with him on other major interpretations. In fact, he disagreed so much it was a wonder, at first glance, that he worked so long with Myrdal. This may have been due to the close relationship he had with colleague Alva Myrdal, which dated back to Frazier's tenure in Copenhagen in the early 1920s. Frazier may have assisted Myrdal more out of admiration for Alva than a respect for Gunnar Myrdal's race relations perspectives. Frazier's friendship with Alva Myrdal resulted in her getting him appointed to a high position in UNESCO during the 1950s. Interview with G. Franklin Edwards, May 1984.

112. The general liberal paradigm of race relations in the interwar and post–World

War II years is premised on optimistic outcomes of multiracialism and thus stresses statistics and statements which emphasize progress and assimilation.

113. Wirth to Keppel, January 5, 1945, Louis Wirth Papers. Since Myrdal left for Sweden in September, 1942, leaving final manuscript preparation in the hands of his staff, there was not time for overall editing.

114. Myrdal to Keppel, June 22, 1942, Louis Wirth Papers; Myrdal to Wirth, July 2, 1942, Louis Wirth Papers.

115. See Myrdal, *An American Dilemma* (1962), pp. lvi–lvii. Wirth's editing skills are also seen in *An American Dilemma*'s methodological appendixes. Although both Wirth and Myrdal had a sociology of knowledge touch, Wirth had the added expertise in race relations which enabled him to apply the valuations issue to the sociological analysis of the Negro problem. His heavy editing or shall we say writing of the methodological appendixes is the only contribution to *An American Dilemma* Wirth claimed after the project was completed. Albert J. Reiss interview, August 1982.

116. Myrdal, *The Political Element in the Development of Economic Theory*, p. 200.

117. Ibid., p. vii.

118. More than anything else, commentators have been impressed with the bulk of *An American Dilemma*, which presents the false impression that bigness is equivalent to thoroughness, coherence, and definitive status. In the 1970s, the Carnegie Corporation unsuccessfully attempted to re-do *An American Dilemma*. As this book goes to press, the National Academy of Science is searching for a director for a well-financed update of the study.

119. Guerin, *Negroes on the March*, p. 18.

8

Philanthropy and Jim Crow in American Social Science: A Theoretical Context

There are three important matters about the pre–World War II foundation financing of social science enterprises that can be expressed in terms of hypotheses: (1) that givers have consciousness and through it produce knowledge; (2) that giving is a generation phenomenon; and (3) that giving is a patrimonial tradition. These hypotheses will be used to give needed theoretical context to empirical points made and implied about philanthropy and Jim Crow in American social science.

GIVERS HAVE CONSCIOUSNESS AND THROUGH IT PRODUCE KNOWLEDGE

The first hypothesis is that funding elites give to create societal change or re-establish order as well as respond to such phenomena. This implies the necessity of reconstructing the world views of financiers and their organizations, in order to understand their giving strategies. This observation is important since official historians of funding institutions such as foundations tend to portray their institutional subjects as passive gatekeepers who at most select beneficiaries from application pools. Since financiers often have their own agendas they frequently create the gate as well as preserve it.

The officers of the Laura Spelman Rockefeller Memorial who were the first foundation administrators to substantially support institutional social science, must be thought of in this way. When Beardsley Ruml became the youthful director of the Memorial in 1923, he designed a funding policy which had an explicit definition of social science, which led him to support social research and institutions that conformed with his beliefs. Ruml concluded that the only way social sciences would be of value to a rapidly urbanizing and industrializing society was that they be practical and geared towards resolving social problems.

The old social science which was speculative social philosophy had to be replaced with social science guided by measurable empirical techniques devoid of theorizing and reformism.

Ruml's positive definition of social science and, indeed, of "scientific" social work, logically influenced his staff selection, internal task organization, and ultimately, the foundation's funding programs. He hired Leonard Outhwaite, a disciple of scientific personnel management, as the race relations program officer. Syndor Walker, an advocate for merging social work schools into academic institutions, was employed to coordinate the scientific social work program. Lawrence Frank was recruited to develop a scientifically based child development program. Ruml was in charge of the domestic and international social science program. These officers along with other staff members were a cohesive, social circle held together through similar ages, educational backgrounds, and definitions of social science and scientific social work.

Ruml's philosophy of social science led him to seek seasoned social scientists who had positivistic approaches. He believed that such research was most beneficial when done in already established institutions. This assumption led him to elite white male universities. The most apparent example of Ruml's selection preferences can be seen in his overwhelming support for his alma mater, the University of Chicago. Social scientists Charles E. Merriam, Ernest Burgess, L. H. Marshall, and Robert E. Park were then embarking on the new social science to which Ruml was attached. It is no wonder that the Chicago Local Community Research Institute demanded so much attention from the Memorial. Charles E. Merriam quickly became the Memorial's in-house social scientist, exemplified in his initial chairmanship of the Memorial sponsored Social Science Research Council.

Ruml's effort to nationalize positivistic social science resulted in his foundation's establishment of the Social Science Research Council and its sponsorship of a fellowship program to develop a generation of empirically oriented social scientists. In each case, Ruml's plan was to create the structures needed to develop the practical social science he felt was the way the human sciences would best fit into American and European life. Meanwhile, in their assigned areas, Outhwaite, Walker, and Frank developed fellowship and research programs and supported researchers and organizations that cultivated scientism. Outhwaite, for instance, established a fellowship program to finance the graduate education of blacks interested in "scientific" race relations research; appropriated funds to the research endeavors of the National Urban League and the Association for the Study of Negro Life; and organized a major conference on scientific race relations research. He was a progenitor of the Fisk University Social Science Department and Charles S. Johnson's directorship of it. Outhwaite also sponsored the race relations research of Chapel Hill sociologist Howard W. Odum, often advising him in the lines of research he should investigate.

The definition of social science Ruml and his staff adhered to ultimately guided their appropriations, which eventually contributed to the institutionalization of a positivistic social science that was divorced from humanistic concerns. The memorial officers contributed to the widely held belief that the social sciences and humanities were distant polar extremes. But the major point of this subsection is that either intentionally or through taken-for-granted assumptions, financiers are creators of markets of ideas. Only retrospectively in their official histories or published annual reports, for instance, do they mystify their contributions and concentrate on the work of their beneficiaries selected through desired formal criteria.

GIVING IS A GENERATION PHENOMENON

As the core of research financing has shifted from individual to organizational patrons in the twentieth century, it has taken on a distinct generational flavor in two ways. We notice that from World War I on, there has been a tendency for giving institutional elites to recruit keepers and appropriators of their funds from the same sociological generation. That is, people who become foundation officers and government agency administrators may not be of the same biological age range, but they share experiences in the same historical milieu which shapes the definition of science. Since giving institutional elites have a vested interest in employing those most knowledgable about the newest paradigms, then drawing from the most contemporary sociological generation makes sense. To do otherwise would ultimately waste funds and lead to the development of outmoded programs which would become an embarassment to the giving institution.

Second, as the twentieth century has progressed, there has been a population explosion of giving organizations that appropriate funds for research. This has stimulated a need for giving institutional elites, and their keepers and appropriators of funds, to coordinate their giving or at least stabilize communication channels to share information about policies and receiving researchers and institutions. Occasional conferences and formal associations have been effective mechanisms to assure that givers in the same field at least know who their institutional and personal competitors and colleagues are and a broad sense about what they are doing. The coordination of giving also conserves capital, since it prevents needless overlap in supporting researchers and their institutions. It also encourages giving institutions to share in sponsoring research.

The need to coordinate giving on an organizational level has contributed to a generation affect. Although certainly there is a great diversity in personal values, world views, and organizational resources, the coordination of giving produces a network which standardizes procedures and general giving philosophies. It creates, in the anthropological sense, a culture of giving in which its participants adhere to similar traditions, values, and norms. This culture is structured in an organizational field which identifies the keeping and appropriating of funds as a career line. This last point is seen in the ease by which administrators of giving institutions exchange personnel. Although in the process of shifting from foundation to foundation or foundation to government agency an individual must make the necessary institutional adjustments, he/she will at least still be participating in the same organizational field, and therefore will know the routines of the giving. All of this can be demonstrated empirically through noting the contours and the personnel of the pre–World War II sponsorship of social science.

Will Alexander of the Atlanta based civil rights organization, the Commission for Interracial Cooperation (1919–1944), was on the Kitchen Cabinet of the General Education Board (1919–1944) and of the Laura Spelman Rockefeller Memorial (1923–1929), as well as vice president (1930–1948) and co-director of the Race Relation Division (1940–1948) of the Julius Rosenwald Fund. His organization, which incidentally had a social research department, received substantial grants from the Laura Spelman Rockefeller Memorial, the General Education Board and the Rockefeller Foundation.

Jackson Davis was the major General Education Board southern programs officer from 1915 to 1947. During this span of time, he was on the Kitchen Cabinet of the Carnegie Corporation and the Laura Spelman Rockefeller Memorial and served on the board of the Phelps-Stokes Fund, becoming the fund's president in 1947 shortly before his death. He was a visiting VIP to South Africa in the mid–1930s under Carnegie Corporation auspices.

Edwin Rogers Embree was a Rockefeller Foundation executive from 1917–1928. In late 1927, Julius Rosenwald, a General Education Board trustee, offered Embree the presidency of his newly organized namesake foundation. While a Rockefeller Foundation executive, Embree was a member of the Laura Spelman Rockefeller Memorial's Kitchen Cabinet.

Charles Spurgeon Johnson, an eminent Chicago trained sociologist, was with the National Urban League during the 1920s before moving to Fisk University, where he became director of the Social Science Department (1928–1946) and then university president (1947–1956). Shortly before leaving the National Urban League, Johnson joined the Kitchen Cabinets of the Laura Spelman Rockefeller Memorial and the Julius Rosenwald Fund. During the 1930s and 1940s, he was invited to join the Kitchen Cabinet of the General Education Board. He became a trustee of the Julius Rosenwald Fund in 1934, and co-director of the foundation's Race Relations Division (with Will W. Alexander) from 1942 to 1948. The financing of Johnson's distinguished Social Science Department came from the Laura Spelman Rockefeller Memorial, the General Education Board, the Julius Rosenwald Fund, and the American Missionary Association.

Charles E. Merriam, father of modern political science, was the major social scientist on the Laura Spelman Rockefeller Memorial's Kitchen Cabinet and was the first chairman of the memorial-sponsored Social Science Research Council. In the early 1930s, he became executive director of the Spelman Fund while Beardsley Ruml served as chairman of the board of trustees. The memorial's generous financing of the Chicago Local Community Research Institute was a consequence of Ruml's admiration of Merriam and James R. Angell.

Beardsley Ruml was an officer with the Carnegie Corporation before moving on to the Laura Spelman Rockefeller Memorial in 1923. During his tenure with the memorial and long after, he served as a member of the Carnegie Corporation's Kitchen Cabinet. It was Ruml who recommended Gunnar Myrdal to Carnegie officers when they were searching for a director for a comprehensive study on the Negro problem. Ruml was one of the first and one of the most influential trustees of Embree's Julius Rosenwald Fund. While a Rosenwald trustee, Ruml served as dean of the Division of Social Science of the University of Chicago and the Spelman Fund's chairman of the board of trustees.

As a final example, Howard W. Odum became the long-time chairman of the University of North Carolina, Chapel Hill, Sociology Department in 1921. The program he established was financed through the Laura Spelman Rockefeller Memorial. After it was absorbed into the Rockefeller Foundation in 1929, the Julius Rosenwald Fund, the Rockefeller Foundation and General Education Board became Odum's institutional sponsors. As the white South's foremost social scientist, Odum served on the Kitchen Cabinets of the Laura Spelman Rockefeller Memorial, the Julius Rosenwald Fund, the Carnegie Corporation, the General Education Board, and the Rockefeller Foundation. He also served as trustee on the Julius Rosenwald Fund.

GIVING IS A PATRIMONIAL TRADITION

The third hypothesis is that the culture and organization of giving is a patrimonial tradition. When focusing on foundations, this seems a commonsensical assertion since the origins, symbolism, and control of foundations are derived from a wealthy donating family. The Julius Rosenwald Fund was founded by Julius Rosenwald and his family. The name of the foundation symbolizes such origins and the foundation's board was controlled informally and formally by the Rosenwald clan. The story repeats itself, more or less, when we turn to the Rockefeller foundations, the Phelps-Stokes Fund, the Carnegie Corporation, the Russell Sage Foundation, the Ford Foundation, the Peabody Education Fund, and the Jeanes Fund. But there were more subtle ways in which foundation giving, in this case to social science, was a patrimonial tradition than the obvious questions of origins, symbolism, and institutional control. We can speculate that this more complex depiction of giving as a patrimonial tradition can be applied to other forms of giving institutions such as government agencies.

No matter how formal or bureaucratic appropriation criteria developed, basically, pre–World War II foundation administrators gave their funds to individuals they trusted. Indeed, we can say with risk of redundancy, that the formal criteria symbolize what giving institution administrators consider to be the ideal traits of those they trust most with their funds. When Edwin Embree spoke of first-rate social scientists, he had in mind his favorite social scientist, Charles S. Johnson. This point about foundations giving their money to those they trust is crucial, since it strips away the ideology of giving, which makes fund appropriating a relationship with impersonal receiving institutions, rather than interpersonal relations between giving institution administrators and sponsored researchers.

We can go a step further in contending that often, particularly when it involves a relationship stretching over many years, the dyadic bond of trust which solidifies between givers and receivers of funds becomes an emotionally tinged friendship. This was evident in the relationship between Will W. Alexander and Leonard Outhwaite, and between Edwin Embree and Charles S. Johnson. Correspondence reveals that over the course of years givers and receivers of funds became more interested in maintaining friendship ties rather than contractual concerns. This makes sense because certainly it is impossible to maintain cold bureaucratic distance in a relationship which requires so much contact and so much mutual trust.

In the process of growing close, we find reciprocal influences occurring between givers and receivers. Such reciprocity is not only symptomatic of deep friendship ties but also provides an important social control mechanism for givers. Giving to favorite beneficiaries avoids serious financial mismanagement and enables financiers to have access to candid knowledge about researchers, institutions and disciplinary trends. In most cases, pre–World War II foundation officers either were not social scientists or were so specialized that they had no intimate knowledge about other disciplines or subdisciplines. Beardsley Ruml, a psychologist, benefited from his friendship with, as well as his patronage of, Charles E. Merriam. Merriam gave Ruml extensive advice about who was doing what in the various social sciences and their professional direction. Howard Odum frequently sent gossipy letters to Ruml and Outhwaite about his fellow sociologists and about the status of sociology. Charles S. Johnson informed Edwin Embree about what was on the minds of black leaders and intellectuals and suggested areas of race-related research.

Thus, patrimonial relationships between givers and receivers minimized errors in appropriation decision making. It also, of course, meant that in many cases concentrated patterns of giving were reflections of how givers and receivers defined what was adequate and inadequate social science: a definition which selected and financed one kind of social science research over others.

Patrimonialism was also the glue of the organization of internal decision-making structures in foundations and the organizational field of giving and receiving. As the organizational field of giving and receiving in the social sciences in the foundation sector evolved through the course of the years between the World Wars, the development of cliques in the network based on intimate friendship subsequently evolved. At times, these cliques functioned as extraordinarily rapid communication channels and showed super efficiency in getting work done. For example, the Edwin R. Embree–Charles S. Johnson–Will W. Alexander clique enabled the Julius Rosenwald Fund to act quickly in responding to regional crisis during the New Deal years and during the racial crisis in the dawn of World War II. The three men pooled their resources, time, and intelligence in doing the field research and writing the reports needed to impact federal policy.

At other times cliques operated as structural clots in the network lines, hindering the funding of research projects. In these cases, members of the sociological generation preferred to reject research projects rather than take the chance of breaking a friendship tie. As we shall see, the friendship which developed between Jackson Davis and Anson Stokes and its unfortunate impact on William E. B. DuBois is a case in point.

There were other cliques that operated to stop research projects and an entire foundation. The Laura Spelman Rockefeller Memorial was "dismantled" by a clique of higher level Rockefeller Foundation officials. Some did not believe the social sciences were sciences, while others were jealous of Ruml and his staff's sudden rise to power in the Rockefeller conglomerate in the 1920s. Whatever the motivations were, they worked throughout the 1920s at trying to get the memorial dismantled and finally won in 1929. It can only be speculated how the contours of social science would have been different if the memorial had been allowed to survive for a decade or two more.

PHILANTHROPY AND JIM CROW IN AMERICAN SOCIAL SCIENCE

Conventional academic wisdom claims that the interwar period was the golden era of race-relations research. Certainly, if philanthropists and foundation administrators had not been so concerned with the Negro problem, the impressive body of scholarship that was created would perhaps have emerged quite differently, if at all. The traditional liberal line insists that the "balanced," "factual" analyses of the Negro problem sponsored by philanthropists and foundations prevented the spread of more conservative paradigms in social Darwinistic or Anglo-Saxonist modes. In this sense, using the abstract empirical tradition in the social sciences to document the dire conditions of blacks was inevitable in the face of more biologically deterministic views which would have disrupted efforts at interracial cooperation. According to this perspective, the liberal philanthropic sponsorship of studies of a descriptive, atheoretical Negro problem was the best recourse in order to usher in rationalism as a means of quieting the racial tensions which never ceased brewing in Jim Crow society.[1]

The liberal approach to the Negro problem in scholarship and in broader political considerations had serious flaws. It fostered the belief that racial gradualism was the wisest strategy due to the "nature of the times" and since "society" was not prepared for more assertive action. Such assumptions tore history from the hands and minds of men and thus conveniently ignored the fact that reality is a social construct. Societal organization is a product of a collective consciousness representative of human interests. Social structures and processes do not appear out of nowhere.

Rather, society seems to evolve according to some impersonal, outside force because through intergenerational socialization, our knowledge about the materialistic foundations of our social being is taken for granted. We often act without knowing why we act. When our actions seem to be contrary to our sensibilities, it is easy to reify our environment and to assume we are creatures of the times rather than creators of it.[2]

The philanthropists and foundation administrators involved in sponsorship of race-relations research engaged in these activities out of choice, not because "society forced them." They had the ability to create or at least to support any societal organization they chose. But for various reasons, ranging from private (or not so private) racist attitudes to fear of repercussions, they mainly chose to promote a race social science embedded in Jim Crow assumptions.[3]

The consequences of this choice helped to institutionalize race-relations research. The primary researchers sponsored—Howard W. Odum and Charles S. Johnson—were true believers in the abstract empirical approach to the Negro problem. Abstract empiricism, bland presentation of race relations facts, was quite functional in a rigidly biracial society, since, when it was applied to race research, it avoided politically sensitive issues.[4] The legitimation of empiricism in social research justified labeling data presentations as science, while theorizing became speculation, if not sensationalism. Empiricism fit nicely into a society in which the handling of racial problems was increasingly assigned to bureaucratic organization more interested in "facts" than in interpretations.[5]

Whether black social scientists were foundation favorites or not, they had to indulge in accommodative abstract empiricism to be heard—more so than did their white colleagues. This was largely based upon the assumption that blacks were naturally subjective. Black social scientists did not receive a great deal of attention in the book review columns of major white social science and history journals, but when they did, most reviewers appeared to be concerned only about whether the authors had engaged in the appropriate abstract empirical rituals. White scholars were criticized for lack of theoretical innovations, but blacks tended to be evaluated on "balance" and quantity of "facts." This double standard emphasizes the assumption, held by foundations and white scholars, that blacks should fulfill race-specific roles geared more toward segregated leadership than creative thinking or contributing to scholarly social science.

For instance, Edwin Embree's and Will Alexander's admiration for positivistic science (since facts "spoke for themselves") had conservative effects on the development of Fisk school paradigms of the black experience. While both applauded Charles S. Johnson's concern for "only the facts," they reinforced prevalent ideas about racial gradualism. Blacks should be patient. In social research, blacks were to be patient fact-gatherers—timelessly marching in step waiting for the day for well-meaning whites to initiate racial integration. The resultant concerns Johnson and his patrons had for method over theory and data documentation over data interpretation produced explanations which had little historical context or relevance and which lacked serendipity. As Jim Crow became legally discredited in the 1950s and the 1960s, much of the work of the Fisk school (Charles S. Johnson, faculty, and graduate students in the Department of Social Science) was useless in explaining social change beyond the stage of racial segregation. Racial integration, that is "social equality," was ontologically impossible in the world views of the foundation patrons of the Fisk school who assumed that most scientific data could be used to promote racial justice in a permanently segregated society. But compared to the Chapel Hill and Chicago schools, the Fisk school used numbers to connote the social conditioning of black oppression.

It may be argued that even in the face of this double standard, we should nevertheless give foundations and philanthropists fair credit for opening the door to the education and placement of an unprecedented number of black social scientists. This argument claims that the results of the actions of men such as Edwin Embree and Leonard Outhwaite in promoting the development of black social scientists should be considered more important than the causes of such efforts, which were embedded in their personal values and priorities. Although the sponsors of black social scientists wanted to maintain sociopolitical control and to support an accomodative form of black leadership, their support actually aided the unraveling of the racial caste order. Foundation boards and administrators did not foresee that the very training and employment of black social scientists, particularly sociologists, would contribute to the discrediting of legal segregation. They did not anticipate consequences of their promotion of Charles S. Johnson and the Fisk University social research center, which led to the documentation of the ills and dynamics of racial oppression. The collection of "facts" gradually developed into an arsenal for civil rights leaders and policy makers who dismantled Jim Crow.[6]

This observation does not negate the fact that philanthropic sponsors of race-relations research attempted to select "safe" blacks in the process of institutionalizing Negro problem research. More radical researchers fell outside the boundaries of what they considered acceptable social scientific reasoning. From the very beginning of foundation and academic patronage of race-relations researchers—blacks in particular—those with blatant integrationist, nationalist, culturally pluralistic, or Marxist perspectives were seldom considered for funding. Scholars like Zora Neale Hurston, Carter G. Woodson, and William E. B. DuBois were not consistently supported by the foundations because their views were considered too radical.[7]

Woodson boldly attacked the African colonial policies of Thomas Jesse Jones in the early 1920s. Later, he paid for his criticisms. Jones attempted to persuade white patrons of Woodson's Association for the Study of Negro Life to withdraw their support. Jones's friend and superior, Anson Stokes, circulated a letter to influential persons pointing out the errors of Woodson's attack, although he also alluded to his respect for the black scholar.[8] From the late 1910s through the late 1920s, Woodson's independence and "difficult" personality were tolerated by philanthropists and foundation administrators, who gave small donations to his organization. But they soon grew weary. Officers of the Rockefeller foundations and the Julius Rosenwald Fund finally began pressuring Woodson to join a black academic institution. He refused, and as a result, philanthropists and foundations refused to assist him, beginning in the late 1930s.[9]

His book, *The Miseducation of the Negro*, published in 1933 was the symbol of Woodson's frustration over the philanthropists' control of black scholars. Of course this insightful expose of white philanthropy was attacked for being "subjective" and "impressionistic." [10]

The most paradoxical example of the philanthropic exclusion of non-accommodative black scholars was William E. B. DuBois. DuBois had a peculiar relationship with philanthropists and foundations. DuBois portrayed himself as a foe of philanthropists and foundations, claiming that he had left Atlanta University because philanthropists were hostile to his radical views. While editor for the NAACP's *Crisis* he periodically lashed out at the policies of foundations. [11]

It is true that philanthropists and foundation administrators viewed DuBois as a rabble-rouser, but this fact must be assessed in its proper context. As radical as he may have been, DuBois needed foundation support in order to carry out major research plans, and occasionally foundation administrators needed him for political reasons. Thus the Slater Fund contributed to DuBois's Negro in American research project at Atlanta University in the early 1900s. [12] DuBois harbored a desire to write a comprehensive Negro Encyclopedia. [13] In the 1920s, Anson Stokes, the Phelps-Stokes Fund Secretary, sponsored Monroe N. Work's Negro Yearbook series of Tuskegee Institute. In the last years of that decade, Stokes decided to organize a Negro Encyclopedia Project. The purpose of the project was to offer a "balanced" overview of Negro history through the participation of prominent white and black scholars and reformers who were true believers of interracial cooperation. [14]

When Stokes began organizing the biracial staff of the Negro Encyclopedia Project, Woodson became infuriated. He claimed Stokes and Thomas Jesse Jones had stolen his idea for an Encyclopedia Africana and had attempted to produce an accommodative reference book which reflected the paternalistic attitudes of the whites chosen to write for the project. [15] Later, he ridiculed the project, describing its staff as white do-gooders who knew nothing about the canons of research. [16] Even though DuBois was a critic of Jones, Anson Stokes asked him to be chief editor of the Negro Encyclopedia Project. DuBois consented, seeing the position as a means to fulfill his dream of writing an encyclopedia. The compromises DuBois was forced to make were characteristic of the dilemma of the radical black scholar prior to World War II. [17] After initial discussion it was decided that blacks would not dominate in the decision-making process. The reasoning was that publication about blacks primarily shaped by blacks would not be able to gain much attention. [18] Only a work involving interracial cooperation—white supervision of black opinion—would be accepted as a valuable scholarly study. [19] DuBois opposed this accommodative stance but was in a small minority against Benjamin Brawley, Robert R. Moton, Thomas J. Woofter, Jr., Will W. Alexander, James Dillard, and other well-known experts on blacks. [20] Thus Woodson was correct in arguing that the project promoted the thought of segregationist social scientists and paternalistic do-gooders, in conformity with Jim Crow traditions.

Originally, Stokes planned to donate the seed money for the encyclopedia and to approach the big foundations for more substantial funds. He spent the 1930s searching unsuccessfully for additional foundation support.[21] His major stumbling block was W.E.B. DuBois. One of Stokes' friends, Jackson Davis of the General Education Board, was deeply interested in the concept of a Negro Encyclopedia, but he along with his foundation's governing board, disapproved of DuBois' radical views.[22] Stokes and Davis twice submitted proposals to the General Education Board, attempting to dilute DuBois's authority. They got him to agree to have a white co-editor (neither Stokes nor Davis believed it was proper for a black to rule over whites) and to resign as editor of *Crisis*.[23] These compromises still did not work, the General Education Board turned down Stokes's project in the late 1930s. Not wanting to jeopardize his friendship with Davis and other foundation administrators, Stokes did not press the issue.

Charles Dollard of the Carnegie Corporation advised Jackson Davis not to have anything to do with DuBois.[24] He did not want to involve his foundation in the Negro Encyclopedia project, not only because of DuBois's contrary attitude, but also because they were about to launch their own study on the Negro Problem—*An American Dilemma*.[25] Given Dollard's antagonism toward DuBois, one might speculate that the Carnegie Study represented, at least in part, an effort to prevent DuBois from making a comparable contribution to race-relations research. DuBois and his co-editor Guy B. Johnson were only able to publish a preliminary volume of the encyclopedia in the 1940s.[26] They were not able to obtain money to do anything more substantial.

The conservatism of philanthropists, foundation administrators, and gatekeepers in the organized social sciences institutionalized an assimilationist concept of white/black relations that stressed asymmetrical cultural adaptation in a formally segregated society. Even in liberal social engineering works (summarized in *An American Dilemma*), more radical paradigms such as those stressing the elite origins of racism, the normality of cultural pluralism, and the independent persistence of race in urban industrial societies were ignored or dismissed. Their authors were excluded from professional consideration in journals, textbooks, and scholarly studies. E. Franklin Frazier's "The Pathology of Race Prejudice," raised so much controversy that he was forced to leave Atlanta where he was teaching and was never again to teach in the South.[27] Mainstream white and black scholars never forgave Oliver Cox for his Marxist perspective on race relations and, more importantly, for his criticism of the Park school and of Gunnar Myrdal, and thus for years he was virtually ignored or ridiculed in professional and social science circles. One review of his *Caste, Class, and Race: A Study in Social Dynamics* claimed:

The attack upon the leading sociologists in this country who have dealt with the Negro indicates certain blind spots in the author's thinking. Again, he treats the question of race in this country in unscientific fashion. As a sociologist Dr. Cox must realize the need to go among the people whom he studies and to make investigations with select groups. However valid some of his criticisms of such eminent sociologists as Park, Burgess, and Frazier may be, they are weakened by the feebleness of the evidence which he can bring against them.

The Marxian tendency in Professor Cox's thinking is constantly evident. This leads him into gross misinterpretations of facts. One may question his view that the State is set up to administer and defend capitalism, or that Fascism and the modern church are on the whole closely related, and naturally so. Not everyone will accept the conclusion that the Negroes in the United States must learn that their interest is primarily bound up with that of the white common people in a struggle for power. Such an angling of material makes it appear that the work is a forum for expounding the author's peculiar political views.[28]

Mainstream scholars, both black and white, who dared to write down radical thoughts found that most of these ideas ended up edited out of published manuscripts, published under pseudonyms, or gathering dust in their files. It was better to be accommodative than to be labeled unscientific, unreasonable, or disloyal to one's patrons. The careless boldness of E. Franklin Frazier, Carter G. Woodson, Oliver Cox, and others was uniformly punished.

Foundation sponsorship of Negro problem research began to decline rapidly in the 1940s and had virtually disappeared by the late 1950s. During the 1940s, the General Education Board curtailed its funding activities dramatically. The Julius Rosenwald Fund was phased out in 1948, while the Carnegie Corporation and the Phelps-Stokes Fund went on to other activities. Foundation officers who had been involved in cultivating race-relations research retired in the 1940s and most died in the 1950s. Researchers who had been foundation "favorites," such as Howard Odum and Charles S. Johnson, either retired or moved out of research by the early 1950s.

If the foundations had continued their sponsorship of Negro problem research and if there had been seasoned researchers to support, there would have been a radical change in focus. Ideologically and politically, post–World War II Americans were being conditioned for a radical change in race-relations thought. Many events between World War I and World War II indicated rising outspoken black discontent with racial caste. The Garvey movement, the Harlem Renaissance, the attraction of blacks to the Communist party, and the activities of the NAACP all suggested this discontent.

During the war, white elites were aware that the old racial order was quickly crumbling and that they had no coherent alternative policies which would put blacks back in their place.[29] The war also provided an impetus for increased black protest and demands for racial integration. White elites also felt international pressures to dismantle Jim Crow in the early 1950s.[30] Unless foundation officers had begun to lobby for the survival of Jim Crow, they would have been forced to advocate integrationist policies. In the 1950s, integrationist-oriented foundations, such as the National Science Foundation, the Ford Foundation and the Fund for the Republic, did arise. The first two were particularly active in the 1960s, in response to that decade's racial problems. They financed research about the Negro problem and the problems of other racial minorities in a society undergoing desegregation. During that time period, the older, big foundations gradually joined those organized after World War II as a new generation of decision-makers began formulating pro-integration funding policies.[31]

This funding tradition mirrors the significant transformation in public policies and opinions regarding racial issues. It helped to legitimate a generation of integration-oriented liberal sociologists, like Gunnar Myrdal, who advocated social engineering as a solution to the Negro problem, which was seen as an unfortunate moral contradiction in an otherwise democratic society. Since this liberal tradition, which is still preferred over more critical paradigms, promotes utopian thinking at the expense of sober observations about persisting racial caste relations, we can testify to the dialectical validity of at least one black adage: What goes around comes around.

NOTES

1. See Morton Sosna, *In Search of the Silent South* (New York, Columbia University Press, 1977); Patrick J. Gilpin, *Charles S. Johnson: An Intellectual Biography* (Ph.D. dissertation, Vanderbilt University, 1973).

2. Peter L. Berger and Thomas Luckmann, *The Social Construction of Reality* (New York: Doubleday and Co., 1967).

3. This thought was inspired by William H. Chafe, *Civilities and Civil Rights: Greensboro, North Carolina and the Black Struggle for Freedom* (New York: Oxford University Press, 1980).

4. Given the reluctance of Rockefeller foundations to finance politically sensitive research, neither the memorial nor the General Education Board supported sociologically oriented studies on blacks other than atheoretical statistical assessments or ahistorical ethnographic analyses. But the Julius Rosenwald Fund, mainly through the prodding of President Edwin Embree, Vice President Will Alexander, and trustee Charles S. Johnson, did occasionally launch into the deep. For instance, it was the Julius Rosenwald Fund's sponsorship of venereal disease control demonstrations that produced Charles S. Johnson's *Shadow of the Plantation* and the foundation's Negro and Economic Reconstruction Project, geared toward southern agrarian reform, that produced several classic race-relations studies. The studies produced from these two projects, which were the Rosenwald Fund's response to the negative impact of the depression and New Deal programs on blacks, created a fad in sociological literature in the early and mid–1930s. They offered southern liberal explanations and documentation resources about black folk life, the plantation South, and southern rural racial stratification. Yet, typical of southern liberal perspectives, these studies failed to address questions about the political economy of caste and the critical dysfunctions of racial segregation. The avoidance of such radical questions was fostered by a disdain for Marxism in foundation and professional sociology circles, especially Marxist interpretations of the South. In the professional sociological literature of the interwar period, Marxist interpretations of the plantation South such as James S. Allen's *The Negro Question in America* (New York: International Publishers, 1936) and Harry Haywood's *Negro Liberation* (New York: International Publishers, 1948) were downplayed or ignored. As we shall see in this chapter, the refusal of the General Education Board to finance Anson Stokes's Negro Encyclopedia Project in the 1930s is illustrative of foundation reluctance to support Marxist-oriented scholars.

5. One is reminded that the publication of *An American Dilemma* in the 1940s moved conservative congressmen to resist inclusion of the social sciences in the National Science Foundation. Roberta Balstad Miller, "The Social Sciences and the Politics of Science: The 1940s," *The American Sociologist* (November 1982):208.

6. John H. Stanfield, "The Cracked Back Door: Foundations and Black Social Scientists," *The American Sociologist* 17 (November 1982):202–203.

7. Anthropologist Zora Neale Hurston was nonaccommodative in the sense of developing normative rather than pathological (i.e., "Negro problem") conceptions of Afro-American experiences. This is one reason why she was deprived of professional recognition during her peak years, the 1920s and 1930s. See Robert E. Hemenway, *Zora Neale Hurston: A Literary Biography* (Urbana, Ill.: University of Illinois Press, 1977).

8. Anson Phelps Stokes, "Confidential Memorandum for Trustees of Phelps-Stokes Fund Regarding Carter G. Woodson's Criticisms of Thomas Jesse Jones," June 26, 1924, Anson Phelps Stokes Papers.

9. Carter G. Woodson correspondence in the General Education Board Archives, Laura Spelman Rockefeller Memorial Archives (hereafter LSRM) and Julius Rosenwald Fund (hereafter JRF) Archives.

10. Carter G. Woodson, *The Miseducation of the Negro* (Washington, D.C.: The Associated Publishers, Inc., 1936).

11. This was especially the case in the 1920s. He also sent occasional criticism of Thomas Jesse Jones to Anson Phelps Stokes during that period of time. William E.B. DuBois folders, Anson Stokes Papers.

12. Atlanta University folders, General Education Board Archives.

13. William E. B. DuBois, *Dusk of Dawn: An Essay Toward an Autobiography of a Race Concept* (New York, Schocken Books, 1968).

14. Anson Phelps Stokes correspondence with Benjamin Brawley and others, Negro Encyclopedia folders, Anson Phelps Stokes Papers and Phelps Stokes Fund Archives, Schomburg Collection on Black Culture.

15. See correspondence in Carter G. Woodson folders, James Welden Johnson Special Collection on Negro Arts and Letters.

16. Carter G. Woodson, Review of *The Encyclopedia of the Negro, Preparatory Volume with Reference Lists, and Reports*, in *Journal of Negro History* 30 (July 1945):339–340.

17. DuBois, *Dusk of Dawn.*

18. Meeting minutes, Negro Encyclopedia folders, Phelps Stokes Fund Archives.

19. Ibid.

20. Ibid.

21. Anson Stokes correspondence in Negro Encyclopedia folders, Phelps Stokes Fund Archives and in Frederick Keppel folders, Anson Phelps Stokes Papers.

22. Jackson Davis conferences with William E. B. DuBois, Anson Phelps Stokes, and Charles Dollard recorded in his diary, General Education Board Archives.

23. Ibid.

24. Ibid.

25. Ibid.

26. DuBois, *Dusk of Dawn.*

27. E. Franklin Frazier, "The Pathology of Race Prejudice," *Forum* 70 (June 1927):856–862; Grace E. Harris, *The Life and Work of E. Franklin Frazier* (Ph.D. dissertation, University of Virginia, 1975, p. 34).

28. Oliver C. Cox, *Caste, Class, and Race: A Study in Social Dynamics* (1948); Williston H. Lofton, Review of *Caste, Class, and Race* by Oliver C. Cox, *Journal of Negro History* 33 (July 1948): 365;*Caste, Class and Race* is being rediscovered in the late 1970s and 1980s more in the area of Cox's Marxist approach than his insightful criticisms of the serious flaws in Park's and Myrdal's race-relations perspectives.

29. Richard Polenberg, *One Nation Divisible* (New York: Viking Press, 1980), pp. 46–126.

30. Ibid., pp. 86–126; Daniel Guerin, *Negroes on the March* (New York: George L. Weissman, 1951).

31. Waldemar A. Nielson, *The Big Foundations* (New York: Columbia University Press, 1972).

Bibliography

ARCHIVAL COLLECTIONS

The following manuscript collections were particularly valuable for developing insights into philanthropists, foundation administrators, and their attitudes toward blacks and the social sciences: Julius Rosenwald Papers, Julius Rosenwald Fund Archives, Laura Spelman Rockefeller Memorial Archives, General Education Board Archives, Charles S. Johnson Special Collection, Howard W. Odum Papers, Phelps Stokes Fund Archives, Edwin R. Embree Papers, and Leonard Outhwaite Papers. The Booker T. Washington Papers and Robert E. Park Papers were the most useful for reconstructing Park's Tuskegee years. The Charles S. Johnson Special Collection, the Howard W. Odum Papers, the General Education Board Archives, and the Laura Spelman Rockefeller Memorial were valuable for exploring how foundations shaped institutional social science in the South. (See the alphabetical list at the end of this section for the location of these archival materials.)

The Charles E. Merriam Papers, particularly copies of minutes of the Interracial Relations Committee of the Social Science Research Council in the 1920s offered supporting data for my statements about the exclusion of blacks from the Social Science Research Council. The Laura Spelman Rockefeller Memorial Archives were also replete with correspondence about the Social Science Research Council, which shaped my impressions. The James R. Angell and the Robert M. Yerkes Papers were most valuable for understanding little-known facts about Beardsley Ruml and about the unique role of James R. Angell in the foundations and social sciences area.

Most of the Carnegie Corporation records on the Myrdal Negro Problem Study have been lost. The surviving records are of uneven quality and value. The most useful records offer background information to the selection of Gunnar Myrdal as project director. Numerous excerpts of surviving records are published in the preface and introduction to his *An American Dilemma*. Materials collected from the General Education Board Archives and the Louis Wirth Papers helped to shed light on the development of the Carnegie Negro Problem Study, particularly on the issue of the roles of Louis Wirth, Horace R. Cayton, Frederick Keppel, Jackson Davis, and Arnold Rose. The Arnold Rose

Papers housed in the University of Minnesota Library were not consulted but do contain documents pertaining to the Negro Problem Study.

The Charles S. Johnson Special Collection and the Julius Rosenwald Fund Archives were instrumental in examining the foundation-sponsored career of Charles S. Johnson. It would have been fascinating to write a deeper comparative analysis of E. Franklin Frazier and the foundations than I have done in this book. But foundation records are strangely silent on E. Franklin Frazier, aside from his memorial scholarship records in the 1930s and minute routine correspondence about his participation in the General Education Board-sponsored American Youth Commission studies on Negro youth. E. Franklin Frazier's Papers, recently made available at Howard University, could be valuable in addressing this issue.

Bureau of Agricultural Economics. National Archives, Washington, D.C.

James R. Angell Papers. Yale University Library, New Haven, Conn.

Ernest W. Burgess Papers. Joseph Regenstein Library, University of Chicago, Chicago, Ill.

Carnegie Corporation of New York Archives. New York, N.Y.

Edwin R. Embree Collection. Rockefeller Archive Center, North Tarrytown, N.Y.

Edwin R. Embree Papers. Berea College, Berea, Ky.

Edwin R. Embree Papers. Yale University Library, New Haven, Conn.

General Education Board Archives. Rockefeller Archive Center, North Tarrytown, N.Y.

E. Franklin Frazier Papers. Howard University, Washington, D.C.

Charles S. Johnson Special Collection. Fisk University, Nashville, Tenn.

James Weldon Johnson Special Collection on Negro Arts and Letters. Beinecke Library, Yale University, New Haven, Conn.

Charles E. Merriam Papers. Joseph Regenstein Library. University of Chicago, Chicago, Ill.

Howard W. Odum Papers, #3167. Southern Historical Collection, Library of the University of North Carolina at Chapel Hill, Chapel Hill, N.C.

Leonard Outhwaite Papers. Rockefeller Archive Center, North Tarrytown, N.Y.

Robert E. Park Papers. Joseph Regenstein Library, University of Chicago, Chicago, Ill.

Rockefeller Foundation Archives. Rockefeller Archive Center, North Tarrytown, N.Y.

Laura Spelman Rockefeller Memorial Archives. Rockefeller Archive Center, North Tarrytown, N.Y.

Julius Rosenwald Fund Archives. Fisk University Library Special Collections, Nashville, Tenn.

Julius Rosenwald Papers. Joseph Regenstein Library, University of Chicago, Chicago, Ill.

Anson Phelps Stokes Papers. Yale University Library, New Haven, Conn.

Phelps Stokes Fund Archives. Schomburg Center for Research in Black Culture, New York, N.Y.

Booker T. Washington Papers. Library of Congress, Washington, D.C.

Louis Wirth Papers. Joseph Regenstein Library, University of Chicago, Chicago, Ill.

Robert M. Yerkes Papers. Yale University Library, New Haven, Conn.

INTERNALIST PERSPECTIVES IN THE SOCIAL SCIENCES

The great persons and the impersonal forces perspectives in the history and sociology of the social sciences literature joins the vast literature on great concepts and paradigms in developing the pervasive internalist approach to the study of the social sciences. The following are selected history and sociology of social science studies that have illustrated one or more internalist perspectives.

Anthropology

Brew, J. O. *One Hundred Years of Anthropology*. Cambridge, Mass.: Harvard University Press, 1968.
De Waal Malefijt, AnneMarie. *Images of Man: A History of Anthropological Thought*. New York: Alfred A. Knopf, 1974.
Douglas, Mary. *Evans-Pritchard*. Sussex: The Harvester Press, 1980.
Evans-Pritchard, Sir Edward. *A History of Anthropological Thought*. London: Faber and Faber, 1981.
Golde, Peggy, ed. *Women in the Field: Anthropological Experiences*. Chicago: Aldine Publishing Co., 1970.
Lowie, Robert H. *The History of Ethnological Theory*. New York: Farrar and Rinehart, Inc., 1937.
————. *Robert H. Lowie Ethnologist: A Personal Record*. Berkeley, Calif: University of California Press, 1959.
Manners, Robert A., and Kaplan, David, eds. *Theory in Anthropology*. New York: Aldine Publishing Company, 1968.
Mead, Margaret. *Ruth Benedict*. New York: Columbia University Press, 1977.
————. *Blackberry Winter: My Earlier Years*. New York: William Morrow & Company, 1972.
Montagu, Ashley, ed. *Frontiers of Anthropology*. New York: G.P. Putnam's Sons, 1974.
Penniaman, T. K. *A Hundred Years of Anthropology*. London: Gerald Duckworth & Co., Ltd., 1965.
Stocking, George W., Jr. *Race, Culture and Evolution: Essays in the History of Anthropology*. New York: The Free Press, 1968.

Economics

Barber, William J. *A History of Economic Thought*. New York: Penguin Books, 1967.
Dobb, Maurice. *Theories of Value and Distribution: Ideology and Economic Theory*. Cambridge: Cambridge University Press, 1973.
Eagly, Robert V. *The Structure of Classical Economic Theory*. New York: Oxford University Press, 1974.
Finkelstein, Joseph, and Thimm, Alfred L. *Economists and Society: The Development of Economic Thought from Aquinas to Keynes*. New York: Harper & Row, 1973.
Heilbroner, Robert. *The Worldly Philosophers*. New York: Simon and Schuster, 1980.
Blaug, Mark. *Economic Theory in Retrospect*. London: Cambridge University Press, 1962.

Political Science

Catlin, George. *The Story of the Political Philosophers*. New York: McGraw-Hill Book Co., 1939.
Gunnell, John G. *Political Theory: Tradition and Interpretation*. Cambridge, Mass: Winthrop Publishers, Inc., 1979.

Hooker, Andrew. *Political Theory: Philosophy, Ideology, Science*. New York: Macmillan Company, 1961.

McIlwain, Charles H. *The Growth of Political Thought in the West: From the Greeks to the End of the Middle Ages*. 1932; repr. New York: Macmillan Company, 1959.

Runciman, W. G. *Social Science and Political Theory*. Cambridge: Cambridge University Press, 1969.

Sait, Edward McChesney. *Masters of Political Thought*, Vol. 3, Boston: Houghton Mifflin Co., 1968.

Psychology

Averill, James R. *Patterns of Psychological Thought: Readings in Historical and Contemporary Texts*. Washington, D.C.: Hemisphere Publishing Corp., 1976.

Boring, Edwin G. *A History of Experimental Psychology*. New York: Appleton-Century-Crofts, Inc., 1950.

Fancher, Raymond E. *Pioneers of Psychology*. New York: W. W. Norton and Company, 1979.

Guthrie, Robert V. *Even the Rat Was White: A Historical View of Psychology*. New York: Harper and Row, 1976.

Hilgard, Ernest R., ed. *American Psychology in Historical Perspective: Addresses of the Presidents of the American Psychological Association*. Washington, D.C.: American Psychological Association, 1978.

Leahey, Thomas A. *A History of Psychology*. Englewood Cliffs, N.J.: Prentice-Hall, Inc., 1980.

Lindsey, Gardner., ed. *A History of Psychology in Autobiography*. Vol. 7. San Francisco: W. H. Freeman and Company, 1980. [Vols. 1–3 edited by Carl Murchinson; Vol. 4 edited by E. G. Boring and others; and Vol. 6 by The Century Psychology Series.]

Lowry, Richard. *The Evolution of Psychological Theory: 1650 to the Present*. Chicago: Aldine-Atherton, 1971.

Murphy, Gardner, and Murphy, Louis B. *Western Psychology: From the Greeks to William James*. New York: Basic Books, Inc., 1969.

Peters, R. S., ed. and abridger. *Brett's History of Psychology*. Cambridge, Mass.: The M.I.T. Press, 1965.

Robinson, Daniel D. *An Intellectual History of Psychology*. New York: Macmillan Publishing Co., 1976.

Watson, Robert I., Sr. *The Great Psychologists*. Philadelphia: J. B. Lippincott Company, 1978.

Wolman, Benjamin B. *Historical Roots of Contemporary Psychology*. New York: Harper & Row, 1968.

Woodworth, Robert S. *Contemporary Schools of Psychology*. New York: the Ronald Press Company, 1948.

Sociology

Atkinson, Dick. *Orthodox Consensus and Radical Alternative: A Study in Sociological Theory*. London: Heinemann Educational Books, Ltd., 1971.

Barnes, Harry E. *An Introduction to the History of Sociology*. Chicago: University of Chicago Press, 1948.

Beal, Owen F. *The Development of Sociology in the United States*. Ann Arbor, Mich.: Edwards, 1944.

Becker, Ernest. *The Lost Science of Man*. New York: George Braziller, 1971.

Becker, Howard, and Barnes, Harry E. *Social Thought from Lore to Science*. Boston: D. C. Heath and Company, 1938.

Bernard, L. L. and Bernard, Jessie. *Origins of American Sociology: The Social Science Movement in the United States*. New York: Thomas Y. Crowell Co., 1943.

Bernstein, Richard J. *The Restructuring of Social and Political Theory*. New York: Harcourt Brace Jovanovich, 1976.

Bramson, Leon. *The Political Context of Sociology*. Princeton, N.J.: Princeton University Press, 1961.

Coser, Lewis. *Masters of Sociological Thought: Ideas in Historical and Social Context*. New York: Harcourt Brace Jovanovich, 1971.

Friedrichs, Robert W. *The Sociology of Sociology*. New York: Free Press, 1970.

Hammond, Phillip E. *Sociologists at Work: Essays on the Craft of Social Research*. New York: Basic Books, Inc., 1964.

Hinkle, Roscoe C., and Hinkle, Gisela J. *The Development of Modern Sociology: Its Nature and Growth in the United States*. New York: Random House, 1954.

Horowitz, Irving I. *Sociological Self-Images: A Collective Portrait*. Beverly Hills, Calif.: Sage Publications, 1969.

Madge, John. *The Origins of Scientific Sociology*. New York: Free Press of Glencoe, 1962.

Odum, Howard W. *American Sociology: The Story of Sociology in the United States Through 1950*. New York: Longman, Green, 1951.

Small, Albion. *Origins of Sociology*. Chicago: University of Chicago Press, 1924.

Turner, Jonathan H. *The Structure of Sociological Theory*. Homewood, Ill.: Dorsey Press, 1974.

EXTERNALIST PERSPECTIVES IN THE SOCIAL SCIENCES

There is a growing literature which offers externalist explanations about the development of the social sciences. Those which particularly link up with internalist issues are valuable references. Historians of economics have long published work stressing the latter approach. The following studies are examples of various externalist views on the development of the social sciences.

Anthropology

Asad, Talal. *Anthropology and the Colonial Encounter*. New York: Humanities Press, 1973.

Economics

Bell, John F. *A History of Economic Thought*. Huntington: Robert E. Krieger Publishing Co., 1980.

Hutchinson, T. W. *The Politics and Philosophy of Economics*. New York: New York University Press, 1981.

Pribram, Karl. *A History of Economic Reasoning*. Baltimore, Md.: Johns Hopkins University Press, 1983.

Roll, Eric. *A History of Economic Thought*. London: Faber and Faber, 1939.

Schumpeter, Joseph A. *History of Economic Analysis*. New York: Oxford University Press, 1954.

Psychology

Gilgen, Albert R. *American Psychology Since World War II: A Profile of the Discipline*. Westport, Conn.: Greenwood Press, 1982.

Sociology

Carey, James T. *Sociology and Public Affairs: The Chicago School*. Beverly Hills, Calif.: Sage Publications, 1975.

Gouldner, Alvin W. *The Coming Crisis of Western Sociology*. New York: Basic Books, 1970.

Schwendinger, Julia and Herman. *Sociologists of the Chair*. New York: Basic Books, 1974.

SELECTED GENERAL REFERENCES

Aptheker, Herbert. *The Negro People in America: A Critique of Gunnar Myrdal's "An American Dilemma."* New York: International Publishers, 1946.

Arnove, Robert F., ed. *Philanthropy and Cultural Imperialism: The Foundations at Home and Abroad*. Boston: G.K. Hall and Company, 1980.

Baltzell, E. Digby. *The Protestant Establishment: Aristocracy and Caste in America*. New York: Random House, 1964.

Blackwell, James E., and Janowitz, Morris. *Black Sociologists: Historical and Contemporary Perspectives*. Chicago: University of Chicago Press, 1974.

Bond, Horace M. *The Education of the Negro in the American Social Order*, rev. ed. New York: Octagon Books, 1965.

Bracey, John H.; Meier, August; and Rudwick, Elliott. *The Black Sociologist: The First Half Century*. Belmont, Calif.: Wadsworth Publishing Company, 1971.

Brazil, Wayne. "Howard W. Odum: The Building Years." Ph.D. Dissertation, Harvard University, 1975.

Carey, James T. *Sociology and Public Affairs: The Chicago School*. Beverly Hills, Calif.: Sage Publications, 1975.

Cayton, Horace R. *The Long Old Road*. New York: Trident Press, 1965.

Chicago Commission on Race Relations. *The Negro in Chicago*. Chicago: University of Chicago Press, 1922.

Cox, Oliver. *Caste, Class, and Race*. New York: Monthly Review Press, 1948.

Drake, St. Clair, and Horace R. Cayton. *Black Metropolis*. New York: Harcourt Brace and Company, 1945.

Dykeman, Wilma, and James Stokely. *Seeds of Southern Change: The Life of Will Alexander*. Chicago: University of Chicago Press, 1962.

Edwards, G. Franklin. *E. Franklin Frazier on Race Relations: Selected Writings*. Chicago: University of Chicago Press, 1968.

Embree, Edwin R. and Julia Waxman. *Investment in People: The Story of the Julius Rosenwald Fund*. New York: Harper Brothers, 1949.

Fee, John G. *Autobiography*. National Christian Association, 1891.

Flexner, Abraham. *The General Education Board: An Account of its Activities, 1902–1914*. New York: General Education Board, 1915.

Fosdick, Raymond. *Adventure in Giving: The Story of the General Education Board*. New York: Harper and Row, 1962.

Frazier, E. Franklin. *The Negro Family in Chicago*. Chicago: University of Chicago Press, 1932.

Gates, Frederick. *Chapters in My Life*. New York: Free Press, 1977.

Gilpin, Patrick. "Charles S. Johnson: An Intellectual Biography." Ph.D. Dissertation, Vanderbilt University, 1973.

Harlan, Louis R. *Booker T. Washington: The Wizard of Tuskegee, 1901–1915*. New York: Oxford University Press, 1983.

Hemenway, Robert. *Zora Neale Hurston*. Urbana: University of Illinois Press, 1977.

Herskovits, Melville J. *The Myth of the Negro Past*. New York: Harper & Brothers, 1941.

Higham, John. *Strangers in the Land: Patterns of American Nativism, 1860–1925*. New Brunswick, N.J.: Rutgers University Press, 1955.

Hinkle, Roscoe C., and Hinkle, Gisela J. *The Development of Sociology: Its Nature and Growth in the United States*. New York, N.Y.: Random House, 1954.

Hofstadter, Richard. *Social Darwinism in American Thought, 1860–1915*. Philadelphia: University of Pennsylvania Press, 1944.

Huizer, Gerrit, and Mannheinm, Bruce, ed. *The Politics of Anthropology*. The Hague: Marion Publishers, 1979.

Hymes, Dell, ed. *Reinventing Anthropology*. New York: Pantheon Books, 1972.

Johnson, Charles S. *The Negro in American Civilization*. New York: Henry Holt and Company, 1930.

———. *Shadow of the Plantation*. Chicago: University of Chicago Press, 1934.

———, Edwin Embree, and Will Alexander. *The Collapse of the Cotton Tenancy*. Chapel Hill: University of North Carolina Press, 1935.

Johnson, Guy B., and Johnson, Guion G. *Research in Service to Society: The First Fifty Years of the Institute for Research in Social Science at the University of North Carolina*. Chapel Hill: University of North Carolina Press, 1980.

Jones, Thomas J. *Negro Education: A Study of the Private and Higher Schools for Colored People in the United States*. Department of the Interior, Bureau of Education, Bulletin 1916, Nos. 38, 39. Washington, D.C.: U.S. Government Printing Office, 1917.

Karl, Barry E. *Charles E. Merriam and the Study of Politics*. Chicago: University of Chicago Press, 1974.

Kennedy, David M. *Over Here: The First World War and American Society*. New York: Oxford University Press, 1980.

King, Kenneth. *Pan Africanism and Education*. London: Oxford University Press, 1971.

Kirby, John B. *Black Americans in the Roosevelt Era: Liberation and Race*. Knoxville: University of Tennessee Press, 1980.

Kirkendall, Richard Stewart. *Social Scientists and Farm Politics in the Age of Roosevelt*. Columbia: University of Missouri Press, 1966.

Kuhn, Thomas S. *The Structure of Scientific Revolutions*. Chicago: University of Chicago Press, 1962.

Ladner, Joyce A. *The Death of White Sociology*. New York: Random House, 1973.

Logan, Rayford. *The Betrayal of the Negro*. New York: Collier Books, 1965.

Lyman, Stanford. *The Black American in Sociological Thought*. New York: Putnam, 1972.

Myrdal, Gunnar. *An American Dilemma*. New York: Harper and Brothers, 1944.

Nielson, Waldemar A. *The Big Foundations*. New York: Columbia University Press, 1972.

Noble, David. *America by Design: Science, Technology, and the Rise of Corporate Capitalism*. New York: A. A. Knopf, 1977.

O'Brien, Michael. *The Idea of the American South, 1920–1941*. Baltimore: The Johns Hopkins University Press, 1979.

———. *American Sociology*. New York: Longman, Green, 1950.

Oleson, Alexandra, and Voss, John, ed. *The Organization of Knowledge in Modern America, 1860–1920*. Baltimore: The Johns Hopkins University Press.

Park, Robert E. *Race and Culture*. New York: Free Press, 1950.

———, and Burgess, Ernest W. *Introduction to the Science of Sociology*. 1921; repr. Chicago: University of Chicago Press, 1970.

———, ———, and R. McKenzie. *The City*. 1925; repr. Chicago: University of Chicago Press, 1970.

Raper, Arthur F. *Preface to Peasantry*. Chapel Hill: The University of North Carolina Press, 1936.

Raushenbush, Winifred. *Robert E. Park: Biography of a Sociologist*. Durham, N.C.: Duke University Press, 1979.

Reid, Ira De. *In a Minor Key*. Washington, D.C.: American Council on Education, 1941.

Reuter, Edward B. *The Mulatto in the United States*. Boston: R. G. Badger, 1918.

———. *Race Mixture*. New York: Whittlesey House, McGraw-Hill Book Co., 1931.

———. *The American Race Problem*. New York: Thomas Y. Crowell Co., 1938.

Ross, Edward A. *The Old World in the New: The Significance of Past and Present Immigration to the American People*. New York: Century Company, 1914.

Schwendinger, Herman, and Schwendinger, Julia R. *The Sociologists of the Chair*. New York: Basic Books, 1974.

Scott, Clifford. *Lester Frank Ward*. Boston: Twayne Publishers, 1976.

Small, Albion, and Vincent, George. *An Introduction to the Study of Society*. New York: American Book Company, 1894.

Solomon, Barbara M. *Ancestors and Immigrants*. Chicago: University of Chicago Press, 1956.

Sosna, Morton. *Search for the Silent South*. New York: Columbia University Press, 1977.

Stone, Alfred H. *Studies in the American Race Problem*. New York: Doubleday, Page and Company, 1908.

Strickland, Arvarh E. *The History of the Chicago Urban League*. Urbana: University of Illinois Press, 1966.

Summer, William G. *Folkways*. Boston: Ginn, 1906.

Sutherland, Robert L. *Color, Class, and Personality*. Washington, D.C.: American Council on Education, 1942.

Takaki, Ronald. *Iron Cages: Race and Culture in Nineteenth Century America*. New York: A. A. Knopf, 1979.

Thomas, William I., and Znanieck, Florian. *The Polish Peasant in Europe and America*. New York: A. A. Knopf, 1918.

Tindall, George. *The Emergence of the New South, 1913–1945*. Baton Rouge: Louisiana State University Press, 1967.

Weiss, Nancy J. *The National Urban League: 1910–1940*. New York: Oxford University Press, 1974.

Werner, Morris R. *Julius Rosenwald*. Glenview, Ill.: Harper and Brothers, 1939.

Wiebe, Robert H. *The Search for Order, 1877–1920*. New York: Hill and Wang, 1967.

Woodward, C. Vann. *Origins of the New South, 1877–1913*. Baton Rouge: Louisiana State University Press, 1951.

Woofter, Thomas J., Jr. *The Basis of Racial Adjustment*. New York: Gin and Company, 1925.

———. *Negro Problem in Cities: A Study*. 1928; repr. New York: Negro University Press, 1969.

———. *Southern Race Progress: The Wavering Color Line*. Washington, D.C.: Washington Public Affairs, 1957.

Yerkes, Robert M., ed. *The New World of Science: Its Development During the War*. New York: The Century Company, 1920.

Index

About the Author

JOHN H. STANFIELD is Associate Professor of Sociology and Afro-American Studies at Yale University. His articles have appeared in *Phylon,* the *Journal of Ethnic Studies,* and *The American Sociologist.*